HEIDEGGER'S
CHILDREN

HEIDEGGER'S CHILDREN

HANNAH ARENDT, KARL LÖWITH,

HANS JONAS, AND HERBERT MARCUSE

• RICHARD WOLIN •

PRINCETON UNIVERSITY PRESS • PRINCETON AND OXFORD

Copyright © 2001 by Princeton University Press
Published by Princeton University Press, 41 William Street,
Princeton, New Jersey 08540
In the United Kingdom: Princeton University Press, 3 Market Place,
Woodstock, Oxfordshire OX20 1SY
All Rights Reserved

Fourth printing, and first paperback printing, 2003
Paperback ISBN 0-691-11479-X

The Library of Congress has cataloged the cloth edition of this book as follows

Wolin, Richard.
Heidegger's children : Hannah Arendt, Karl Löwith, Hans Jonas,
and Herbert Marcuse / Richard Wolin.
p.   cm.
Includes bibliographical references and index.
ISBN 0-691-07019-9 (hardcover : alk. paper)
1. Heidegger, Martin, 1889–1976—Influence.   2. Jewish
philosophers—Germany—History—20th century.   I. Title.

B3279.H49 W63 2001
193—dc21   2001032105

British Library Cataloging-in-Publication Data is available

This book has been composed in Dante Typeface

Printed on acid-free paper. ∞

www.pupress.princeton.edu

Printed in the United States of America

5   7   9   10   8   6   4

FOR

JÜRGEN HABERMAS

IN ADMIRATION AND GRATITUDE

Do not become anxious, you German republicans; the German revolution will not take place any more pleasantly and gently for having been preceded by the Kantian critique, Fichtean transcendental idealism, or even natural philosophy. Through these theories revolutionary forces have built up which only await the day on which they may break loose, filling the world with horror and awe. Kantians will appear who want nothing to do with mercy even in the phenomenal world; they will plough up without pity the very soil of our European life with sword and axe, in order to eradicate every last root of the past. . . . Armed Fichteans will arise, whose fanaticism of will can be restrained neither through fear nor through self-interest. . . . More terrible than all will be the natural philosophers, who will participate actively in any German revolution, identifying themselves with the very work of destruction. If the hand of the Kantian strikes swift and sure because his heart is not moved by any traditional reverence; if the Fichtean courageously defies all danger because for him it does not exist at all in reality; so the natural philosopher will be terrible, for he has allied himself to the primal forces of nature. He can conjure up the demonic powers of ancient German pantheism and that lust for battle that we find among the ancient Germans will flame within him.

HEINRICH HEINE, *History of Philosophy and Religion in Germany* (1834)

• CONTENTS •

Preface
xi

PROLOGUE

"Todesfuge" and "Todtnauberg"
1

ONE

Introduction: Philosophy and Family Romance
5

TWO

The German-Jewish Dialogue: Way Stations of Misrecognition
21

THREE

Hannah Arendt: *Kultur*, "Thoughtlessness," and Polis Envy
30

FOUR

Karl Löwith: The Stoic Response to Modern Nihilism
70

FIVE

Hans Jonas: The Philosopher of Life
101

TEN YEARS ago I wrote a book, *The Politics of Being*,[1] on Martin Heidegger's political thought. At the time, it was far from my intention to expend further energies on matters Heideggerian. Yet it seemed increasingly clear that if one is interested in the fateful intersection between politics and the history of ideas in our time, an encounter with Heidegger's "case," in all its tortured complexities, is indispensable. Thus I argued—at the time, distinctly against the grain—that the philosopher's enlistment for the Nazi cause, far from being casual or unpremeditated, was deeply rooted in specifically German intellectual traditions to which Heidegger stood as a type of self-proclaimed heir. My intention was not to "finish with" Heidegger, but to alert interpreters to the historico-political depth dimension of his thought. To many *German* critics and disciples, this so-called depth dimension was, for cultural and linguistic reasons, more or less self-evident and, hence, less controversial. On this side of the Atlantic, owing to the predominance of ahistorical and text-immanent readings of Heidegger's philosophy, such claims proved more contentious and, in certain quarters, unwelcome.

At that time, the first-wave North American reception of Heidegger had undergone a major paradigm shift. The time of reverential exegesis of the early "existential" Heidegger had passed. Instead, it was the later Heidegger of the "Letter on Humanism"—the unyielding critic of "man" and "reason" who once proclaimed that *"reason is the most stiff-necked adversary of thought"*—who had seized the imagination of American interpreters. Confidence in Western ideals was at an all-time low due to cold-war cynicism and the apocalypse in Vietnam. Heidegger's philosophical attack against "reason" and "modernity" in the name of "Being" and *"poesis"* dovetailed surprisingly well with the alienated orientation of a younger generation of scholars. Ironically, Heidegger's powerful critique, which took its cues from the pre-Socratics and the "primordial" (*das Ursprüngliche*), meshed seamlessly with an emergent postmodern *Zeitgeist* that wished to bid "farewell to reason" and the modern age, with its attendant horrors and catastrophes. Thus, a strange marriage of convenience was arranged between Heidegger and postmodernism; a marriage brokered in Paris, where French intellectuals, frustrated by orthodox Marxist dogmatics, perceived in Heideggerianism a more ruthless and unforgiving critique of the modern West. Among North American continental philosophers, this intellectual mood ultimately gave rise to an exotic merger between Heidegger and Derrida, producing a potent new breed of *Heideggerian Derridians* or *Derridian Heideggerians*. At the time, I was little aware of how the volatility of this new breed would complicate attempts to ponder the political implications Heidegger's doctrines.

Shortly after *The Politics of Being*, appeared I decided to pursue the interpretive tack I had initiated there with a documentary complement, *The Heidegger Controversy: A Critical Reader.*[2] My intention was to make available to an English-speaking readership Heidegger's key political texts from the 1930s (which, remarkably, had remained untranslated), along with perceptive commentaries concerning the philosophical stakes of Heidegger's ill-fated political involvement. When Jacques Derrida strenuously objected to the inclusion of a brief interview (despite the fact that permission to reprint it had been readily granted by the original publisher), *The Heidegger Controversy* itself became an object of controversy.

Of course, the publishing dispute itself was merely the tip of the iceberg. "L'Affaire Derrida," as it came to be known, was, as the Freudians might say, highly overdetermined. As it turned out, Derrida and his supporters utilized the occasion to respond to a variety of events that had, justly or unjustly, besmirched the repute of deconstruction: first, the de Man affair, in which it was revealed that Derrida's chief transatlantic benefactor had compromised himself as a collaborator in Nazi-occupied Belgium; then, the revelations concerning the depths and extent of Heidegger's own activities on behalf of the Nazis—insinuations that, for decades, had been successfully parried by Heidegger and a battery of faithful disciples. Yet the more recent charges, buttressed by the publication of well-researched biographies by Victor Farias and Hugo Ott, seemed both undeniable and genuinely incriminating. Since "deconstruction," as a critique of metaphysics and reason, openly proclaimed its own Heideggerian pedigree, it felt implicated amid the rising tide of political scrutiny. Ultimately, "L'Affaire Derrida" metamorphosed into a strange referendum on the "cultural left." Devotees of postmodernism felt obliged to cast their lot with Derrida, whose detractors, for their part, had long made up their own minds. Sadly, but predictably, in view of our fad-ridden scholarly *Zeitgeist*, expressions of intellectual independence were few and far between.

As usual, what suffered amid the rising tide of accusations and counter-accusations were central matters of substance pertaining to the evaluation of Heidegger's philosophical legacy. To paraphrase Jean Baudrillard, one might say that, regrettably, the real debate never took place.

Following *The Politics of Being* and *The Heidegger Controversy*, *Heidegger's Children* represents a final installment in my effort to come to grips with Heidegger's ambiguous and powerful intellectual legacy. In part, it is a study in what Harold Bloom called "the anxiety of influence." My four protagonists—Hannah Arendt, Karl Löwith, Hans Jonas, and Herbert Marcuse—all were Jewish and were also for a time "convinced Heideggerians." Even Marcuse, who hailed from the political left, continued to idolize his fallen Master. Late in life, he dreamed of returning to Freiburg, where he studied with Heidegger during the late 1920s, and giving a lecture with Heidegger looking on approvingly from the gallery.[3] All four would go on to become major thinkers in their own right and would be faced with the conundrum of how to reconcile their youthful philosophical allegiances with the "totalitarian turn" in Heidegger's thought circa 1933. All four, moreover, thought of themselves as assimilated Germans rather than as Jews. Yet this self-understanding would be severely put to the test by the antidemocratic—not to mention anti-Semitic—turn taken by German politics in the early 1930s.

In Chapter 7, "*Arbeit Macht Frei*: Heidegger as Philosopher of the German 'Way,'" I explicitly return to the vexed question of Heidegger and politics. The occasion for reassessing his political thought was the recent publication of a fascinating lecture course offered immediately following the philosopher's resignation as Nazi rector of Freiburg University in spring 1934. Announced in the university catalogue as a course on "Logik" (as it turns out, a great misnomer), the lectures contain Heidegger's systematic reflections on the "ontological import" of Nazism: an appraisal of the movement's "essential" significance when viewed from Heidegger's standpoint of the "history of Being." The material is significant insofar as it contains not occasional political musings—since Heidegger had already resigned from the rectorship, he no longer had cause to dissemble his true sentiments and kowtow to the regime—but a systematic articulation of Heidegger's own positive "metapolitical" standpoint. Far from being a Nazi tract, the lectures systematically ponder a number of key political concepts—"Volk," "labor," and "historicity"—to demonstrate hidden affinities between Nazism and Heidegger's own philosophy of existentialism.

The book that follows evolved out of a number of independent, yet related, projects. Two of the chapters—"Hannah Arendt: *Kultur*, 'Thoughtlessness,' and Polis Envy" and "Hans Jonas: The Philosopher of Life"—first appeared as articles in *The New Republic*. Both have been substantially revised. I owe a tremendous debt to *The New Republic's* literary editor, Leon Wieseltier, for his confidence in my ability to convey at times ponderous philosophical themes to a broadly educated public. The assignments I have undertaken for *The New Republic* have been compelling exercises in the virtues of intellectual communication. They have helped me unlearn (in the constructive sense) the debilities of scholarly specialization, whereby what matters is one's ability to interact with a handful of fellow cognoscenti. Expert training no doubt has its merits and place, but it can also readily lose sight of matters of broad public importance. In today's academy, the arcane nature of much debate, reinforced by a forbidding linguistic exclusivity, has led to a kind of crippling self-ghettoization. One of the ironies of the present situation is that the academic left, trumpeting the virtues of "relevance," has defensively rallied around a type of discursive hermeticism. Ironically, whatever grains of truth this discourse might have to purvey are lost in advance by virtue of its willful rhetorical impenetrability.

I owe an equal debt of gratitude to my editor at Princeton University Press, Brigitta van Rheinberg, who has nursed this project along from embarrassingly inchoate beginnings. I initially conceived the book as a series of loosely related essays. Much of its final focus and coherence are the direct result of Brigitta's gentle and timely prodding. There is no doubt in my mind that were it not for her astute editorial guidance, the end result would have been inferior. I would also like to thank my copyeditor, Jody James, for her promptness and professionalism. Thanks are due to my research assistant, Martin Woessner, for his perceptive comments on the manuscript.

Lastly, I would also like to acknowledge the insightful feedback I received on an earlier version of the manuscript from Michael Ermarth of Dartmouth University and William Scheuerman of the University of Minnesota, both of whom are extremely well versed in the ruses and complexities of the German intellectual tradition. At different points, their remarks proved indispensable in helping me rethink key aspects of my argument. In the end, the strengths and weaknesses they were able to identify in the manuscript version provided me with a much-needed external touchstone.

I have dedicated this book to Jürgen Habermas. I first met him twenty years ago in Berkeley, where he presented a series of remarkable lectures that were ultimately published as *The Theory of Communicative Action*, volumes I and II. For me personally, and I'm sure for many others in the overflowing lecture hall, these lectures marked an intellectual turning point. As a product of the 1960s and a disciple of Hegelian-Marxism, I had until then been a convinced Adornoian who viewed *Negative Dialectics* as a type of philosophical holy writ. I was persuaded that Adorno, in describing late capitalism as a "totally administered world" and a "context of delusion," had more or less delivered the final word. Listening to Habermas's reconstruction of modern social theory from Durkheim to Parson caused the scales to fall from my eyes. I came away from his stimulating presentations with a keen awareness of how much ground the first generation of Critical Theorists had unwittingly ceded to the enemy camp by (à la Max Weber) narrowly identifying "reason" with "instrumental reason" or "positivism." I also came away with a renewed appreciation of the valuable potentials for reform, contestation, and critique residing in existing democratic societies—a lesson that, I fear, has taken too long to learn for many of my generational *compagnons de lutte*.

Ten years later, our paths crossed again when Professor Habermas was gracious enough to serve as academic host during my tenure as an

Alexander von Humboldt Fellow in the Department of Philosophy at the University of Frankfurt. During this year, I probably learned more about German intellectual traditions than it would be possible to recount. It was also from this period that my investigations concerning matters Heideggerian date. This dedication, to the man who has done so much to remind his countrymen and women about the importance of "democratic norms" that Americans too often take for granted, is then a modest way of repaying an enormous intellectual and personal debt.

Let me also seize this occasion to acknowledge the generosity of Professor Habermas's successor, Axel Honneth, who was kind enough to host me during a return trip to Frankfurt (also under the auspices of the Humboldt Stiftung) three years ago, at which point my conception for a book on "Heidegger's children" first took shape.

New York City
July 2001

HEIDEGGER'S
CHILDREN

"Todesfuge" and "Todtnauberg"

I N 1967, the Jewish poet and Holo-
caust survivor Paul Celan visited Martin Heidegger's famous ski hut in
the heart of Germany's Black Forest. It was there that, forty years
earlier, the German philosopher had written *Being and Time*, one of the
milestones of twentieth-century existentialism.[1] For the Heideggerian
faithful, the tiny cabin still functions as an obligatory pilgrimage site. A
day earlier, Celan had delivered a reading to an overflow crowd at
Freiburg University. When poet and philosopher met for the first time
following the reading, a journalist suggested that they pose together for
a photograph. Celan demurred. Heidegger's Nazi past stood in the
way. After all, the philosopher had never publicly distanced himself
from his political misdeeds. Though Celan admired Heidegger's philosophy, he was not about to provide the philosopher with the political
absolution he so desperately sought. Celan biographer John Felstiner
has glossed the situation as follows: "It is clear that an encounter with
the man who under Hitler was Rector at Freiburg in 1933–34, who in
1935 declared Nazism's 'inner truth and greatness,' who in 1936 still
signed his letters *Heil Hitler!*, had his classes give the salute, and sported
a swastika pin, and who paid party dues until 1945—an encounter with
this man had to be fraught, especially given Heidegger's silence about
it all since the war."[2]

In the poem "Todtnauberg"—after the site of Heidegger's hut—
Celan recalls how he signed the cabin log book with "hope of a thinking man's coming word in the heart"—a word of contrition. But his
hopes met with stony silence. From the philosopher's lips came no
words of remorse. To add further irony to an already tense situation,
Tod is the German word for death, and "Todesfuge" ("Death Fugue") is

the poem that, following the war, catapulted Celan to international literary renown.

Toward the end of the poem, Celan, a former concentration camp inmate, makes a portentous declaration: *"Death Is a Master from Germany."*[3] They are by far the most quoted words of Celan's luminous *oeuvre*. The poem's remarkable opening lines bear citing:

> Black milk of daybreak we drink it at evening
> We drink it at midday and morning we drink it at night
> We drink and we drink
> We shovel a grave in the air there you won't lie too cramped

Undoubtedly, the linguistic overlap between "Todesfuge" and the name of the ex-Nazi Heidegger's mountain retreat proved unsettling to the world-weary poet. The composition of "Todtnauberg" must have stood as the negative confirmation of a lifetime of experience. Like so many Central European Jews, Celan, who hailed from Bukovina, Rumania, had as a youth vigorously imbibed German cultural traditions. He viewed Germany, as did Heidegger, as a nation of *Dichter und Denker*—a nation of writers and thinkers. It was the land of *Geist* and *Bildung*, a culture that prided itself on the values of spiritual inwardness and the tasks of self-cultivation. It was the nation of Goethe, Schiller, and Hölderlin—poets who, during the epoch of German classicism, elevated native German traditions to the rank of world literature. In her famous treatise *De l'Allemagne* (1809), Madame de Staël could, following two decades of war and revolution, chastise her countrymen for not being more like the Germans; for while the French were preoccupied with all manner of political excess, including the folly of world conquest, the Germans had produced a literary efflorescence unequaled since the days of classical antiquity.

How, though, were writers and thinkers of German-Jewish provenance to reconcile their biographical allegiances to German culture with the grim horrors those traditions had yielded a little more than a century later? This was the problem Celan confronted time and again in his poetry. It also forms one of the essential leitmotifs of *Heidegger's Children*: the way in which Heidegger's most gifted students—many of whom were Jewish—strove to confront their profound indebtedness to German intellectual traditions given the obscene uses to which those traditions had been put during the Nazi era. There can be no doubting the fact, moreover, that the misbegotten marriage between Nazism and *Kultur* was actively encouraged by the mandarin professorate, which quite frankly saw the regime as a golden opportunity to put paid to the chaos of the "liberal system" and reassert the value of authentic German traditions.[4]

In Celan's case, the dilemma of which strands of German culture had been contaminated and which ones had survived relatively unscathed manifested itself as much in the formal structure of his poetry—abrupt disjunctions and tortured neologisms—as in its content per se. In the manner of a postapocalyptic bricoleur, Celan attempted to wrest consolation and meaning from a language that had been used for unspeakably reprehensible purposes. It was a theme that must have been in the forefront of his thoughts during his visit to Heidegger's Schwarzwald lair when, during his audience with the German sage— the heir apparent to the literary traditions Celan revered—he waited with "hope of a thinking man's coming word" for a gesture of reconciliation that never materialized.

Like so many Germans of his generation, Heidegger never engaged in a serious attempt to work though the sins of the German past. In this respect, he certainly didn't make the task of his Jewish "children"— several of whom implored him in the postwar period to make a public and forthright break with those dalliances and flirtations during the Nazi era that continued to mar his reputation—any easier.[5] Instead, in those relatively few passages of his immense corpus where he condescends to address the horrors of the war the Nazis had unleashed, one finds only evasions and rationalizations—as in the lecture from the late 1940s in which Heidegger tastelessly equates "the manufacturing of corpses in gas chambers" with "mechanized agriculture."[6]

Three years following his disappointing encounter with Heidegger, Celan met with a fate that was sadly all too familiar to Holocaust survivors: he took his own life by drowning himself in the Seine.

Introduction:

Philosophy and Family Romance

Dilemmas of Discipleship

THE PROTAGONISTS of *Heidegger's Children*—Hannah Arendt, Hans Jonas, Karl Löwith, and Herbert Marcuse—were non-Jewish Jews who thought of themselves as proverbial "Germans of Jewish origin." As philosophically trained intellectuals, they expected to find salvation and meaning not in the traditions of Jewish cultural belonging but in the hallowed Germanic ideals of *Geist* and *Bildung*. All four were trained by Germany's greatest philosopher, Martin Heidegger. Although Heidegger was virtually unpublished until the landmark appearance of *Being and Time* in 1927, his talents as a lecturer and teacher had already gained him considerable renown.

Heidegger's Jewish students were among his very brightest. Each of the protagonists in question carved out a distinctive niche in the world of twentieth-century philosophy and letters. Hannah Arendt is probably the twentieth century's greatest political thinker.[1] At an advanced age, Hans Jonas achieved renown as Germany's premier philosopher of environmentalism. Herbert Marcuse gained fame—and notoriety—as a philosophical eminence of the Frankfurt School as well as a mentor to the New Left. (At one point in the late 1960s, he was denounced by the Pope himself.) Karl Löwith, upon his return to Germany in 1956, became one of the leading philosophers of the postwar era. Moreover, Heidegger's own mentor, Edmund Husserl, to whom the philosopher dedicated *Being and Time*, was also Jewish. In light of Heidegger's zealous involvement with Nazism during the early 1930s, the attendant ironies—the Nazi rector of Freiburg University, a former assistant to Husserl, who was in turn surrounded by talented Jewish disciples—are considerable.

However, the inconsistencies in Heidegger's attitude are less profound than they may appear on first view. Among Heidegger's Jewish "children," none were practicing Jews. As assimilated Jews devoted to the allurements of *Geist*, the manifestly Jewish dimension of their personae was in most cases imperceptible. Löwith, in fact, was a convert to Protestantism. Jonas had some Jewish education as a youth and, late in life, published several influential texts on the theme of post-Holocaust theology. Yet, in his major *philosophical works*, traces of Jewish influence are negligible. For a time during the 1930s, Arendt worked with Youth Aliyah, a Paris-based organization that helped send Jewish children to Palestine. Yet, following the Jewish Agency's 1943 Biltmore declaration rejecting a two-state solution to the question of Palestine, she became one of Zionism's most vocal critics. And although as we shall see, Heidegger's worldview was by no means free of the everyday anti-Semitism that seethed beneath the surface of the liberal Weimar Republic, he never subscribed to the racial anti-Semitism espoused by the National Socialists. To him this perspective was philosophically untenable, insofar as it sought to explain "existential" questions in reductive biological terms. For Heidegger, biology was a base exemplar of nineteenth-century materialism—a standpoint that needed to be overcome in the name of *"Existenz"* or *"Being."*

This book is a careful study of Heidegger's Jewish students—their intellectual orientations, doctrines, and political convictions. As such, it oversteps the customary disciplinary boundaries among philosophy, politics, and intellectual history. What is it that such a study has to teach us?

To begin with, there is much to learn about the conditions that governed the global dissemination of Heidegger's ideas, especially in the postwar period when he had been banned from teaching due to his political fall from grace during the early 1930s. Since his students' attitudes were often instrumental in determining how Heidegger's views would be received, *Heidegger's Children* is in part a study in reception history. In contemporary scholarship, the idea that there can be no absolute separation between a body of thought and its reception has become commonplace. Long before such notions became fashionable, the philosopher and critic Walter Benjamin formulated a related insight: *"The work is the death of the intention."*[2] Once objectified, doctrines and ideas tend to defy the will of their author, taking on a life of their own. Often, commentary and interpretation outstrip proprietary assertions of authorial intention: rarely are authors the best judges of their own work. Thus, by observing the peregrinations of Heidegger's gifted Jewish students, one simultaneously gains new insight into both the richness and the limitations of his manner of thinking.

Insofar as his Jewish protégés went on to become celebrated thinkers in their own right, *Heidegger's Children* is also a study in the "anxiety of influence."[3] Heidegger's impact as a teacher and mentor was, according to most extant accounts, inordinately profound. Few scholars who experienced his mesmerizing lectures and seminars remained untransformed. By the same token, students who fell under his powerful philosophical shadow often had difficulty extricating themselves and establishing an independent intellectual identity—a dilemma that even his most gifted students were forced to confront. Needless to say, such problems were compounded in the case of his extraordinarily talented Jewish students, men and women who often first experienced their Jewish identity in the crosshairs of German anti-Semitism. For these students, the dilemmas of intellectual individuation proved doubly fraught, insofar as Heidegger's doctrines had fallen within the orbit of contamination circumscribed by the "German catastrophe" in ways that were both readily intelligible and ineffable since, often, what was at issue was a quintessentially Heideggerian *habitus* or *gestus*. At the same time, as eyewitnesses to Germany's shocking political devolution, Heidegger's "children" were able to offer invaluable firsthand testimony concerning the spiritual conditions responsible for the collapse. Yet that privileged proximity often proved existentially and philosophically troubling, for how much of what they had imbibed as students of German thought and culture had been tainted by the *Bacillus teutonicus*? Many would continue to pose similar questions until the end of their lives.

In the aftermath of Hitler's seizure of power and Heidegger's brief, though concerted and incriminating complicity with the regime, his "children" sought to philosophize *with Heidegger against Heidegger*, thereby hoping to save what could be saved, all the while trying to cast off their mentor's long and powerful shadow. In this respect, *Heidegger's Children* is the story of the search for new beginnings undertaken by his Jewish disciples. But the task would prove a difficult one, for Heidegger's children were as much his contemporaries as they were his juniors. Fundamentally, they were shaped by the same momentous political and cultural transformations that formed Heidegger's own worldview. Hence, rarely did their efforts to circumvent the parameters of his immense gravitational influence prove successful. To wit, *all accepted, willy nilly, a series of deep-seated prejudices concerning the nature of political modernity—democracy, liberalism, individual rights, and so forth—that made it very difficult to articulate a meaningful theoretical standpoint in the postwar world.* Though all came to reject specific features of Heidegger's doctrine (his later, quasi-mystical *Seinsgedanke*, or philosophy of Being, was a frequent target of attack), at base they shared much of his conservative revolutionary "diagnosis of the times." Often, the reception of Heidegger the philosopher has led commentators to neglect his extremely influential status as a *Zivilisationskritiker*, or "critic of civilization." But the two aspects of his persona cannot be divorced; an airtight separation between philosopher and *Weltanschauung* is impossible to maintain.[4] In Heidegger's view—and this was a perspective that his disciples largely shared—the modern age was an era of "absolute sinfulness" (J. G. Fichte). As such, any and every means was justified to drive it into the abyss. For the "front generation," to which both Heidegger and his children belonged (Heidegger, Löwith, and Marcuse actually served in the First World War), a distinct flirtation with nihilism was a corollary of the conviction that widespread destruction was required before anything of lasting value could be built.[5]

Heidegger's Children also returns to the question of how to account for the uncanny ideological affinities between Heidegger the thinker and the political movement known as National Socialism. In Chapter 7, I have sought to address this question explicitly, taking as my point of departure the recent publication of a disturbing 1934 lecture course in which Heidegger delivers his own brief on behalf of a starry-eyed "ontological fascism"—Nazism in the service of the *Seinsgedanke* or idea of "Being." Prior to the 1980s, it still seemed plausible to deny that there was a causal nexus between Heidegger's philosophy and Nazism. Following the pathbreaking biographical studies by Hugo Ott and Victor Farias, however, the reality of Heidegger's turn to Hitler as the charismatic leader capable of redeeming humanity from a fate of unremitting nihilism has been convincingly established.[6] At the same time, it would be foolish to claim that Heidegger's political *lapsus*, however egregious, would somehow disqualify his immense philosophical achievement. Instead, to state the obvious, the truth of the matter lies somewhere between these two extremes. Each of Heidegger's Jewish disciples was compelled to confront this conundrum: how Germany's greatest philosopher—and the man who was heir to so much that was distinctive and admirable about the German spirit—could willingly embrace a political movement that seemed to represent the wholesale negation of philosophy and culture. In this context, it is worthwhile to invoke the reflections of Herbert Marcuse who, in a 1948 letter to Heidegger, formulated the problem in the following way:

> A philosopher can be deceived regarding political matters; in which case he will openly acknowledge his error. But he cannot be deceived about a regime that has killed millions of Jews— merely because they were Jews—that made terror into an everyday phenomenon, and that turned everything that pertains to the ideas of spirit, freedom, and truth into its bloody opposite; a regime that in every respect imaginable was the deadly caricature of the Western tradition that you yourself so forcefully explicated and justified.[7]

In this passage, Marcuse emphasizes something that is important to keep in mind: Nazism was a tyranny unlike prior tyrannies, a historically unprecedented form of political terror. To be sure, its gruesome endpoint—Auschwitz—was not foreseeable from its quasi-Chaplinesque beginnings; but those beginnings—*Gleichschaltung*, mass arrests, concentration camps, and convulsive anti-Semitism—were egregious enough. To his discredit, Heidegger never renounced this obscene terminus, the death camps that have become emblematic of twentieth-century industrialized mass murder. His philosophical ruminations on this problem, moreover, were myopic and largely beside the point. In his view, the genocidal politics of the Nazis were attributable to the evils of "technology," the distortions of the "modern world-picture," the post-Cartesian "will to will," or the "forgetting of Being." Thus, his contorted, "metapolitical" explanations stressed everything but the obvious: the peculiarities and distortions of German historical development that had from the outset facilitated Nazism's political success.

Heidegger's "Fall"

Had it not been for Heidegger's fateful political lapse of 1933 when, with great fanfare, he joined the Nazi Party and assumed the rectorship of Freiburg University, biographers might have scant material to work with. Heidegger was studiously averse to traveling outside his native home in Baden. In the early 1930s, he twice turned down offers to teach at the University of Berlin with resounding affirmations of the virtues of provincialism. One such account, "Why We Remain in the Provinces," reads like a parody of the German discourse of "blood and soil."[8]

Yet Heidegger's dalliances with Nazism, though short-lived, have made biographical considerations central to the evaluation of his intellectual worth. Heidegger resigned as Nazi rector of Freiburg University after a year in office, but by then sufficient damage had been done. He had effectively delivered the university over to the aims and ends of the "German Revolution." On the lecture stump, he proved an effective propagandist on behalf of the new regime, concluding one speech by declaring: "Let not ideas and doctrines be your guide. The *Führer* is the only German reality and its law."[9]

In May 1933, Heidegger sent a telltale telegram to Hitler expressing solidarity with recent *Gleichschaltung* legislation. There were instances of political denunciation and personal betrayal. Moreover, Heidegger remained a dues-paying member of the Nazi Party until the regime's bitter end. He continued to open his classes with the so-called "German greeting" of "Heil Hitler!" In 1936, he confided to Löwith that his "partisanship for National Socialism lay in the essence of his philosophy"; it derived, he claimed, from the concept of "historicity" (which stressed the importance of authentic historical commitment) in *Being and Time*.[10]

As the rector of Freiburg University, Heidegger was charged with enforcing the anti-Semitic clauses of the so-called "Law for the Preservation of a Permanent Civil Service," which effectively banned Jews from all walks of government service, including university life. Despite his later disclaimers, in his capacity as rector Heidegger faithfully executed these laws, even though it meant banning Husserl, to whom he owed so much, from the philosophy faculty library. In the eyes of Hannah Arendt, this action, which had affected the septuagenarian phenomenologist so adversely, made Heidegger a "potential murderer."[11] At the time, Husserl complained bitterly in a letter to a former student about Heidegger's growing anti-Semitism: "In recent years [he] has allowed his anti-Semitism to come increasingly to the fore, even in his dealings with his groups of devoted Jewish students," observes Husserl. "The events of the last few weeks," he continued (referring to Heidegger's joining the Nazi Party as well as the recent university ban on Jews), "have struck at the deepest roots of my existence."[12]

In 1929, Heidegger had already complained that Germany was faced with a stark alternative: "the choice between sustaining our *German* intellectual life through a renewed infusion of genuine, *native* teachers and educators, or abandoning it once and for all to *growing Jewish influence* [*Verjudung*]—in both the wider and narrow sense."[13] According to a former student, the philosopher Max Müller, "From the moment Heidegger became rector, he allowed no Jewish students who had begun their dissertations with him to receive their degree."[14] He dashed the hopes of one doctoral candidate with the callous declaration: "You understand, Frau Mintz, that I cannot supervise your promotion because you are a Jew."[15] In an unsolicited letter in which he tried to block the academic appointment of Eduard Baumgarten (nephew of the sociologist Max Weber), Heidegger complained that Baumgarten hailed from a "liberal democratic" milieu, had become "Americanized" during a stay in the United States, and associated with "the Jew [Eduard] Fränkel."[16]

With the regime's fall, Heidegger paid dearly for his transgressions. A university denazification commission found that by lending the prestige of his name and reputation to the regime in its early months, Heidegger had helped to legitimate it in the eyes of other German scholars. During the proceedings, an especially damning letter of evaluation was provided by the philosopher Karl Jaspers, who claimed that Heidegger's philosophy was "unfree" and "dictatorial." "I think it would be quite wrong," concluded Jaspers, "to turn such a teacher loose on the young people of today, who are psychologically extremely vulnerable."[17] Heidegger was stripped of his right to teach and granted emeritus status. The man who thought of himself as the greatest philosopher since Heraclitus did not take the verdict well. For nearly two months, he was hospitalized for depression. According to recent reports, at one point he even attempted to take his own life.[18]

Heidegger's children were forced to confront the painful fact of their mentor's political misdeeds. In light of the immense esteem in which they held him, the process proved difficult, protracted, and, at times, disorienting. As youths they firmly believed that, by casting their lot with the Freiburg sage, they were riding the crest of the philosophy of the future. They felt, as did Heidegger's other disciples, that his novel philosophy of "existence" put paid to the stale academicism of the reigning German school philosophies—neo-Kantianism, Hegelianism, and positivism. His abrupt conversion to Nazism took almost all of his students, Jewish and non-Jewish, by surprise. However, if one carefully reconstructs the ideological components of his early philosophy of existence, his political turn seems less than a total break.[19] In a concluding Excursus, *Being and Time: A Failed Masterpiece?*" I have examined Heidegger's philosophical path prior to the composition of his great work of 1927, in order to show that indeed the "anticivilizational" (*zivilisationskritisch*) elements of his thinking, far from being a later accretion, were firmly embedded in his project from the very outset.

Following 1933, his Jewish students were forced to ponder, under the stress and hardship of exile, whether there was something integral to *Existenzphilosophie* that triggered Heidegger's Nazi allegiance. Perhaps Hannah Arendt's initial response was the most extreme: by her own admission, she abandoned philosophy for a period of twenty years.[20] As late as 1964, the author of *The Human Condition* still bridled at being referred to as a "philosopher." ("Political thinker" was the term she preferred.) Among her fellow students, there was general agreement that Heidegger's philosophical "radicalism" was in part the catalyst behind his political excesses. Paradoxically, the element that accounted for his greatness—his insistence on breaking with all inherited philosophical paradigms and traditions—also proved his undoing. His students realized that when uncompromising intellectual radicalism is transposed to the realm of politics and society, the results can be calamitous.

Thereafter, a difficult process of coming to terms with the German intellectual past ensued. It was Karl Löwith, Heidegger's first dissertation student, who pursued this project at greatest length. Convinced that Nazism reflected a spiritual malaise afflicting not only Germany but the West as a whole, he sought out the intellectual roots of the crisis in the nineteenth century, when educated men and women abandoned the balance of German classicism (Goethe and Hegel) for the extremes of existentialism, scientism, and nihilism.[21] Both Jonas and Arendt also perceived a Faustian-nihilistic strain in Western humanism—the loss of a sense of proportion and "limit"—that seemingly propelled the modern age headlong toward the abyss. For both thinkers, the dangers of nihilism that had been dramatically exposed by Nazism had not been laid to rest by the Allies' triumph of May 8, 1945. Instead, they lived on in the manifestations of modern technology: the risks of nuclear annihilation, environmental catastrophe, and interplanetary disorientation. Thus, in the opening pages of *The Human Condition*, Arendt gave eloquent voice to the fears of a generation:

> In 1957, an earth-born object made by man was launched into the universe, where for some weeks it circled the earth according to the same laws of gravitation that swing and keep in motion the celestial bodies—the sun, the moon, and the stars. . . . But . . . it was not pride or awe at the tremendousness of human power and mastery which filled the hearts of men, who, when they looked up from the earth toward the skies, could behold there a thing of their own making. The immediate reaction . . . was relief about the first "step toward escape from men's imprisonment to the earth." . . . The banality of this statement should not make us overlook how extraordinary in fact it was; for although Christians have spoken of the earth as a vale of tears and philosophers have looked upon their body as a prison of mind or soul, nobody in the history of mankind has ever conceived of the earth as a prison for men's bodies or shown eagerness to go literally from here to the moon.[22]

In *The Imperative of Responsibility* (1984), Jonas set forth a series of parallel reflections concerning the threat to human existence posed by the uncontrollable momentum of modern technology:

> My main fear relates to the apocalypse threatening from the unintended dynamics of technical civilization as such, inherent in its structure, whereto it drifts willy-nilly and with exponential acceleration: the apocalypse of the "too much," with the exhaustion, pollution, desolation of the planet. . . . Darkest of all is the possibility . . . that in the global mass misery of a failing biosphere . . . "everyone for himself" becomes the common battle cry, [and] one or the other desperate side will, in the fight for dwindling resources, resort to the *ultima ratio* of atomic war.[23]

In the context at hand, there is another point worth stressing: how difficult it would be for former Heideggerians to escape the Master's influence entirely, despite valiant efforts. After all, Arendt and Jonas could hardly have chosen a more representative Heideggerian theme than the alienating effects of "planetary technology" on modern society.[24]

Among our four protagonists, Herbert Marcuse stands out as something of an exception. Whereas Arendt, Jonas, and Löwith remained more or less within a Heideggerian philosophical trajectory, Marcuse's commitment to critical Marxism and the political left produced a significantly different intellectual orientation. Hence, whereas Arendt, Jonas, and Löwith frequently took their normative and political bearings from classical antiquity (as did Heidegger, who endowed the "Greek beginning" with unmatched historical significance), Marcuse, under the influence of Marx and Hegel, projected his Golden Age into the future in the form of a classless society. At the same time, given his strong Hegelian influences, Marcuse's Marxism was distinctly heterodox: he corresponded with the surrealists (from whom he derived his notion of "the Great Refusal"), published widely on Freud, and wrote an important critical study of Soviet Marxism. In light of these nonconformist interests, it is perhaps no great surprise that during the late 1920s he was preoccupied with the idea of a "Marx-Heidegger" synthesis and wrote a habilitation thesis on "historicity" under Heidegger's direction.

Yet, if one digs beneath the surface, one detects in Marcuse's political thought a palpable indebtedness to the tradition of Jewish Messianism that became a rite of passage for Central European Jewish intellectuals who came of age circa World War I. Whereas by 1900, postrevolutionary promises of universal equality had gone far toward alleviating the plight of Western European Jewry, the assimilationist dreams of their Central European counterparts seemed all but dashed amid recurrent waves of virulent anti-Semitism. Consequently, for Central European Jewry, the "liberal option" seemed to have played itself out. Socialism and Zionism appeared as the only viable political alternatives. Thus, at a time when hopes for assimilation dwindled, the only possibilities seemed to lie either in political radicalism or the pursuit of an authentic Jewish identity elsewhere. The historical dynamic behind this approach has been well described by Anson Rabinbach:

> In the years approaching the First World War, the self-confidence and the security of German Jewry was challenged by a new Jewish sensibility that can be described as at once radical, secular and Messianic in both tone and content. What this new Jewish ethos refused to accept was above all the optimism of the generation of German Jews nurtured on the concept of *Bildung* as the German Jewish mystique. They were profoundly shaken by political anti-Semitism and the anti-liberal spirit of the German upper classes, which for them called into question the political and cultural assumptions of the post-emancipation epoch. Especially irksome was the belief that there was no contradiction between *Deutschtum* and *Judentum*; that secularization and liberalism would permit the cultural integration of Jews into the national community.[25]

The classical representatives of the sensibility described by Rabinbach were Ernst Bloch and Walter Benjamin, and it was largely via their influence that themes of Jewish political Messianism surfaced in Marcuse's work. In his preface to *The Theory of the Novel*, Georg Lukács coined the term "romantic anticapitalism" to describe a generation of Central European intellectuals who had been traumatized by Europe's rapid industrial expansion as well as the aftereffects of the Great War. "The standpoint of their work," noted Lukács, "aimed at a fusion of 'left' ethics and 'right' epistemology. . . . From the 1920s onwards this view was to play an increasingly important role. We need only think of

Ernst Bloch's *Geist der Utopie* (1918, 1923) and *Thomas Münzer als Theologe der Revolution*, of Walter Benjamin, even of the beginnings of Theodor W. Adorno, etc."[26] Marcuse's unbending revolutionary longings and sweeping critique of the inadequacies of modern industrial civilization make him a direct heir to the aforementioned group, even though his Messianic inclinations were always tempered by other intellectual influences and traditions—above all, a rather unmessianic, Hegelian belief in the power of "reason in history."

Heidegger's Breakthrough

Heidegger's Children also addresses the fate of one of the dominant currents of twentieth-century intellectual life: existentialism—an intellectual trend set in motion by the publication of Heidegger's 1927 masterpiece, *Being and Time*. On few occasions has a work of philosophy had such an immediate and far-reaching impact. Even prior to its appearance, when Heidegger was still an assistant professor in Marburg during the mid-1920s, philosophy students from all over Germany packed his lecture courses and seminars. With the publication of *Being and Time*, however, quantity was transformed into quality and the worldwide dissemination of his doctrines began in earnest. Appropriating the influences of Kierkegaard, Nietzsche, and Dilthey (not to mention literary sources as diverse as Tolstoy, Dostoyevsky, and Rilke), Heidegger had in *Being and Time* fundamentally recast the terms of philosophical thought. In comparison with his unassimilable neologisms and theoretical daring, all previous paradigms and precepts appeared hopelessly outmoded.

Given the centrality of *Being and Time* to the intellectual narrative that follows—for Heidegger's children, the encounter with this work and the radical critique of the historical present it purveyed became in many ways a defining life-experience—I have decided to include an Excursus that reviews Heidegger's original motivations for having written it. As we now know, the conditions surrounding its inception were anything but straightforward. Instead, its composition was overdetermined by a number of circumstantial variables—biographical, confessional, cultural, and historical—whose importance has only recently come to light. In attempting to reconstruct the key stages of Heidegger's early development, I have relied extensively on the recently published lecture courses from the *Collected Works* edition (*Gesamtausgabe*), which shed indispensable light on the genesis of what remains one of the landmark works of modern thought.

Since Descartes, epistemological concerns had been the focal point of modern philosophy. By returning to the "question of Being" in the opening pages of *Being and Time*, Heidegger cast aspersions upon this entire post-Cartesian conceptual lineage. Epistemology's success had gone hand in hand with the rise of modern science. Yet this legacy had triumphed, it seemed, at the expense of the more basic human concerns. Following Nietzsche's ruthless debunking of democracy, morality, and religion, the blandishments of Western humanism, appeared to offer little more than false consolation. Their empty assurances and assertions, it seemed, represented merely the window-dressing for the predicament of modern nihilism. By forthrightly posing the question of nihilism, Nietzsche established the discursive parameters for a subsequent generation of philosophers and literati. As he memorably phrases the problem in *The Will to Power*:

> Nihilism stands at the door: whence comes this uncanniest of all guests? . . . What does nihilism mean? *That the highest values devaluate themselves.* The aim is lacking; "why?" finds no answer. . . . *Radical nihilism* is the conviction of an *absolute untenability of existence when it comes to the highest values one recognizes*; plus the realization that we lack the least right to posit a beyond or an in-itself of things that might be 'divine' or morality incarnate.[27]

With these observations, Nietzsche appeared to seal the fate of traditional approaches to philosophy. He referred to his new method as "philosophizing with a hammer." He claimed his books were "assassination attempts" and "dynamite," having little to do with drawing-room notions of what it meant to do philosophy. During the 1930s, Heidegger devoted a multivolume lecture course to Nietzsche, whose thought he regarded as a key to understanding the dilemmas of the modern age. Already, in the early 1920s, the encounter with Nietzsche had left him convinced that the traditional concepts of philosophy were inadequate to the momentous tasks of the historical present: the problems of technology, mass society, and social "leveling" that had been apocalyptically set forth in Spengler's powerful treatise on *The Decline of the West*.

Dasein was Heidegger's response to the missteps of transcendental philosophy. Heidegger rejected Descartes's point of departure—*res cogitans* or "thinking substance"—because it harbored too many substantive and misleading preconceptions. To take disembodied subjectivity as philosophy's starting point predisposed one to follow a certain line of questioning that led to a class of predictable and fruitless responses. The neologisms preferred by Heidegger, culled from colloquial German, indicated his strong preference for a nonscientific new beginning whose point of departure would be Dasein's irreducible "situatedness" or "Being-in-the-world." Unlike the theoretical "subject" of modern epistemology, Heideggerian Dasein was defined more by its moods, its capacity for silence in the face of idle talk, its "Being-toward-death," than by its capacities for "clear and distinct ideas" (Locke) or syllogistic reasoning.

It would be foolish to deny the fruitfulness of Heidegger's existential démarche. It offered a method of addressing life, or Being-in-the-world, that surpassed in many respects the theoretical standpoint of philosophy qua epistemology. With the advent of logical positivism, whose heyday coincided with Heidegger's youth, philosophy was at risk of shriveling to the status of a handmaiden to scientific inquiry. Heidegger's existential approach presented a constructive antidote to this perilous foreshortening of philosophy's purview and scope.

Today, philosophy departments are ruled by the methods of linguistic analysis. Yet this school of philosophy represents another manner of narrowing philosophy's influence and range. The existential concerns that occupied pride of place in Heidegger's rich phenomenological inquiries seem banished from philosophy's horizon. History and social criticism, too, seem to have forfeited their place. Wittgenstein claimed that language games must be understood as "forms of life," but he leaves us without a way of evaluating their respective merits and deficiencies, for as "forms of life," all language games make sense internally. Thus, the goals of philosophy should be *therapeutic* rather than *substantive*. The elimination of misunderstandings, rather than the establishment of positive goals or agendas, is the end toward which

thought should aspire. Philosophy should, we are told, place more
trust in common sense or everyday linguistic practice. As a perceptive
critic has remarked:

> Linguistic philosophy is conceived not merely as therapy or eutha-
> nasia, but also as prophylaxis, and as a prophylaxis against a neces-
> sarily ever-present danger. . . . This is the Night Watchman theory
> of philosophy: it has no positive contribution of its own to make,
> but must ever be on guard against possible abuses that would
> interfere with, or confuse, genuine knowledge.[28]

One of the grave inadequacies of the linguistic approach is that it
lacks a capacity for strong evaluation, for making conceptual distinctions of far-reaching significance.[29] Its quietism seems well captured indeed by Wittgenstein's dictum that "philosophy leaves everything as it
is." Moreover, with philosophy's professionalization, a corresponding
measure of specialization has taken hold. Prospects of reconnecting
philosophy with the lifeworld or "everydayness"—the experiential basis
of human society—so that it might thereby become meaningful once
again, seem increasingly remote.

Heidegger sensed the shortcomings of traditional philosophy and developed his paradigm of *Existenz* to offset them. The promise of his
approach continues to merit our serious attention. Yet this scrutiny
must not be allowed to devolve into hagiography or uncritical devotion—constant temptations when one is confronted with a thinker of
Heidegger's singular talents. Heidegger believed his philosophy was
able to capture and convey an experience of the "primordial" (*das
Ursprüngliche*); as such, it was viscerally opposed to superficialities of
modern thought. Yet he was often unable to explain *why* the primordial itself was valuable, or why it was intrinsically superior to the more
contemporary philosophical approaches he deemed misguided. Providing "rational accounts" of his positions and preferences was never
Heidegger's forte. Despite its merits, his approach, too, possesses distinct limitations. Too often, it glorifies "immemorial experiences" and
"unreason." It remains suffused with an antidemocratic sensibility that
Heidegger himself perversely viewed as a badge of distinction. All of
these prejudices played a role in his delusional political misstep of 1933.
His supporters—on the whole, an adulatory lot—have yet to disen-

tangle the intellectual threads that precipitated his Nazi involvement. Until they do, their attempts to perpetuate his legacy will remain afflicted by many of the same oversights and conceptual imbalances. Thus, like a Greek tragedy—though on a smaller scale—the sins of the father will be visited upon the daughters and sons.

The German-Jewish Dialogue:

Way Stations of Misrecognition

Heidegger's Children is a tale of German-Jewish experience, especially among Germany's *Bildungsbürgertum* or educated middle-class elite. It helps chronicle what might be called—albeit, with the advantage of historical hindsight—the delusions of Jewish assimilationism, for Heidegger's children were non-Jewish Jews who first discovered their Jewishness amid the traumas of political anti-Semitism as institutionalized under the Third Reich.

For decades, gifted historians and critics have debated the nature of the German-Jewish experience in the aftermath of Auschwitz. Although the relevant literature continues to mount, and there can be no doubting its quality, some fifty years after the Holocaust almost all the existing narratives remain deeply unsatisfactory. No matter what explanatory tack or perspective one chooses, troublesome and contradictory propositions intervene to upset the prospects for consensus. The issue that continues to defy comprehension may be stated as follows: How could the extermination of the European Jews have been conceived and enacted by the very nation where, going back to the middle of the nineteenth century, Jews had been the most successfully integrated? As one historian has formulated the problem: "It is one of the great paradoxes and cruel ironies of recent times that the most calamitous epoch in the turbulent history of the Jews of Europe followed upon or grew out of the phase of their greatest emancipation, acculturation, and assimilation."[1]

Commentators have described the fifty-year period prior to Hitler's seizure of power as the Golden Age of European Jewry. It was at this point that Jews, taking advantage of the new liberal climate of opinion, began to shed their separate identity and integrate themselves within the mainstream of European civic, cultural, and professional life. They accomplished this end within a remarkably short time and with an astonishing degree of success. Within two generations, Jews emerged from the restrictions of ghetto life to assume leading positions in the professions, arts, and sciences. Rabbi Leo Baeck, a leading representative of the "science of Judaism," viewed modern Germany as the locus of the third golden age of Judaism, following Hellenistic Judaism prior to the destruction of the second temple and Sephardic Judaism before the expulsion from Spain. Prior to the Nazi era, thirteen out of thirty-three German Nobel prizes had been won by Jews. With the collapse of the Second Empire (1918), the last professional restrictions still in force against Jews were lifted. Enjoying full civic equality under the Weimar Republic, Jews thrived in large numbers and in ways that were unprecedented. The list of Jewish artists and writers who flourished during these years reads like a who's who of German cultural excellence: Franz Kafka, Sigmund Freud, Edmund Husserl, Max Horkheimer, Walter Benjamin, Theodor Adorno, Ernst Bloch, Georg Lukács, Alfred Döblin, Kurt Tucholsky, Arnold Schönberg, Gustav Mahler, Max Reinhart, Fritz Lang, Siegfried Kracauer, Karl Mannheim, Karl Kraus, and Joseph Roth—to list only the better known figures. In his classic study, *Behemoth: The Structure and Practice of National Socialism*, political scientist Franz Neumann set forth the provocative claim that "paradoxical as it may seem . . . *the German people are the least anti-Semitic of all*"—implying that anti-Semitism had been foisted upon an unwilling German populace by ruthless Nazi leaders.[2] Yet Jewish cultural preeminence was a source of bitter resentment among the German lower-middle class, a factor that played a far from negligible role in German Jewry's ultimate demise.

Despite these considerable successes, Jewish assimilation often came at a steep cost: for the declared precondition for Jewish acceptance by mainstream German society was the renunciation of one's Jewishness. Thus, in many cases, identification with the German virtues of *Kultur* and *Geist* mandated an abandonment of traditional Jewish concerns. Indeed, with respect to things German, many Jews became *plus royaliste que le roi*. The writer Ludwig Strauss went so far as to declare that "in a study of Goethe one finds one's Jewish substance."[3] The Zionist leader Kurt Blumenfeld once described himself as "a Zionist by grace of Goethe."[4]

When in 1782 Wilhelm Dohm published his liberal treatise *On the Civic Improvement of the Jews*, he made it clear that tolerance could be extended toward Jews only insofar as they would agree to abandon their atavistic religious practices. As the old saying went: "For the Jews as individuals, everything; for the Jews as a people (i.e., as Jews), nothing." Hence, for those who sought a way out of the ghetto, "Being a Jew became a liability, an embarrassment, a fact not to be mentioned if it could be helped."[5] When Freud, a self-declared unbeliever, posed the question: "What is there still Jewish about you if you have given up all those things that you have in common with your fellow Jews?" he could only respond: "Still a great deal, probably the main thing"—but he was never able to articulate precisely what that "thing" was.[6]

Kafka, who endowed the idea of civilization qua "dis-ease" with new eschatological meaning, once remarked that getting rid of his father's Jewishness was to him "the most effective act of piety one could perform."[7] Among the many gradations of meaning his stories and novellas encompass, the profound disorientation of Central European Jewish consciousness circa World War I is surely among the most prominent. No longer Jewish in the traditional *shetl* sense, in but not *of* the culture of their adoptive European homelands, Central European Jews were caught in a no-man's-land of identity crisis and nonbelonging. As one commentator has noted: "Without a conscious appreciation of religion, the guiding force of Jewish tradition was lost, the sense of being connected with, of being one link in the chain of generations that extended backward to the beginnings of civilized life on earth, of being part of a people of timeless significance—the People of God."[8] The great mass of assimilated Central European Jewry wagered everything on the prospect of acceptance by their non-Jewish brethren. How were they to know that, in losing the bet, they would come perilously close to forfeiting their existence as a people?

Kafka's writings gave consummate expression to the modern Jew's existential perplexity, despite the vast improvements in the quality of Jewish life in the postemancipation era. Like few of his co-religionists, he possessed keen insight into the lot of what he disparagingly referred to as the "typical Western Jew," with whom he nonetheless identified, and whom he once described in the following terms: "This means, expressed with exaggeration, that not one calm second is granted me; everything has to be earned, not only the present and the future, but the past too—something after all which perhaps every human being has inherited, this too must be earned, it is perhaps the hardest work."[9] Many Jews discovered that, while there was no question of going back to the ghetto, the path toward social acceptance remained blocked. Baptized Jews found themselves cut off from their traditional roots, yet shunned by their non-Jewish countrymen. Offspring of affluent Jewish families, so assimilated as to be indistinguishable from their gentile neighbors, found that conversion or a mixed marriage would forever bar them from their parental home. When World War I broke out, Jews viewed enlistment as a proof of national sentiment and volunteered in droves. Out of 120,000 who served, 12,000 died in battle. At stake in a German victory, declared Leo Baeck in the spirit of 1914, was "European culture and humanity."[10]

Kafka formulated his own dilemma as a Czech-born, German-speaking Jew in terms of what he called "three impossibilities": "The impossibility of not writing, the impossibility of writing in German, the impossibility of writing differently." (On occasion, he would add as a "fourth impossibility": "the impossibility of writing.")[11] Whereas the progressivist doctrines of liberalism suggested that Jewish efforts to assimilate would be repaid with professional success and broad social acceptance, the realities of Central European life decreed a different, more sinister outcome.

Even the so-called "Golden Age" of German-Jewish relations was marred by ominous portents and developments. Anti-Semitism, which, according to enlightened opinion, was a medieval atavism destined to be swept away by the march of progress, gained a new and potent hold on European political life. Racial anti-Semitism burgeoned into an ideology that claimed to hold the key to the antagonisms and contradictions of modern life in its entirety. In an age of disbelief, it took on a quasi-eschatological cast. Saul Friedländer has coined the phrase "redemptive anti-Semitism" to describe its functional status as a worldview in which Jews were perceived as responsible for the iniquities of modern civilization *in toto*. "From the eighteenth century on,"

Friedländer observes, "new conspiracy theories pointed to threats from a number of occult groups: Freemasons, Illuminati, Jesuits. . . . Within this array of occult forces, the Jews were the plotters par excellence, the manipulators hidden behind all other secret groups that were merely their instruments."[12] Given the fractious nature of German political life, in which confessional, cultural, and regional divisions frequently outweighed allegiances to Berlin, anti-Semitism's potential as a unifying political force could hardly be underestimated.

For the anti-Semites, only the Jews' wholesale removal would be a cure appropriate to the virulence of modernity qua "dis-ease." Prior to the war, Vienna's anti-Semitic mayor, Karl Lueger, gave voice to the standard complaints against disproportionate Jewish influence in contemporary European life when he intoned:

> In Vienna there are as many Jews as there are grains of sand on the seashore; wherever you go, nothing but Jews; if you go to the theater, nothing but Jews; if you take a walk in the Ringstrasse, nothing but Jews; if you enter the Stadtpark, nothing but Jews; if you go to a concert, nothing but Jews; if you go to a ball, nothing but Jews; if you go to the university, nothing but Jews. We are not shouting *Hep, hep, hep*, but we strongly object to the fact that in the place of the old Christian Austrian Empire a new Kingdom of Palestine should be arising.[13]

In 1912, Pan-German League president Heinrich Class published a celebrated pamphlet, *If I Were the Kaiser*, in which he set forth a program for the complete elimination of Jews from German public life—civil service, politics, the professions, banking, and commerce—that in many respects foreshadowed the anti-Semitic legislation decreed by the Nazis at Nuremberg. As World War I drew to a close and German defeat became imminent, Class urged a "ruthless campaign against Jewry, against which the all too justified wrath of our good, but misled, people must be directed."[14] As the "ideas of 1914"—polemically directed against those of "1789" and central to the ideology of the "German way"—were radicalized with the defeat of four years hence, the conception of the Jews as a "domestic enemy" gained acceptance among nationalistically inclined Germans.

Thus, when the elegist of the German "front experience," Ernst Jünger, observed in 1930 that, "The Jew can play a creative role in nothing at all that concerns German life, neither in what is good nor in what is evil," he merely gave voice to the widespread conviction that, in spite of their efforts to assimilate, Jews could never become "real" Germans.[15] Jünger thereby perpetuated a credo that had been articulated eighty years earlier by Richard Wagner in "Das Judentum in der Musik": since Jews dwelled parasitically among other nations, they were devoid of authentic "culture"; hence, they could never be genuinely creative. As is well known, Wagner concluded the essay prophetically by observing that the only solution to the troublesome Jewish question would be (following the precedent of Ahasverus) the Jews' *annihilation* (*Untergang*).[16]

In the mid-1930s, the legal philosopher Carl Schmitt, who in his earlier work emphasized the importance of racial homogeneity (*Artgleichheit*) and the need to annihilate the "domestic enemy," opened a conference of German jurists with the declaration: "We need to liberate the German spirit from all Jewish falsifications, falsifications of the concept of spirit which have made it possible for Jewish emigrants to label the great struggle of Gauleiter Julius Streicher as something unspiritual."[17] Hitler had initiated the process of Jewish de-emancipation shortly after his seizure of power. To German Jews, it seemed like merely another temporary setback on the long march out of the ghetto. Who could have suspected that anything as unthinkable as a "Final Solution" lay in store?

Following the *Anschluss*, Wittgenstein, who hailed from an assimilated, upper-crust Viennese family, remarked that the laws of the Third Reich had finally succeeded in turning him into a German Jew.[18] It was a reaction shared by a good number of assimilated Jews who experienced their own Jewishness for the first time under the sign of Nazi persecution. Yet, as the Zionists frequently argued, Jews who voluntarily exchanged their traditional allegiances for the trappings of improved social standing were often deluded about the social implications of their success. Consequently, as the 1930s unfolded, many assimilated Jews were unprepared for the tragic course of the events that followed—though in one of history's sad ironies, it was often the better-off, assimilated Jews who were able to buy their way out of Hitler's Germany, while their impoverished brethren perished in great numbers.

Often, the assimilated Jew's inordinate attachment to things German functioned as an elaborate compensatory mechanism, an ersatz religion. As Isaiah Berlin has aptly observed, viewed psychologically, the passion with which Jewish intellectuals and artists identified with German traditions was often "the result of an inadequate sense of kinship and a desire to have the rift forgotten; since the more insurmountable it was, the greater was the desire to overcome it, or to behave as though it did not exist."[19] In the words of Gershom Scholem: "The unending Jewish demand for a home was transformed into *the illusion of being at home. . . .* During the generations preceding the catastrophe the German Jews . . . distinguished themselves by an astounding lack of critical insight into their own situation."[20] In contrast with the standard efforts to celebrate Jewish influences on German culture as a process of mutual enrichment, Scholem perceived a one-way street that ultimately redounded to Judaism's distinct disadvantage. He hyperbolically characterized the frequently romanticized "German-Jewish symbiosis" as a series of "continuous bloodlettings, through which the Jews lost their most advanced elements to the Germans."[21] Echoing Scholem's resignation, the historian Dan Diner described German-Jewish relations as an example of *"negative symbiosis."*[22]

In a similarly skeptical vein, a more recent chronicler of German-Jewish relations has questioned the mutuality of the German-Jewish dialogue. After all: How can there be a dialogue when one of the parties refuses to listen?

> The disappearance of the ghettos, the granting of civil rights to Jews, their entry into society, and their adoption of the German language gave rise to a German-Jewish culture, which, however, was never the result of a genuine symbiosis. Instead of inaugurating a dialogue between Jews and Germans, assimilation led immediately to a *Jewish monologue*, which took place in the Germanic world, was expressed in the German language, and was nourished by the German cultural legacy, but which, in fact, was carried on in a void.[23]

With the benefit of hindsight, it is easy for latecomers to glean portents of doom that were indiscernible to those experiencing the events firsthand. When all is said and done, Fritz Stern's critical gloss on the

German-Jewish nexus seems fair-minded, as well as psychoanalytically apt: "The spiritual stance of German Jewry can perhaps best be described by the word *ambivalence*: ambivalence about themselves, ambivalence about the Germans, ambivalence about their role in German life."[24]

Conventional wisdom has it that the Weimar Republic facilitated a triumph of "outsiders"—modernists, socialists, and Jews; that, for Jews, the sudden dismantling of cultural and legal barriers resulted in an unprecedented integration within the parameters of German society, giving rise to a Jewish cultural renaissance that assumed predominantly secular hues. But this description, while accurate in part, hardly captures the whole story.

In Germany, during the 1920s, Jewish culture itself experienced a remarkable resurgence. To the chagrin of German Jewry, in the aftermath of the Great War, decades of rabid political anti-Semitism gained a new lease on life. (Widespread acceptance of the "stab-in-the-back" myth represented only one index thereof.) Whereas during the first half of the nineteenth century, Jews had been shunned because of their "backwardness," as assimilation progressed they were scorned as parvenus who had lost touch with their own traditions. Confronted with these painful circumstances and developments, for many German Jews, dreams of successful integration went up in smoke. In fact, one may justifiably speak of a process of *dissimilation*: a conscious abandonment of the delusory promises of assimilation and a corresponding quest for a meaningful Jewish identity.[25]

The dissimilation process began in the years prior to World War I. Circa 1900, Martin Buber challenged Jews to rise to the challenge of a "Jewish Renaissance," which he defined as "the resurrection of the Jewish people from partial life to full life."[26] A few years later, he published a collection of Hasidic tales from eighteenth-century Poland, a summons to Jewish authenticity that had enormous resonance. Throughout the nineteenth century, as Jews strove to abandon their rituals and traditions in order to assimilate, the *Ostjuden* had represented a type of anachronistic embarrassment. But the persistence of anti-Semitism spurred a reassessment of their relation to the dominant culture. Hence, increasingly, it was the assimilated, Germanized Jews who were adjudged inauthentic, devoid of genuine Jewish selfhood, and their "primitive" Eastern European brethren who now seemed to embody an authentic Jewish spirit. From them, their well-adapted German co-religionists stood to learn much.

The Jewish Renaissance during the Weimar years was a phenomenon that assumed diverse cultural hues. Buber and Franz Rosenzweig sought to recast Jewish thought in existential terms that would meet the spiritual needs of Central European Jewry. The tradition of Jewish mysticism underwent a revival. In Frankfurt, Rosenzweig became the inaugural director of the *Freies Jüdisches Lehrhaus*, which focused on the needs of adult education. Through Lehrhaus course offerings, many assimilated Jews experienced the sacred texts of Judaism—Torah and Talmud—for the first time. There was even a resurgence of literature and painting dealing with indigenous Jewish themes. As the Zionist author Moritz Goldstein implored fellow Jews on the eve of World War I: "The Jewish drama, the Jewish novel has not yet been written. The creation of a new type of Jew—not in real life, but in literature—is of utmost importance in this respect. We all see life, people, and nature as our artists present them to us. . . . Jewish writers, to work!"[27] Ismar Schorsch has summarized these developments as follows: "If one sector of the community is indeed best accounted for in terms of spiritual bankruptcy, the behavior of another sector constituted a dramatic polar opposite, whose singular achievement was to deepen and culminate the development of a distinct Jewish subculture in a relatively open and voluntaristic setting."[28] During the 1930s, as Hitler consolidated his grip on power and Nazi anti-Semitic measures expanded, the search for a meaningful Jewish identity became an urgent cultural imperative among Germany's remaining Jews, who had been banned from virtually all walks of German civic life. Soon it became clear that all hopes for a *modus vivendi* with the Third Reich were chimerical. But, of course, for most of Central European Jewry, this realization came too late.

FIG. 1. Hannah Arendt in 1933.

Hannah Arendt:

Kultur, "Thoughtlessness," and Polis Envy

Explaining Totalitarianism

IN 1945, Thomas Mann gave a memorable speech at the Library of Congress entitled "Germany and the Germans." Attempting to come to grips with the so-called German catastrophe—which, had it been confined to the Germans alone, might not have been nearly so catastrophic—he observed: "There are not two Germanys, an evil and a good, but only one, which through devil's cunning, transformed its best into evil."[1] Mann realized that the horrors of Nazism could not be attributed to an arbitrary instance of mass hypnosis. The problem was not just Hitler or "Hitlerism," but the fact that a vast majority of Germans had consciously and willingly met their infamous Führer halfway. Hitler's seizure of power was not some kind of unforeseeable "industrial accident" or *Betriebsunfall*, as postwar Germans were fond of claiming, that befell the nation from outside and that left German traditions unscathed. Instead, the genocidal imperialism that the Nazis unleashed upon Europe represented the consummation of certain long-term trends of German history itself. It was in this spirit that Mann, in "On Germany and the Germans," implored his countrymen not to go too easy on themselves. Instead they needed to plumb the depths of their national patrimony, from Herder to Heidegger, in order to ferret out and confront those specifically German delusions that facilitated disaster.

Both Hannah Arendt and Martin Heidegger set forth accounts of the

German calamity. Both were adamant about interpreting Nazism primarily as a European phenomenon rather than as typically German, an approach that has certain merit. After all, Germany was far from alone in opting for a fascist-authoritarian solution to the political ills of the interwar period. At the same time, this position's interpretive weakness lies in the fact that it systematically underestimates the Germanic specificity of the Third Reich.

To say that Arendt's explanation was the more successful, despite its flaws, is hardly controversial. In many respects, Heidegger's own narrative was simply delusory, a retrospectively contrived psychological prophylaxis against his own enthusiastic support for the regime. In Heidegger's view, everything that came to pass—the war, the extermination camps, the German dictatorship (which he never renounced per se)—was merely a monumental instance of the "forgetting of Being," for which the Germans bore no special responsibility. After the war, he went so far as to insist that German fascism was unique among Western political movements in that, for one shining moment, it had come close to mastering the vexatious "relationship between planetary technology and modern man." In Heidegger's estimation, therein lay the "inner truth and greatness of National Socialism." But ultimately "these people [the Nazis] were far too limited in their thinking," he claimed.[2] Pathetically, Heidegger was left to replay in his own mind the way things might have been had Hitler (instead of party hacks) heeded the call of Being as relayed by Heidegger himself. Nazism might thereby have realized its genuine historical potential. Fortunately, the world was spared the outcome of this particular thought experiment.

Arendt set forth her account in *The Origins of Totalitarianism*, a work that deservedly earned her an international reputation. In *Origins*, Arendt identified the most important phenomenon of twentieth-century politics. As a form of political rule, totalitarianism was a *novum* whose structures and practices were unprecedented. The regimes of Stalin and Hitler differed qualitatively from traditional tyrannies, which, as a rule, left a compliant civil population in domestic peace. Not so these modern dictatorships, which, in keeping with a spirit of total mobilization, demanded the active complicity of their subjects. The images of these regimes most likely to endure are the choreographed mass rallies staged by Hitler and Mussolini, immortalized in films like Riefenstahl's *Triumph of the Will*. In these spectacles, pliable human material was to be sculpted (to employ one of Mussolini's pet metaphors) into a form suitable for totalitarian rule.

Arendt captured the predominant features of the totalitarian experience as no one had before. But her analysis contained glaring weaknesses that left subsequent generations of scholars confused. Her account was divided into three main headings: anti-Semitism, imperialism, and totalitarianism. She scorned the traditional method of causal historical explanation—the idea that certain historical circumstances were produced by determinant antecedent variables—as deterministic. Instead, in the tradition of the *Geisteswissenschaften*, she held that whereas the natural sciences "explain," in the writing of history we seek to "understand." She thus characterized anti-Semitism and imperialism as "elements" that, at a certain point, "crystallized" into modern totalitarian practice.

Yet what it was that catalyzed this mysterious process of crystallization remained murky in her account. To wit: there have been numerous historical formations in which the elements of anti-Semitism and imperialism had been prominent, though nothing resembling totalitarianism emerged. Historically speaking, there have been only two genuinely totalitarian societies: Nazi Germany and the Soviet Union under Stalin.[3] In both cases, concentration camps were emblematic. *Origins*, however, suffered from a massive imbalance. Part III on totalitarianism dealt almost exclusively with National Socialism. The discussion of Stalinism was appended as though it were an afterthought. Moreover, whereas National Socialism and its horrendous crimes would be inconceivable without anti-Semitism, which was the linchpin of Nazi ideology, in the worldview of Bolshevism it played a negligible role. If, then, one of the essential elements is entirely absent in one of the main instances of totalitarian rule, what kind of explanatory power might the model as a whole retain?

Moreover, in *Origins* Arendt's "Jewish problem"—that is, her problem with her own Jewish identity—was apparent in a way that foreshadowed the terms of the Eichmann controversy some twelve years hence. Already the lines between perpetrators and victims had been blurred. The Jews were faulted for being an apolitical people—as if that were a lot they had chosen. Arendt concluded that, in many instances, the Jews had foolishly brought historical persecution upon themselves.[4] Jewish arrogance, in the form of the myth of the chosen people and the "in-group–out-group" mentality in which it found historical expression, played a prominent role in her narrative. From this perspective, it would not require too large a logical leap to arrive at the rather perverse judgment that, in certain respects, the Jews deserved their fate, just as the protagonists of Greek tragedies can be said to have deserved their fate. Although Arendt had not yet explored the complex interrelationship between the Jewish Councils, collaboration, and (non-) resistance, in many respects the theoretical groundwork for some of the more controversial features of the Eichmann book had been established.

A Dangerous Liaison

Not only did Arendt have a Jewish problem, she also had a "Heidegger problem." In many respects, the two were integrally related. The amorous liaison during the 1920s between Heidegger and Arendt has been public knowledge for years. The contours of their affair, however, have remained an object of speculation. The recently published Heidegger-Arendt correspondence offers important insight into the dynamics of their libidinal entanglement—and an "entanglement" it was.

At the time their affair began in 1925, Heidegger was a thirty-five-year-old father of two who had already acquired the reputation, despite a scanty publication record, as a philosophical *wunderkind*. He was known colloquially as the "magician of Messkirch" (Heidegger's birthplace), and students from all over Germany flocked to his courses in droves. To avoid the crunch, he scheduled his lectures at the crack of dawn. Karl Löwith once described Heidegger's seductive podium persona as follows:

> We gave Heidegger the nickname "the little magician from Messkirch." . . . He was a small dark man who knew how to cast a spell insofar as he could make disappear what he had a moment before presented. His lecture technique consisted in building up

an edifice of ideas which he then proceeded to tear down, presenting the spellbound listeners with a riddle and then leaving them empty-handed. This ability to cast a spell at times had very considerable consequences: it attracted more or less pathological personality types, and, after three years of guessing at riddles, one student took her own life.[5]

At the time, Arendt was a far cry from the proud New York intellectual warrior she would become later in life. She was a frail eighteen-year-old from the East Prussian city of Königsberg. Though she hailed from a well-to-do, assimilated Jewish family, Hannah experienced her share of hard knocks at an early age. Her father died a prolonged, horrible death from syphilis in 1913, his agonies extending from Arendt's second to seventh year. Several months before her father's death, her beloved maternal grandfather also died. A few years later, her mother remarried. Overnight, the precocious young Hannah acquired two half-sisters with whom she had precious little in common. Her sense of displacement was no doubt acute. In an impassioned, youthful autobiographical tract portentously titled "The Shadows," she lamented her "helpless, betrayed youth."[6]

The liaison between Arendt and Heidegger was dangerous because, in the idyllic university town of Marburg, Heidegger could have been dismissed from his teaching position had the lovers been found out. Heidegger had already acquired a considerable reputation, in the Socratic tradition, as a seducer of youth. His wife, Elfride, was notoriously jealous, especially of the train of female students who were mesmerized by Heidegger's spell. She was also a notorious anti-Semite. In the 1920s, she once suggested to Günther Stern—soon to become Arendt's first husband—that he enlist in a local Nazi youth group. When Stern replied that he was Jewish, Frau Heidegger merely turned away in disgust.

Heidegger and Arendt were an unlikely couple: she, the fetching young Jewish woman from a Baltic-cosmopolitan milieu; he, the Schwarzwalder, a lapsed Catholic and convinced provincial. According to Elzbieta Ettinger, Arendt's exotic Eastern features "stood in stark contrast to the Teutonic Brunhildas he was close to: his mother and his wife."[7] In one of his more fatuous texts of the 1930s, "Why We Remain in the Provinces," Heidegger delivered a humorless encomium to the joys of provincial life. Today, the essay reads like a parody: "Let us stop all this condescending familiarity and sham concern for Volk-character and let us learn to take seriously that simple, rough existence up there."[8] As a rule, this *völkisch* mentality went hand in hand with a broadly shared anti-Semitism. Unfortunately, Heidegger remained true to the stereotype. In his infamous 1933 Freiburg University rectoral address, he was at pains to eulogize the "forces that are rooted in the soil and blood of the [German] Volk."[9] A letter of reference from 1929 shows him lamenting the rampant "Jewification" ("Verjudung") of the German spirit—some four years prior to the advent of Nazi rule. And in a recently unearthed letter from 1933, Heidegger proffers a crude ideological denunciation of the Jewish philosopher Richard Hönigswald:

> Hönigswald comes from the neo-Kantian school which stands for a philosophy that is tailor-made for liberalism. The essence of man is dissolved into a free-floating consciousness and this, in the end, is thinned down to a general, logical world-reason. On this path, on an apparently rigorous scientific basis, the path turns away from man in his historical rootedness and his national [*volkhaft*] belonging to his origin in earth and blood [*Boden und Blut*]. Together with this goes a conscious forcing back of all metaphysical questioning, and man is counted as nothing more than a functionary of an indifferent, general world-culture. This is the fundamental stance from which Hönigswald's writings stem.[10]

This letter portrays a worldview that, if not quite Nazi, was capable of reconciling itself seamlessly with National Socialist aims and goals.

Some commentators have pointed to Heidegger's dalliance with Arendt, combined with his cordial relationships with other Jewish students, as evidence of a philo-Semitic streak. Yet Heidegger had no compunction about serving on the board of the Academy for German Law with the likes of Julius Streicher, chief purveyor of Nazi anti-Semitic pornography and editor of *Der Stürmer*. The board's president, Hans Frank, was the future German governor of Poland. Later, both Streicher and Frank were convicted at Nuremberg of "crimes against humanity." The Academy's avowed credo was to reestablish the basis of German law in accordance with the principles of "Race, State, Führer, Blood, [and] Authority." Heidegger labored in the company of such men until 1936, a good two years after he had resigned his Freiburg rectorship. By then he had severed ties with all of his former Jewish students.[11]

It seems that Heidegger's relationship with Arendt, while not without tenderness, was profoundly exploitative. Given their discrepancies in age, social standing, and background, it could hardly have been otherwise. It was Heidegger who initiated the affair. Arendt, an impressionable eighteen-year-old, was clearly awestruck by this formidable embodiment of *Geist*, a man nearly twice her age. Ettinger reconstructs the prehistory of their acquaintanceship as follows:

That Hannah Arendt was drawn to [Heidegger] is not surprising. Given the powerful influence he exerted on his students it was almost inevitable. Neither her past—that of a fatherless, searching youngster—nor her vulnerable, melancholic nature prepared her to withstand Heidegger's determined effort to win her heart. She shared the insecurity of many assimilated Jews who were still uncertain about their place, still harboring doubts about themselves. By choosing her as his beloved, Heidegger fulfilled for Hannah the dream of generations of German Jews, going back to such pioneers of assimilation as Rahel Varnhagen.[12]

The two met clandestinely (usually in Arendt's Marburg student garret), at Heidegger's urging, in accordance with the demands of his schedule. Inevitably, the demands of secrecy became confusing and burdensome to both. Approximately a year after the affair began, Arendt decided to transfer to another university. She viewed the move as an act of self-sacrifice on Heidegger's behalf. As she explained in a letter, she reached this decision, "because of my love for you, to make nothing more difficult than it already was."[13] But it seems that Heidegger was also pressuring her to leave, while hoping that they could continue their surreptitious rendezvous under circumstances in which the likelihood of their being discovered would be diminished. To facilitate this end, Heidegger arranged for Arendt to study with his friend Karl Jaspers in Heidelberg.

Though Arendt's departure from Marburg was nominally voluntary, she was clearly wounded by Heidegger's callous treatment. It was as though he had repaid her intimacy and trust by summarily banishing her. Upon moving to Heidelberg, she retaliated by refusing to provide him with her new address. At this point, Heidegger seized the initiative and sent one of his students, Hans Jonas, to seek her out. Arendt's trysts with Heidegger continued for another two years at forlorn whistle-stops along the Marburg-Heidelberg railway line. Shortly after Heidegger received his permanent appointment at Freiburg in 1928, he abruptly broke off the affair. In response to the bitter news, Arendt ended her letter with a melodramatic premonition: "'And with God's will / I will love you more after death.'"[14] But her threat, if it actually was one, was never carried out. The following year, she married Günther Stern (soon to become Günther Anders).

To the very end, however, Arendt remained in Heidegger's thrall. In 1974, the year before her death, she wrote to him, in barely sublimated code: "No one can deliver a lecture the way you do, nor did anyone before you."[15] And when they reconciled following the war, Heidegger confided to Arendt that she had been "the passion of his life."[16]

Negative Symbiosis

Inevitably, in the late 1920s, Arendt's Jewish problem came to the fore, as it would for so many other assimilated German Jews. For many, the realization that, in the eyes of their German acquaintances, they were more Jewish than German—despite their ardent attempts at acculturation—came as a shock. It must have been especially painful to discover their own Jewishness for the first time via the acid bath of anti-Semitism. To express this dilemma in Sartrian terms, their Jewishness had been "constituted" by the gaze of anti-Semites.[17] Suddenly, they were forced to confront the fact that the lives they were leading had been predicated on a series of illusions—above all, the illusion that they were as German as any of their non-Jewish fellow citizens. The process of disillusionment was particularly bitter for well-educated Jews, who labored under the delusion that German culture or *Bildung* was the great equalizer, their "entry ticket" to the privileges of German society.

Arendt's biography fit squarely within this mold. She, too, had be-

lieved that, if one only tried hard enough to internalize the virtues of
Geist, the doors to German society would magically open: "Jews who
wanted 'culture' left Judaism at once, and completely, even though
most of them remained conscious of their Jewish origins," she once
remarked.[18] As she told an interviewer in 1964: "As a child I did not
know that I was Jewish. . . . The word 'Jew' was never mentioned at
home when I was a child. I first met up with it through anti-Semitic
remarks . . . from children on the street. After that I was, so to speak,
'enlightened.'" When in the course of the same interview she was
asked what remained of her German upbringing, she responded:
"What remains? The language remains."[19] Thirty years prior to Auschwitz, Kafka, with preternatural foresight, arrived at a considerably
more ambiguous verdict concerning the virtues his native tongue: "Yes-
terday it occurred to me that I did not always love my mother as she
deserved and as I could, only because the German language prevented
it. The Jewish mother is no 'Mutter,' to call her 'Mutter' makes her a
little comic. . . . 'Mutter' is peculiarly German for the Jew, it unconsciously contains, together with the Christian splendor, Christian
coldness."[20]

Arendt characterized problems of Jewish identity as "perplexing,
troubling, and evasive."[21] She described her Jewishness as an indubitable
fact. As she put it: "I belong to [the Jewish people] as a matter of
course, beyond dispute or argument."[22] But whether Jewishness had
much significance for her beyond this ontological "being-so-and-not-
otherwise" is doubtful. As Richard Bernstein has pointed out, the preceding declaration "is not to answer to the question of Jewish identity,
but to evade it."[23] Indeed, beyond such perfunctory declarations of a
shared existential fate—a Jewish counterpart to the German idea of
Schicksalgemeinschaft (a "community of fate")—her reflections on matters of Jewish identity are notably lacking in substance. As a rule, Arendt adhered to a problematic separation between "Jewishness" qua
brute ontological datum and "Judaism" qua religion—an idea that, she
admits frankly, never held much of an attraction for her. What it is that
remains of "Jewishness" when one has jettisoned "Judaism" was a matter she never addressed.

In the eyes of their fellow Germans, those Jews who avidly pursued
Bildung never shed their taint as social climbers or parvenus. The more

successfully Jews integrated themselves within the framework of German society, the more strident—and politically well-organized—grew their anti-Semitic detractors. Whereas an earlier generation of anti-Semites had decreed that the criterion for admission to German society was that Jews relinquish their "national peculiarities"—essentially, that they become Germans instead of Jews[24]—for a later generation, that demand no longer sufficed. Instead, according to the new doctrine of racial anti-Semitism, try as they might, Jews as a nation or race could never become German. Illustrative of this trend was the fact that Wilhelm Marr's inflammatory 1879 tract, *The Triumph of Judaism over Germanism*, went through twelve editions in six years. As Marr declared, giving voice to the new racialist credo: "There must be no question of parading religious prejudices when it is a question of *race* and when the differences lie in *blood*."[25] Ironically, whereas previously Jews had been criticized for remaining too attached to their medieval rites and ghetto mores, during the Second Empire they were scorned for having abandoned their traditional Jewish backgrounds and trying to "pass for German"—in essence, for being a people without an identity.

The leading representatives of German classicism—Kant, Herder, Goethe, and Wilhelm von Humboldt—viewed *Bildung* as a sublime cosmopolitan-democratic ideal; its substance was, in principle, accessible to everyone who persevered, Germans and Jews alike. Jewish intellectuals and religious leaders revered the classical period as a golden age of German spiritual life; they gave themselves body and soul to its precepts and promises. German Jews were allegedly "Jewish by the grace of Goethe," an edition of whose collected works had, for liberal Jews, become a standard bar mitzvah gift. As late as 1915, the philosopher Hermann Cohen expressed this trust as follows: "Every German must know his Schiller and his Goethe and carry them in his heart with the intimacy of love. But this intimacy presupposes that he has won a rudimentary understanding of Kant."[26]

Yet a later generation of Germans emphatically turned their backs on the universal designs of *Bildung*, shamelessly glorifying instead the virtues of German particularism. The historian Heinrich von Treitschke, who coined the infamous slogan, "The Jews are our misfortune," vigorously lent his energies and reputation to the anti-Semitic campaigns of the *Gründerzeit*. For von Treitschke, the attacks against the Jews were merely a "brutal but natural reaction of German *national* feeling against a foreign element."[27]

Many Jews believed—in retrospect, naively—that World War I presented a golden opportunity to prove their loyalty as German citizens. Instead, they met with recriminations, the infamous wartime census, and the "stab-in-the-back" myth—all of which were a sad harbinger of trends to come.

With the economic collapse of 1929 and the Nazis' stunning electoral success of the following year, the demise of the fragile Weimar Republic became imminent. A turning point in the course of German history had occurred. The rationalizations of earlier years abruptly ceased to hold and, for Jews, a wholesale reorientation was required. During the 1920s, anti-Semitism had become an article of faith among Germany's so-called "national revolutionaries." Ernst Jünger gave voice to a belief that was widely shared when, doing von Treitschke one better, he remarked circa 1930 that, "To the same extent that the German will gains in sharpness and shape, it becomes increasingly impossible for the Jews to entertain even the slightest delusion that they can be Germans in Germany; they are faced with their final alternatives, which are, in Germany, either to be Jewish or not to be."[28]

How, then, might one evaluate this momentous transformation from traditional, religion-based anti-Semitism to its modern, mass-political variant? The historian Peter Pulzer aptly summarizes these developments as follows: "The audience's vague and irrational image of the Jew as the enemy probably did not change much when the orators stopped talking about 'Christ-slayers' and began talking about the laws of blood. The difference lay in the effect achieved. It enabled anti-Semitism to be more elemental and uncompromising. Its logical conclusion was to substitute the gas chamber for the pogrom."[29]

Caritas *and* Existenz

In 1928, Arendt wrote a dissertation, under Jaspers' supervision, on Saint Augustine's concept of love. The essay represented an orthodox phenomenological reconsideration of Augustine's doctrines. Faithful to the training she had received from Heidegger and Jaspers, the demigods of German *Existenzphilosophie*, she gave existential questions pride of place in her study. Arendt addressed the quandary of how one might reconcile a theory of this-worldly, neighborly love with Augustine's conviction that an authentic relation to the world must be thoroughly mediated by one's relationship to God. With this focus, Arendt attempted to work through the problem of "Being-with-others"—a key category in *Being and Time*—as it pertained to Augustine's doctrines.[30]

The pathos of Augustine's conversion experience bore marked affinities with the concerns of existentialism. It resonated in Heidegger's notion of "authentic resolve" as well as in Jaspers' concept of the "limit-situation." In a post-Nietzschean, atheological spirit, however, both thinkers tried to translate such religious sentiment into secular terms. For Heidegger, it pertained, above all, to the isolated individual's authenticity in confronting his or her own existential nothingness or death.

Arendt's work also contains an implicit critique of Heidegger, both as a philosopher and as a person. In a footnote, Arendt faults her mentor (and former paramour) for his impoverished phenomenological understanding of the concept of "world." For Heidegger, she suggests, "world" has become an utterly impersonal and loveless notion. As such, his description of it threatens to backslide into the "objectivating" discourse that *Being and Time* sought to surmount. Thus Arendt declares that, for Heidegger, "world" has become *"ens in toto*, the decisive How, according to which human existence relates to, and acts toward, the *ens"*—a characterization that, in her view, barely transcends what it means to be "ready-to-hand." Conversely, her stated aim in the dissertation is to develop a dimension of "world" that Heidegger has neglected: *"the world conceived as the lovers of the world* [view it],"[31] adumbrations of which she claims to find in the early Christian ideal of *caritas*, which figures prominently in the *Confessions*. Given the intensity of their affair and the trauma of their parting, the autobiographical implications of Arendt's focus are not hard to discern.

Arendt published the dissertation in 1929 to mixed reviews. Theologians were put off by her unwillingness to take the existing literature into account. All in all, it is a strikingly un-Arendtian document; the inflections of her mature philosophical voice are barely audible. It is the work of a disciple, narrowly textual in orientation and focus, devoid of the originality that would characterize her subsequent work. In certain respects, the work stands out as an embarrassing testimonial to the delusions of assimilationism. It was written at a point in Arendt's life when she still entertained hopes of a university career amid the woefully conservative milieu of German academic mandarins.[32]

Some commentators have claimed that the Augustine study foreshadows Arendt's mature philosophical concerns. It contains, for example, hints of her concept of "natality"—the uniquely human capacity to establish new beginnings. Yet, on closer inspection, the argument for intellectual continuity proves difficult to sustain; for whereas the later Arendt is known primarily as a philosopher of "worldliness," such concerns are hard to reconcile with an orientation as manifestly otherworldly as Augustine's. Moreover, Augustine's commitment to the values of transcendence undermines Arendt's attempt to interpret his doctrine in terms that are meaningful from the standpoint of human intersubjectivity or community. In *Love and Saint Augustine*, Arendt seeks to develop a notion of neighborly love in conjunction with a doctrine for which "worldliness" is the equivalent of "temptation." For Augustine, love of one's neighbor must never be intrinsic or for its own sake. Such love would merely be sinful. Instead, neighborly love, the virtues of human community, must always be mediated by our all-encompassing relationship to God. As Arendt herself recognizes: "This very faith will thrust the individual in isolation from his fellow individuals in the divine presence. . . . Faith takes man *out of the world*, that is, out of a certain community of men, the *civitas terrena*."[33] The notion of community that Arendt discovers in Augustine is morbid and oblique, drenched in a veil of theological tears: it is that mournful community of the fallen or sinful who can trace their lineage back to the first sinner, Adam. As Arendt expresses it: "Humanity's common descent is its common share in original sin. This sinfulness, conferred with birth, necessarily attaches to everyone. There is no escape from it. It is the same in all people. The equality of the situation means that all are sinful."[34]

The conceptual divide separating this *Jugendschrift* from Arendt's later concerns has been best articulated by the philosopher herself. In *The Human Condition* (1958), she openly polemicizes against the "worldlessness" of the early Christian *civitas dei*—as exemplified by the work of Augustine—in contrast with the genuine human achievements of "plurality" and "publicness":

> To find a bond between people strong enough to replace the world was the main political task of early Christian philosophy and it was Augustine who proposed to found not only Christian brotherhood but all human relationships on charity. . . . The bond of charity between people, *while it is incapable of founding a public realm of its own*, is quite adequate to the main Christian principle of *worldlessness* and admirably fit to carry a group of *essentially worldless people through the world.*[35]

Moreover, in Arendt's subsequent study of Rahel Varnhagen, a Berlin Jew, she developed withering critiques of both the delusions of "introspection"—the psychological corollary to "worldlessness"—and the false consciousness of Jewish assimilationism. There can be no doubt about the fact that such criticisms were meant as a harsh rejection of Arendt's own youthful Germanophilia. Thus, for compelling biographical reasons, her polemical repudiation of the Augustine study could hardly have been more explicit. After all, in Augustine it is only via introspection—"the turn to the inner voice of conscience," as he puts it—that we begin to abandon the temptations of worldliness in favor of the eternal life of salvation. Conversely, in the Varnhagen study, Arendt associated introspection with a meretricious and self-deluded *worldlessness*. As a psychic mechanism of denial, introspection preserves a semblance of inner autonomy while endorsing a fatal indifference to worldly concerns. Ultimately, it represents a form of narcissistic self-deception: "Lying can obliterate the outside event which introspection has already converted into a purely psychic factor. Lying takes up the heritage of introspection, sums it up, and makes a reality of the freedom that introspection has won."[36]

Rahel Varnhagen: From Parvenu to Pariah

Following the traumatic breakup with Heidegger, Arendt bid an unsentimental farewell to German philosophy. Heidegger's brusque rejection undoubtedly enhanced her sense of Jewish inferiority. In her own mind, she must have wondered what role her Jewishness had played in their parting. As the Weimar Republic tottered toward the brink of collapse, many issues must have been confused in her mind. German philosophy, which she had once assumed to be her calling, now seemed fully implicated in the deteriorating political situation. On a personal level, Arendt was shocked at the remarkable ease with which the leading representatives of German *Kultur* had, overnight, metamorphosed into convinced Nazis and anti-Semites. In 1933, after Heidegger had become Nazi rector of Freiburg University and assumed responsibility for instituting anti-Jewish decrees, Arendt sent him an accusatory letter. In a later interview, she expressed her profound disillusionment with her fellow German intellectuals in unequivocal terms:

> The problem . . . was not what our enemies did but what our friends did. In the wave of *Gleichschaltung* [the Nazification of German society], which was relatively voluntary—in any case, not yet under the pressure of terror—it was as if an empty space formed around one. I lived in an intellectual milieu, but I also knew other people. And among intellectuals *Gleichschaltung* was the rule, so to speak. But not among the others. And I never forgot that. I left Germany dominated by the idea—of course somewhat exaggerated: Never again! I shall never again get involved in any kind of intellectual business. I want nothing to do with that lot.[37]

In retrospect, it would seem that she conceived this indictment with Heidegger's case foremost in mind.

Arendt's circumstantially compelled confrontation with her own heretofore repressed Jewish identity led to a dramatic shift in her intellectual interests. As soon as she had finished the Augustine dissertation, she began research on a biographical study of the Enlightenment *maitresse de salon*, Rahel Varnhagen. The book's subtitle, "The Life of a Jewess," was indicative of Arendt's new area of concern. Only in hindsight, and in light of what we now know about her star-crossed romance with Heidegger, does the profoundly autobiographical tenor of the Varnhagen book become clear.

Varnhagen's story was that of a woman who, like Arendt, had for a long time struggled to keep her Jewish identity at a distance through the rationalizations and delusions of *Innerlichkeit* or "inwardness." In the end, however, she learned—like her biographer—to reconcile herself to her pariah status as a Jewish woman in the midst of an unaccepting and at times actively hostile Gentile society. Rahel's dying words, as recounted by Arendt, were: "The thing which all my life seemed to me the greatest shame, which was the misery and misfortune of my life—having been born a Jewess—*this I should on no account now wish to have missed.*"[38]

A widely accepted Enlightenment precept held that the Jews, a backward and uncultured people, could only gain acceptance once they shed their Jewishness, an ungainly medieval atavism. According to Arendt, Prussian Jews of Rahel's day suffered from a type of collective false consciousness: "Jews did not even want to be emancipated as a whole; all they wanted was to escape from Jewishness, as individuals if possible."[39]

The turning point in Rahel's life came early—just as it had for Arendt by virtue of her encounter with Heidegger. In her struggle to gain acceptance in a semi-enlightened Prussian society, Rahel decided on a solution that was fairly common among Jewish parvenus of the day: baptism and intermarriage.

With her assimilationist dreams rapidly fading, Rahel found herself an eminently suitable beau in the person of Count Karl von Finckenstein, an occasional visitor to her salon. Soon, the two were betrothed. Varnhagen's expectations for a new life as Countess von Finckenstein—a life of unblemished social acceptance—were high. Suddenly and unexpectedly, however, their engagement fell through. It seems that his immediate family disapproved of the prospective bride. More importantly, von Finckenstein felt ill at ease in the overtly bourgeois salon ambience, where titles counted for naught, and where *what* one was mattered more than *who* one was. In this latter respect, the Count—Rahel's ticket to social respectability—had precious little to show for himself.

Little interpretive genius is required to appreciate how profoundly Arendt must have identified with her literary protagonist and co-religionist. Rahel, a self-described *Shlemihl*—neither rich, nor beautiful, and a Jew—was the archetype of the Jewish "pariah," a Weberian characterization that would become the leitmotif for Arendt's understanding of the diaspora experience.[40] Nor does it require much of an imaginative leap to appreciate the painfully autobiographical terms in which Arendt viewed the von Finckenstein episode. The parallel with Heidegger's courtship of her, which also ended in an excruciatingly abrupt parting of the ways, must have struck her as uncanny. In all of these respects, Varnhagen must have appeared to Arendt as an eerily perfect *doppelgänger*. Even their responses to the dilemmas of pariahhood—quiescent acceptance followed by vigorous self-affirmation of Jewishness—mesh to a tee.

But there is another aspect of the Varnhagen volume that merits scrutiny in light of Arendt's aggrieved relations with Heidegger. The study opens with a heavy-handed and sustained polemic against the delusions of German romanticism: against the perils of a sensibility for which the values of "inwardness" have been transformed into the highest aim of life. Expressed in the idiom of Arendt's later philosophy, the romantic cult of interiority suffered acutely from a lack of "worldliness." Her unsparing critique of the aberrations of the German intelligentsia—the delusions of *Geist*—contains some of the most impassioned writing of her entire *oeuvre*:

> Sentimental remembering is the best method for completely forgetting one's own destiny. It presupposes that the present itself is instantly converted into a "sentimental" past. . . . The present always first rises up out of memory, and it is immediately drawn into the inner self, where everything is eternally present, and converted back into potentiality. Thus the power and autonomy of the soul are secured. Secured at the price of truth, it must be recognized, for without reality shared with other human beings, truth loses all meaning. Introspection and its hybrids engender *mendacity*.
>
> Introspection accomplishes two feats: it annihilates the actual existing situation by dissolving it in mood, and at the same time it lends everything subjective an aura of objectivity, publicity, extreme interest. In mood the boundaries between what is intimate and what is public become blurred; intimacies are made public, and public matters can be experienced and expressed only in the realm of the intimate—of gossip.[41]

Rahel Varnhagen: The Life of a Jewess thus embodies an uncompromising rejection of the false hopes of Arendt's youth. She zealously dismisses her girlhood delusion—one shared by Rahel—concerning the

egalitarian nature German *Kultur*: a sphere in which people were purportedly judged on the basis of merit rather than rank or ethnicity.
These were the illusions that had collapsed for Varnhagen in the aftermath of her breakup with von Finckenstein. They came to grief for
Arendt following her rejection by Heidegger amid a rising tide of German anti-Semitism. Inevitably, these two circumstances—one highly
personal, the other political—must have been maddeningly conflated
in Arendt's mind.

The passionate tenor of Arendt's Varnhagen critique helps us make
sense of her embittered renunciation, in the aforementioned interview,
of German intellectuals and intellectual life—"Never again! I shall
never again get involved in any kind of intellectual business." For it was
the intellectuals who had betrayed her, turning against her almost overnight, in solidarity with the new regime. The Nazis were her declared
enemies. Her philosophical intimates—Germany's spiritual elite, those
steeped in the virtues of inwardness, the cultured heirs to Goethe,
Hölderlin, and Rilke—were the ones from whom she least expected
betrayal.

All of these dilemmas must have crystallized for Arendt in May 1933.
It was then that she learned of Heidegger's sensational entry into the
Nazi Party, as well as of his pro-Nazi rectoral address, which concluded
with a blusterous ode—in good romantic tradition—to the "Glory and
Greatness of the New [German] Awakening." But the worst was still to
come. Later that same year, Freiburg's new "Rector-Führer," stumping
on behalf of the new regime, would end his speeches with rhetorical
flourishes such as: "Let not doctrines and ideas be the rules of your
Being. The Führer alone *is* the present and future German reality and
its law," punctuated by a "threefold Sieg Heil!" Some thirteen years
later, when Arendt first tried to assess Heidegger's Nazism in the pages
of *Partisan Review*, she tellingly observed that Heidegger's *"whole mode
of behavior has exact parallels in German Romanticism"*; he was "the last
(we hope) romantic—as it were, a tremendously gifted Friedrich Schle-
gel or Adam Mueller."[42] In other words, Heidegger's case epitomized
the risks of romantic "worldlessness," along with the concomitant
megalomania and delusions of grandeur. Following the war, Thomas
Mann also looked to the debilities of romanticism to account for Germany's descent into barbarism: above all, romanticism's fascination

with "a certain dark richness of soul that feels very close to the chtho-nian, irrational, and demonic forces of life"; a fascination that led to "hysterical barbarism, to a spree and a paroxysm of national arrogance and crime, which now finds its horrible end in national catastrophe, a physical and psychical collapse without parallel."[43] But, needless to say, there are profound limits to explanations of Nazism that remain con-fined to the parameters of *Geistesgeschichte*.

"A Confirmation of an Entire Life"

Arendt and Heidegger reconciled upon her return to Germany in 1950. The reunion transformed her from one of his harshest critics into one of his most staunch defenders. At the time, Heidegger remained banned from German university life. His reputation irreparably dam-aged as a result of his status as a Nazi collaborator, he stood in desper-ate need of a reliable publicist and goodwill ambassador. Arendt fit the bill. As a Jewish intellectual with an international reputation and a leading critic of totalitarianism, her support could help parry the persis-tent accusations concerning Heidegger's Nazism. Arendt was ecstatic about their reunion. She believed that she had recovered the dreams of her youth, the worse for wear, perhaps, but recovered nevertheless. "That evening and that [next] morning," she wrote, "are *a confirmation of an entire life*. In fact, a never-expected confirmation."[44]

Arendt became Heidegger's de facto American literary agent, dili-gently overseeing contracts and translations of his books. In a moment of desperation, Heidegger, elderly and cash-poor, contemplated auc-tioning off the original manuscript of *Being and Time*. Unworldly in matters of *Geld*, where was he to turn for advice? To a Jew, of course. Arendt dutifully complied, consulting a Library of Congress expert and offering detailed counsel.

In her correspondence with Jaspers immediately following the war, Arendt's characterizations of the Freiburg sage had been relentlessly critical. She derogated Heidegger's lectures on Nietzsche as "absolutely horrible [and] chatty." And further: "That life in Todtnauberg [in Ger-many's Black Forest], this railing against civilization, and writing *Sein* with a 'y' is in reality a kind of mouse hole into which he withdrew, assuming with good reason that the only people he will have to see are pilgrims filled with admiration for him; no one is likely to climb 1200 meters just to make a scene."[45] In the aforementioned *Partisan Review* essay, she lambasted Heidegger's philosophy, faulting his "fundamental ontology" for having regressed behind Kant's notion of human autonomy. "Heidegger's ontological approach," charged Arendt, "hides a *rigid functionalism* in which Man appears only as a conglomerate of modes of Being, which is in principle arbitrary, since no concept of Man determines his modes of Being."[46]

Following their reconciliation, however, her tone changed abruptly. Thereafter, she systematically downplayed the gravity and extent of Heidegger's Nazi past. In her contribution to a *Festschrift* commemorating Heidegger's 80th birthday, Arendt went out of her way to dispute the relationship between Heidegger's philosophy and his enlistment for Hitler. Gone were the earlier impassioned inculpations of romantic inwardness—that quintessentially German spiritual mania, for which the world could remain a hovel, so long as the thinker's palace of ideas remained intact. Absent, too, was any trace of her earlier critical portrayal of Heidegger as "the last (we hope) romantic." Arendt instead meekly copped a plea on behalf of her embattled mentor. In an abrupt and contradictory turnabout, she claimed that Nazism was a "gutterborn" phenomenon and, as such, had nothing to do with the life of the mind. She readily bought into the myth that Heidegger had practiced "spiritual resistance" against the regime during his lecture courses of the 1930s—a myth that has been effectively refuted by Heidegger biographer Hugo Ott. And, in a poorly veiled rejoinder to Adorno's powerful critique of Heidegger in *The Jargon of Authenticity* (in a 1963 article, Adorno had claimed that Heidegger's philosophy was "fascist to its innermost core"), she added that, whereas Heidegger had taken certain "risks" in defiance of the regime, "The same cannot be said of the numerous intellectuals and so-called scholars . . . who rather than speaking of Hitler, Auschwitz, and genocide . . . have recourse to Plato, Luther, Hegel, Nietzsche or even Heidegger, Jünger, or Stefan George, in order to remove the dreadful phenomenon from the gutter and adorn it with the [rhetoric of] the human sciences or intellectual history."[47] According to this new interpretive tack, the realm of German *Kultur*, on whose mantle Arendt had hung the hopes of her youth, bore no responsibility for the German catastrophe. To her, of course, Heidegger was the living embodiment of both that realm and her youthful hopes. In her correspondence, Arendt proffered an even more spirited defense of her embattled mentor, one that at times bordered on blind loyalty. She characterized Heidegger's 1933 rectoral address as a text that, "though in spots unpleasantly nationalistic" was *by no means an expression of Nazism.*" "I doubt," she continued, "that Heidegger at that time had any clear notion of what Nazism was all about. But he learned comparatively quickly, and after about 8 or 10 months, his whole 'political past' was over."[48]

How did Heidegger repay such blind devotion? Sadly, but true to form, he remained psychologically incapable of acknowledging the fact that his former student mistress had blossomed into an intellectual of world stature. When the German translation of *The Origins of Totalitarianism* appeared in the early 1950s, Heidegger responded with months of icy silence—a resounding non-response. And several years later, when Arendt proudly sent him the German edition of *The Human Condition*, which she had wanted to dedicate to Heidegger ("it owes you just about everything in every regard"), she commented ruefully in a letter to Jaspers:

> I know that he finds unbearable that my name appears in public, that I write books, etc. Always, I have been virtually lying to him about myself, pretending the books, the name, did not exist, and I couldn't, so to speak, count to three, unless it concerned the interpretations of his works. Then, he would be quite pleased if it turned out that I can count to three and sometimes to four. But suddenly I became bored with the cheating and got a punch in the nose.[49]

After they reestablished contact after the war, Arendt tried to engage Heidegger in a dialogue about the European catastrophe—in particular, about the tragic fate of European Jewry. In response, Heidegger, true to form, served up his usual array of specious metaphysical obfuscations. Imploring Arendt to comprehend "Being" without reducing it to the terms of conventional secular "history," he continued by observing: "the fate of Jews and Germans has its own truth that cannot be reached by our historical reckoning. When evil has happened and happens, then Being ascends from this point on for human thought and action into mystery; for the fact that something is does not mean that it is good and just."[50] As Seyla Benhabib has observed with reference to Arendt's failure to respond to such blatant mystifications: "In [this] episode of their correspondence Arendt's readiness to indulge Heidegger's cultivated sense of his own political naïveté takes a toll on her forthrightness."[51]

Hitler's Banal Executioners

In 1963, Arendt published *Eichmann in Jerusalem*. She never fully recovered from the scandal that ensued as a result of a brief discussion in which she implied that the behavior of Jewish Council officials was on a par with that of the Nazi executioners. She claimed that, had the Jewish leaders refused to cooperate with the Nazis, more Jews would have survived; we now know that claim to be untenable. In certain cases, collaboration bought precious time. However, her argument represented a tasteless equation of victims and executioners. Moreover, her account neglected to convey the unspeakable duress under which the Jewish leaders were required to function—by any standard, a grave omission.

Steering clear of historical complexities, Arendt contended that, for a Jew, "this role of the Jewish leaders in the destruction of their own people is undoubtedly *the darkest chapter of the whole dark story*." She went on to discuss "the totality of the moral collapse the Nazis caused in respectable European society—not only in Germany but in almost all countries, not only among the persecutors *but also among the victims*."[52]

In *Eichmann in Jerusalem*, Arendt relied extensively on Raul Hilberg's magisterial work, *The Destruction of the European Jews*. Though Hilberg's work was pathbreaking in many respects, it was far from flawless. The treatment of the role of the Jewish Councils was one of its major deficiencies. Hilberg relied primarily on non-Jewish sources that often portrayed Jews according to the basest of anti-Semitic stereotypes: Jews were pliable and servile, easily compromised by appeals to self-interest.

Thus, according to Hilberg, *Judenrat* (Jewish Council) collaboration was a fairly simple affair, the consummation of an ingrained Jewish predisposition to acquiesce in the face of persecution. However, this simplistic portrayal of the Jewish response has become increasingly difficult to maintain in view of mounting evidence compiled by more recent research.

The strategy of the Jewish Councils was to exchange goods and labor in the hope of saving Jewish lives. Under the circumstances, it seemed a reasonable approach. It was a course that proved effective until the final deportations, when, without warning, all other options disappeared. Moreover, such negotiations sought to take advantage of tensions among the German high command over whether the exploitation of Jewish labor for war aims or the anti-utilitarian logic of the "Final Solution" should prevail.

Like Hilberg, Arendt failed to distinguish the various stages of Jewish cooperation with their Nazi persecutors. These gradations, however, are crucial to evaluating Jewish culpability. During the initial mass deportations, many *Judenrat* leaders refused to hand over Jewish lives when commanded to do so by the Nazis. When confronted with Jewish intransigence, the SS either arrested the Jewish leaders or executed them on the spot. Often, the Nazis then proceeded to hand-pick a second generation of Jewish leaders, about whose willingness to cooperate there could be no doubt. It was largely under this Nazi-selected second regime of *Judenrat* officials that the deportations proceeded. As Yehuda Bauer observes in *A History of the Holocaust*: "The histories of most ghettoes can be divided . . . into two periods: before and after the first mass murders."[53] In the eastern Galician town of Stanislawow, for example, three successive *Judenrat* leaders were executed because of their refusal to hand over Jews.

In *Judenrat: The Jewish Councils in Eastern Europe under Nazi Occupation* (1972), Isaiah Trunk demonstrated conclusively how Jewish "collaboration," far from being voluntary, was predominantly a product of German coercion. On almost all occasions, the Nazis forced the Jews to establish the councils, coerced Jews to serve on them, and compelled their cooperation, often upon pain of the most brutal reprisals. Moreover, circumstances permitting, many of the councils supported Jewish resistance activities. Some, such as the Warsaw ghetto council, were democratically organized. In Arendt's unsympathetic portrayal, however, such crucial distinctions were flattened out.

Few would deny that corruption existed among segments of the Jewish leadership. As Gershom Scholem observed: "Some among them were swine, others were saints. There were among them also many people in no way different than ourselves, who were compelled to make terrible decisions in circumstances that we cannot even begin to reproduce or construct." What he found troubling in Arendt's account was what he called "a kind of demagogic will-to-overstatement." As Scholem comments, "I do not know whether they were right or wrong. Nor do I presume to judge. I was not there."[54]

As Michael Marrus has aptly observed, as the Eichmann polemic unfolded, "it became apparent how thin was the factual base on which [Arendt] had made her judgments." He concludes with the following sober caveat: "The Jewish negotiations with the Nazis . . . were in retrospect, pathetic efforts to snatch Jews from the ovens of Auschwitz as the Third Reich was beginning its death agony. Yet it should be mentioned that, however pathetic, these efforts seemed sensible to some reasonable men caught in a desperate situation."[55]

Generally speaking, Arendt's broad condemnation of the Jewish leadership displayed little comprehension of—let alone sympathy toward—the contingencies and extremes of a set of dire historical circumstances. Concerning Rumkowski's corrupt reign in the Lodz ghetto, it has often been pointed out that, had Soviet troops arrived a few months sooner, he would have gone down in history as a hero instead of a traitor.[56]

At times, Arendt's insensitivity to the dimensions of the Jewish tragedy was striking. In a spirit of German-Jewish arrogance, she described Eichmann's Israeli prosecutor, Gideon Hausner, as "a Galician Jew [who] . . . speaks without periods or commas . . . like a diligent schoolboy who wants to show off everything he knows . . . ghetto mentality"—the ultimate slight from a high-born Jew. She imprudently referred to the Berlin Jewish leader Leo Baeck (the head of the *Reichsvereinigung der deutschen Juden*) as the "Jewish Führer," characterized Eichmann as a "convert to Judaism," claimed that Jewish cooperation "was of course the cornerstone of everything he [Eichmann] did," and, on countless occasions, stooped to compare the nationalist aspirations of Zionism and National Socialism—thereby suggesting a macabre equation of victims and perpetrators.[57] Her suggestion that, in the 1930s, the Zionists and Nazis shared a common vision and worked hand in hand—at one point, she went so far as to describe the 1930s as Nazism's "pro-Zionist period"—seemed spiteful and insensitive.[58] Finally, in a letter to Jaspers, she expressed the tasteless opinion that, "Ben Gurion kidnapped Eichmann only because the reparation payments to Israel were coming to an end and Israel wanted to put pressure on Germany for more payments."[59]

She supplemented this lack of empathy for the victims with the contention that the man on the witness stand, Adolf Eichmann—second only to Himmler and Heydrich in responsibility for the Final Solution—was "banal." Accepting Eichmann's own calculated denials at face value, she argued that he possessed little awareness of his own culpability. She came to the conclusion that Eichmann's crimes were devoid of "intentionality." Instead, Eichmann was merely a cog in a massive bureaucratic machine in which wrongdoing had become the norm—hence, his "banality." Hilberg, whose study in many respects pioneered the "functionalist" account of the Holocaust, took offense at the suggestion that Eichmann's character could be adequately described in such terms:

[The "banality of evil"] is certainly a description of her thesis about Adolf Eichmann and, by implication, many other Eichmanns, but is it correct? In Adolf Eichmann, a lieutenant colonel in the SS who headed the Gestapo's section on Jews, she saw a man who was "déclassé," who had led a "humdrum" life before he rose in the SS hierarchy, and who had "flaws" of character. She referred to his "self-importance," expounded on his "bragging," and spoke of his "grotesque silliness" in the hour when he was hanged, when—having drunken a half-bottle of wine—he said his last words. She did not recognize the magnitude of what this man had done with a small staff, overseeing and manipulating Jewish councils in various parts of Europe . . . preparing anti-Jewish laws in satellite states and arranging for the transportation of Jews to shooting sites and death camps. She did not discern the pathways that Eichmann had found in the thicket of the German administrative machine for his unprecedented actions. She did not grasp the dimensions of his deed. There was no "banality" in this "evil."[60]

The most forceful accusation Arendt could mobilize against Eichmann and his fellow perpetrators was the charge of "thoughtlessness"—a characterization that seriously misapprehended the nature of Nazi ideology, its power as an all-encompassing worldview. In Arendt's view, the Nazis were less guilty of "crimes against humanity" than they were of "an inability to think"—a charge which, if taken at face value, risks equating their misdeeds with those of a dim-witted child. Moreover, Arendt's reliance on "banality" and "thoughtlessness" as central explanatory concepts signified a remarkable change of heart in relation to *The Origins of Totalitarianism*, where she had pointedly characterized National Socialism as an incarnation of "radical evil"—that is, as far from banal. Ironically, it was Arendt herself who had convincingly shown in *Origins* that one of the hallmarks of totalitarian regimes was that they made resistance all but impossible.[61]

Perhaps Arendt's greatest failing as an analyst of the Jewish response to Nazism was that, regarding the most tragic hour of modern Jewish history, she came off seeming hard-hearted and uncaring. Even a stalwart supporter such as the historian Hans Mommsen was forced to avow, in the Preface to the German edition of *Eichmann in Jerusalem*, that "The severity of her criticism and the unsparing way in which she argued seemed inappropriate given the deeply tragic nature of the subject with which she was dealing." Moreover, concludes Mommsen, the Eichmann book "contains many statements which are obviously not sufficiently thought through. Some of its conclusions betray an inadequate knowledge of the material available in the early 1960s."[62]

Arendt never seemed to understand what all the fuss was about. She complained that the "Jewish Establishment" was orchestrating a conspiracy against her. She attributed the bad press she was receiving in Israel to the fact that the same Ashkenazi types who had manned the Jewish Councils were pulling the strings behind the scenes. Arendt viewed herself as superior to those Eastern Jewish ghetto-dwellers who in her account had acquiesced in their own destruction. She identified herself with European intellectual traditions that were more refined and sublime—the tradition of *Geist*. She had studied—and fallen in love—with Martin Heidegger, one of its leading representatives. Could it have been those allegiances—uncanny and subterranean—that in some way led her to purvey such calumnies about the Jews in the *Eichmann* book? Could such remarks have been meant to absolve the Messkirch magician of his crimes on behalf of a regime that sought to wipe out the Jews, by insinuating that, in certain respects, they were no better than the Nazis?

Functionalism Revisited

The idiosyncrasies of Arendt's relationship to Judaism would remain a matter of limited biographical interest were she not one of the leading interpreters of totalitarianism and the Holocaust. However, her "banality of evil" thesis, as articulated in the *Eichmann* book, has been become the cornerstone of the so-called "functionalist" interpretation of Auschwitz. For this reason alone, the historiographical and political stakes involved in reassessing her legacy are immense.

According to the functionalist approach, the Holocaust was primarily a product of "modern society." In his analysis of revolutionary France, Tocqueville had already shown how the democratic leveling characteristic of modernity was conducive to despotism.[63] Social leveling produced a dangerous asymmetry between atomized individuals, who had suddenly been deprived of their traditional social standing (the estates), and the centralized power of the democratic leader. In *Origins*, Arendt built on Tocqueville's approach to explain the system of organized terror—and the corresponding inability of atomized masses to resist—that was one of the predominant features of totalitarian society.

The functionalist approach emphasizes the role of bureaucracy in producing a qualitatively new, impersonal form of industrialized mass death. Thus, at a certain point, the "machinery of destruction" (Hilberg) begins to take on a life of its own. Since the bureaucratic perpetrators operate at a remove from the actual killing sites, they are impervious to the horror unleashed by their actions. From Arendt's perspective, the Nazis' misdeeds were "crimes without conscience."

The nature of the killing process, which had been organized in accordance with modern principles of bureaucratic specialization and the division of labor, meant that the executioners were unaware that they had done anything wrong. As Arendt explains:

> Just as there is no political solution within the human capacity for the crime of administrative mass murder, so the human need for justice can find no satisfactory reply to the total mobilization of a people for that purpose. *Where all are guilty, nobody in the last analysis can be judged.* For that guilt is not accompanied by even the mere appearance, the mere pretense of responsibility. So long as punishment is the right of the criminal—and this paradigm has for more than two thousand years been the basis of the sense of justice and right of Occidental man—guilt implies the consciousness of guilt, and punishment evidence that the criminal is a responsible person.[64]

According to Arendt, the Nazi perpetrators displayed neither "consciousness of guilt" nor a sense of personal responsibility for the crimes they had committed. She described the Nazi henchmen as "co-responsible irresponsibles" insofar as they were simply cogs in a "vast machine of administrative mass murder."[65] The uniqueness of the Holocaust lay in the creation of a new, peculiarly modern type of mass murderer: the *Schreibtischtäter* or desk murderer.

Consequently, for Arendt, Auschwitz had few implications for German history or German national character: "In trying to understand what were the real motives which caused people to act as cogs in the mass-murder machine, we shall not be aided by speculations about German history and the so-called German national character," she confidently remarked.[66] "The mob man, the end-result of the 'bourgeois,' is an international phenomenon; and we would do well not to submit him to too many temptations in the blind faith that only the German mob-man is capable of such frightful deeds."[67] Therefore, to punish the Germans collectively as a people, as some were inclined to do, would be misguided and senseless. Rather than being a specifically *German* crime, Nazi misdeeds were symptomatic of the ills of *political modernity in general*. They were of universal significance and, as such, could have happened anywhere. In fact, one of their distinguishing features was that they had been perpetrated neither by fanatics nor by sadists, but by normal "bourgeois." In this connection, Arendt invoked Heidegger's notion of "inauthenticity" to account for the perpetrators' mediocrity cum bureaucratic conformism. The malefactors, she argued, were typical representatives of mass society. They were neither Bohemians, nor adventurers, nor heroes. Instead, they were family men in search of job security and career advancement. As Arendt affirms in "Organized Guilt and Universal Responsibility," the average SS member is:

a "bourgeois" with all the outer aspect of respectability, all the habits of a good *paterfamilias* who does not betray his wife and anxiously seeks to secure a decent future for his children; and he has consciously built up his newest terror organization . . . on the assumption that most people are not Bohemians nor fanatics, nor adventurers, nor sex maniacs, nor sadists, but, first and foremost *jobholders and good family-men*. . . . Himmler's over-all organization relies not on fanatics, nor on congenital murderers, nor on sadists; it relies entirely upon the normality of jobholders and family-men.[68]

"Organized Guilt and Universal Responsibility," which Arendt wrote in 1945, contains the germ of her controversial "banality of evil" thesis. Nevertheless, in *The Origins of Totalitarianism*, Arendt described Nazism—its bureaucratic-administrative underpinnings notwithstanding—as a form of "radical evil." The unspeakable horror of the events in question was still fresh. However, when she reformulated her thesis in the context of her report on the Eichmann trial—an event that became the occasion for a major reassessment of Nazism's criminal essence—Arendt's "functionalist" approach provoked shock and indignation.

There is certainly much that one can learn about the Final Solution by focusing on the bureaucratic nature of the killing process. Of course, there are scholars who would be quick to mention that the mobilized killing units in the East, the so-called *Einstazgruppen*, were found by the Nuremberg Military Tribunal to be responsible for the deaths of nearly two million Jews—and these deaths were anything but bureaucratic.

However, the functionalist thesis, as articulated by Arendt and others, tells only part of the story. What it fails to explain is the specificity of *this particular genocide*. Why was it that the Nazis explicitly targeted European Jews for extermination?[69] To be sure, other groups had been victims of persecution and even annihilation. But concerning the centrality of anti-Semitism to the Nazi worldview there can be no doubt. Inevitably, an explanatory framework pitched at such a level of generality risks losing touch with the specificity of the phenomenon it seeks to comprehend. According to the functionalist approach, the extermination of the Jews could have happened anywhere. But the fact remains that it did not. It was not only the result of a brutal and impersonal "machinery of destruction"; it was also the product of the proverbial "peculiarities of German history."

The main weakness of the functionalist approach is that it tends to underplay one of the most salient features of Nazi rule: ideology—specifically, the ideology of anti-Semitism. It would be difficult to imagine a regime more focused on total ideological control than was Nazism during its twelve-year reign. The horrors of Auschwitz are not explicable in strictly functionalist terms. Not all societies characterized by the predominance of "instrumental reason" are predisposed toward genocide. The distinctive feature of Auschwitz was not bureaucratic administration. Instead, it was the fact that modern bureaucratic methods were placed in the service of a fanatical and totalizing racist ideology. Unfortunately, Arendt ruled out such considerations a priori as a result of her idiosyncratic focus on the bourgeois *paterfamilias*, which, some eighteen years later, would reemerge as the linchpin of her "banality of evil" thesis.

Ultimately, Arendt's methodological decision to concentrate on the bureaucratic aspects of Nazism, not to mention her astounding (though hardly unique) claim that "the crimes that had been committed at Auschwitz *said nothing about German history or German national character,*" itself needs explaining. Although in her response to Scholem concerning the *Eichmann* book, she denied having hailed from the milieu of the German left, she was not being entirely honest. It was clear that the influence of Heinrich Blücher—an ex-communist, autodidact, and non-Jew—on her thinking about totalitarianism and the course of European history was enormous, perhaps to such an extent that Arendt herself could barely recognize it.[70] A December 1963 letter from Jaspers indicates that the banality of evil concept was originally Blücher's: "Heinrich suggested the phrase 'the banality of evil' and is cursing himself for it now because you've had to take the heat for what he thought of."[71] An excessive emphasis on the "structural" features of the Nazi dictatorship has been a distinguishing feature of left-wing fascism analysis, from Franz Neumann to Raul Hilberg to Hans Mommsen. Conversely, the blind spot of this approach has been the ideological elements that derive from the "superstructure" instead of the sociological "base."

But perhaps there is another biographical reason why Arendt opted for a functionalist approach. By emphasizing the "universal" constituents of the Final Solution at the expense of their specifically German qualities, she also managed to avoid implicating her country of origin—and thereby, narcissistically, herself. Perhaps it would have been psychologically difficult for Arendt to admit that Auschwitz was in fact a German invention, for such an avowal would have implicated her own early intellectual attachments as an assimilated German Jew, not to mention those of friends, professors, and so forth. Margaret Canovan puts her finger on the problem when she observes: "*By understanding Nazism in terms not of its specifically German context but of modern developments linked to Stalinism as well, Arendt was putting herself in the ranks of the many intellectuals of German culture who sought to connect Nazism with Western modernity, thereby deflecting blame from specifically German traditions.*"[72] In a similar vein, Steven Aschheim points out that, "Arendt appears almost as a philosophical counterpart to the analyses of the more staid conservative German historians such as Gerhard Ritter and Friedrich Meinecke, who argued that the rise of Nazism had less to do with internal, 'organic' German development than with the importation of essentially alien and corrupting modern mass practices and ideologies."[73]

Arendt's supporters have long sought to make her "banality of evil" thesis plausible by pointing out that, though Eichmann himself may have been banal, the evil for which he was responsible certainly was not.[74] The problem is that such helpful corrections remain at odds with the dominant tenor of Arendt's narrative. By choosing "A Report on the Banality of Evil" as the subtitle of her book, she opened the floodgates of misunderstanding. Arendt certainly did not consider the Nazis' crimes to be banal. But by relying on a generalizing narrative emphasizing the centrality of *Schreibtischtäter*, she confused the issue. Time and again she insisted that Eichmann was not a monster, that he was "terribly and terrifyingly normal"; yet one suspects that she had been

duped by his unassuming courtroom demeanor. Moreover, while re-
writing her story, she came across some fairly damning countervailing
evidence: prosecutor Gideon Hausner's revelation that Israeli psychiatr-
ists had found Eichmann to be "a man obsessed with a dangerous and
insatiable urge to kill," "a perverted, sadistic personality."[75] Yet she decided to discount these claims and her thesis remained unaltered.

Thus Arendt selected a narrative framework for understanding the
Holocaust that was consistent with her own profound cultural-bio-
graphical ambivalences as an assimilated German Jew. In her efforts to
fathom the Jewish catastrophe—from *Origins* to *Eichmann*—one detects
a profound unwillingness to face up to questions of German responsibility. It is as though Arendt looked everywhere except the place that
was most obvious: the deformations of German historical development
that facilitated Hitler's rise to power. In her mind, all hypotheses other
than this one were worth exploring: Jewish political immaturity, the
excrescences of political modernity, the rise of mass society, bureaucracy, even "thoughtlessness." That the Final Solution to the Jewish
question was conceived, planned, and executed by fellow Germans was
a fact that remained psychologically insupportable. Hence, nowhere
was it accorded its due in her reflections and analyses. Dan Diner suggests provocatively that, in the last analysis, "her line of argument
seems to have more in common with the self-exonerating perspective
of the perpetrators, than with the anguish of the victims."

> Arendt tends towards a kind of universal extremism, which de-
> realizes historical actuality. In her mind, Auschwitz becomes possi-
> ble everywhere, although it turned out to have been executed by
> Nazi Germany. This tendency in juxtaposing the historical reality
> and the universal possibility of Auschwitz at reality's expense, is a
> pervading undercurrent in Hannah Arendt's argumentation. Such
> universalization tends to deconstruct the event—and to offend the
> victims.[76]

Action and Intimacy

Arendt's "action-oriented" framework, as suggested by *The Human Condition*, has of late been uncritically celebrated as a type of panacea for

the ills of political modernity: the instrumentalization of politics by "interests" and the colonization of the political by "society." But such interpretations, decontextualized to a fault, underestimate the significant extent to which her political thought is rooted in the visceral antimodernism of Germany's *Zivilisationskritiker* of the 1920s.[77] This indebtedness, one might say, constitutes the "political unconscious" of Arendt's mature thought; and it is in these terms that her intellectual affinities with Heidegger's philosophical framework remain profound. Although this "critique of modernity" had adherents on both left and right sides of the political spectrum (the "romantic anti-capitalists" identified by Lukacs in *The Theory of the Novel* were its left-wing corollaries), there is no doubt that its most vocal proponents, such as Heidegger, decisively cast their lot with the political right.

The starting point for these critics of civilization was a rejection of "mass society" in all its forms. Heidegger's condemnation of "everydayness" in *Being and Time* was merely a philosophically outfitted expression of this standpoint.[78] But ultimately the concept of "mass society" remains too undifferentiated to do justice to the plurality of forms assumed by modern democracies. In those societies in which civil libertarian and parliamentary traditions remained strong, the values of "individualism" (in Durkheim's sense) and civic consciousness predominated. Thus, it would be unjust to equate democratic rule with "mass society" *tout court*. The ideology of German exceptionalism (the proverbial *Sonderweg*) frequently subtended the "critique of civilization" as elaborated by right-wing luminaries such as Spengler, Moeller van den Bruck, Carl Schmitt, and others. Although this critique certainly contained an element of truth in the case of nations such as Germany, where the transition to modern political and economic forms tended to be violent and abrupt, in other cases such characterizations were merely polemical and erroneous.

Arendt's filiations with this intellectual guild—filiations that are largely mediated through the work of Heidegger—echo clearly in her pejorative characterizations of "society," which in her later philosophy becomes a figure for the ills of modern civilization *simpliciter*. As she remarks tellingly in *The Human Condition*: "the unconscious substitution of the social for the political betrays the extent to which the original Greek understanding of politics has been lost."[79] Today, Arendt continues,

We see the body of peoples and political communities in the image of a family whose everyday affairs have to be taken care of by
a gigantic, nation-wide administration of housekeeping. The scientific thought that corresponds to this development is no longer
political science but "national economy" or "social economy" or
Volkswirtschaft, all of which indicate a kind of "collective housekeeping"; the collective of families economically organized into
the facsimile of one super-human family is what we call "society,"
and its political form is the "nation."

Missing in this dismissive portrayal of "the social" is Marx's brilliant,
youthful description of the creative dimension of labor qua praxis in his
Paris Manuscripts: labor as an essential form of human self-fulfillment,
a manifestation of "species-being"; labor qua practical-critical "human
sensuous activity."[80] Whereas the antidemocratic ontological tradition
denies that self-fulfillment through praxis can ever be achieved by "the
many," the Hegelian Marxist tradition refuses to rest content with a
situation in which happiness was accessible only to the privileged few.
Thus, as another one of Heidegger's children, Herbert Marcuse, glossed the relationship between labor and human self-realization: "Labor
is man's 'act of self-creation', i.e. the activity through and in which man
really first becomes what he is by his nature as man. He does this in
such a way that this becoming and being are there *for himself*, so that
he can know and regard himself as what he is (man's 'becoming-
for-himself'). . . . Labor understood in this way, is the specifically human 'affirmation of being' in which human existence is realized and
confirmed."[81]

Missing, too, in Arendt's account of the social is an awareness of the
exponential growth of human intimacy as nourished by the bourgeois
family, a process coincident with the modern separation between "public" and "private." Once again, her reliance on deprecatory Greek eval-
uative concepts, for which the "private sphere" is definitionally devoid
of any higher significance and meaning, proves a major analytical hindrance. In modern life, the family-induced cultivation of the potential
for intimacy is an indispensable precondition for the development of a
variegated and rich personality. The family is the crucible for the development of modern individualism, as portrayed in the novel and psycho-

analysis, where all individual life histories or stories are intrinsically interesting. One commentator has described the monumental transvaluation of the intimate sphere, following the transition from traditional to modern societies, in the following perceptive terms: "What changes is not that people begin loving their children or feeling affection for their spouses, but that these dispositions come to be seen as a crucial part of what makes life worthy and significant." In opposition to the diffuse nature of affective ties in traditional societies, dominated by the extended family, in the modern family—the proverbial "haven in a heartless world"—emotional bonds are accentuated and enriched. Thus, in the latter part of the eighteenth century, "the affectionate family undergoes an intensification and comes to be seen self-consciously as a close community of loving and caring, in contrast to relations with more distant kin and outsiders, which are correspondingly seen as more formal or distant."[82] Accompanying this new appreciation of intimacy, one finds a Protestant-induced emphasis on the intrinsic value of *ordinary life* or everydayness, whose character was celebrated as far back as the seventeenth century by Milton: "To know / That which before us lies in daily life / Is the prime wisdom."[83]

Arendt's narrative perceives none of these modern virtues or advances.[84] Instead, in her account, under conditions of modernity we have mainly "a society of property-owners, as in Locke, or a society relentlessly engaged in a process of acquisition, as in Hobbes, or a society of producers, as in Marx, or a society of jobholders, as in our own society, or a society of laborers, as in socialist and communist countries."[85] She argues that by privileging the concerns of "society," modern political thought (Hobbes, Locke, and their heirs) has abetted the eclipse of the political. Similarly, in *On Revolution* she reductively attributes the French Revolution's Jacobin *dérapage* of 1792–94 to the predominance of the "social question," although we now know that in fact the social welfare demands of the *sans culottes* and the sanguinary practices of the Committee of Public Safety operated at cross-purposes.[86] Arendt views totalitarianism as an outgrowth of modern mass society. While this insight is descriptively accurate in part, it fails to explain why certain mass societies develop in a totalitarian direction, whereas others do not. Here, too, the strength of civil libertarian and parliamentary traditions seems to be the decisive variable.

In hazarding these summary analytical judgments, Arendt betrays a number of antiquarian normative biases that often fail to do justice to the nature of political modernity. For example, the purported link between democracy and tyranny, which seemed compelling in Plato's day, is, as we have seen, far from universally applicable in modern times. To claim that the predominance of the "social question" (matters of economic justice) under conditions of modernity breeds political regression is also false; it represents a misleading transposition of Aristotelian ethics (a denigration of the *oikos* or "household" qua realm of necessity and a corresponding elevation of political "action" qua freedom) to a modern political framework.[87] In fact, one could readily stand Arendt's argument on its head and claim that one of modernity's distinct political *successes* consists in having *broadened* questions of first-generation rights (civic and political equality) to encompass second-generation rights (social equality), at least among so-called developed countries.[88] As attentive critics have pointed out, "The actual political reemergence and reinstitutionalization of these [neo-Aristotelian] values would require an almost total rupture with all existing institutions."[89]

The normative moorings of Arendt's harsh critique of modern politics—an exotic blend of Aristotle and the German *Zivilisationskritiker* of the 1920s—reveal an anti-democratic bias that limits its diagnostic value for the political present. By expanding the boundaries of political inclusion, modernity has in many respects successfully combated the elitist and exclusionary orientations of traditional politics. In light of these facts, claims about the "eclipse of the political" (the very real problems of modern mass democracy notwithstanding), promoted toward different ends by both Arendt and Carl Schmitt, seem distinctly exaggerated.

Political Existentialism

In 1933, in response to Karl Jaspers' query as to how he could consider someone as uncultured as Hitler fit to rule Germany, Heidegger responded: "It's not a question of culture. Look at his beautiful hands!"[90] In other words: the potencies and allure of charismatic rule have nothing to do with reason or cultivation. They defy a strictly rational accounting. Instead, at issue are qualities of personal authenticity—the virtues of political existentialism.

Hannah Arendt became the ultimate political existentialist. Her political thinking followed what one might describe as a "left Heideggerian" course: she transposed the revolutionary energies that Heidegger praised in right-wing revolutionary movements to the ends of the political left. Thus, Arendt identified profoundly with the experience of the workers' council movement.[91] But this allegiance led her to devalue the workings of normal parliamentary process and instead to overvalue of the glories of revolutionary activism. Both Heidegger and Arendt sought to surmount the mediocrity and routine of "mass society" by embracing the virtues of "action." As a result of their shared mistrust of the political capacities of average men and women, the political thought of both remained profoundly elitist and undemocratic.

In Heidegger's case, the concrete historical outcome of this taste for "revolutionary action" is well known: his enlistment for Hitler in 1933. His disillusionment with Nazism dates from the moment when the movement abandoned its original revolutionary élan—the Röhm purge of June 1934—and consolidated itself qua regime. Heidegger's philosophical justifications of his Nazi engagement are of more than passing interest insofar as his intellectual radicalism exerted an enduring influence on Arendt's mature political thought.

His lecture courses following the Nazi seizure of power show the extent to which he was enamored of the Nazi *Führerprinzip* or leadership principle. As he declaims in the lectures on Hölderlin: "The true and only Führer points by virtue of his Being to the realm of the demigods."[92] Heidegger partook of Burckhardt's view that democracy was responsible for the downfall of the ancient polis. To his way of thinking, it went without saying that, "The true is not for everyman but only for the strong."[93] His Grecophilia was of Nietzschean inspiration. In stark contrast to the social-leveling characteristic of the modernity, with the Greeks the principles of "rank and domination" occupied pride of place.

His justification of revolutionary activism can perhaps best be seen in his panegyric to "the great creators" (*die grossen Schaffenden*): an elite cadre of authentic "leader types"—poets, thinkers, and statesmen—who stand in a privileged relation to Being. Via the violence of their

works, they are charged with the task of redeeming the mass of humankind from the nihilism of the historical present. An existential van-
guard, they constitute, as it were, the shock-troops of Being. Heidegger
characterizes them as follows: "the violent ones . . . who use force to
become pre-eminent in historical Being as creators, *as men of action*."
"Without statute" or formal limits on their power, they represent a
self-justifying elite who ultimately become laws unto themselves.[94]

Arendt's political thought offers us a parallel, if slightly left-leaning,
version of Heideggerian revolutionary vitalism. The Master's emphasis
on authentic leader-types is, moreover, fully preserved. "Only the vulgar will condescend to derive their pride from what they have done,"
Arendt observes in *The Human Condition*. She continues, quoting Isak
Dinesen: "'great people themselves are judged by what they are.'"[95]
According to Arendt, "The political way of life never has been and
never will be the way of the many." The primary fallacy of the "democratic mentality of an egalitarian society is that it tends to deny the
obvious inability and conspicuous lack of interest of large parts of the
population in political matters as such."[96] In a Heideggerian vein, she
bemoans the fact that in contemporary democratic societies, "authentically political talents can assert themselves only in rare cases." Conversely, with the rule of a self-selecting political elite:

> The joys of public happiness and the responsibilities for public
> business would then become the share of those few from all walks
> of life who have a taste for public freedom and cannot be "happy"
> without it. Politically, they are the best, and it is the task of good
> government and the sign of a well-ordered republic to assure
> them of their rightful place in the public realm. To be sure, such
> an "aristocratic" form of government would spell the end of gen-
> eral suffrage as we understand it today; for only those who as
> voluntary members of an "elementary republic" have demon-
> strated that they care for more than their private happiness and
> are concerned about the state of the world would have the right
> to be heard in the conduct of business of the republic.[97]

Arendt seemed untroubled by the fact that such avowedly aristocratic strictures willingly consign the majority of citizens to an entirely
marginal political existence—as indicated, for example, by her quaint

argument for the elimination of "general suffrage." She thereby reintroduces, on vitalist-existential grounds, the distasteful distinction between active and passive citizens. The political elites Arendt reveres manifest a superior aesthetic capacity to reveal and display themselves in public. In her view, such capacities are definitive of authentic political "action." As Canovan has observed: "As we explore [Arendt's] theory, the action and self-disclosure that apparently started as general human capacities seem to be narrowed down until they become rare human achievements"—a statement that captures the elitist biases of Arendt's political theory in general.[98]

In Arendt's central philosophical work, *The Human Condition*, her embrace of political existentialism is unequivocal. There she unabashedly proffers an aestheticized politics: it is not so much the *ends* of politics that matter—such an emphasis would be woefully prosaic and utilitarian. Instead, it is certain "aesthetic" or "theatrical" qualities that count above all: speaking and acting in public is the means whereby political actors reveal their authenticity. As Arendt remarks in a Nietzschean-aristocratic vein: "action can be judged only by the criterion of *greatness* because it is in its nature to break through the commonly accepted and reach into the extraordinary, where whatever is true in common and everyday life no longer applies because everything that exists is unique and *sui generis*."[99] For Arendt, as well as for Heidegger, politics is primarily a matter of *existential self-affirmation*: a terrain of virtuoso performance and individual bravado, a proving grounds for authenticity. Her emphasis on political *agon*—the depiction of politics as a sphere in which an "action-oriented elect" might distinguish themselves—is remarkably antidemocratic. It is a paradigm that is devoid of altruism. For this reason, her perspective is irreconcilable with the values of political solidarity that are so essential to the concept of democratic citizenship. Instead, Arendt identifies with Nietzsche's quest for a "great politics."[100]

Arendt lamented, in an antiquarian-Homeric spirit, the loss in the modern world of "the shining glory of immortal fame which may follow the great deed."[101] Like her mentor from Messkirch, she suffered profoundly from "polis envy"—a tendency to view modern political life as a precipitous fall from the glories of a highly mythologized Periclean heyday.

FIG. 2. Karl Löwith, Florence, 1925. Photo courtesy of J. B. Metzlersche Verlagsbuchhandlung and Carl Ernst Poeschel Verlag, Stuttgart 1986.

Karl Löwith:

The Stoic Response to Modern Nihilism

We find ourselves more or less at the end of the modern rope.
. . . To ask earnestly the question of the ultimate meaning of
history takes one's breath away; it transports us into a vacuum
which only hope and faith can fill.
KARL LÖWITH, Introduction to *Meaning in History* (1947)

One repays a teacher badly if one remains a student.
FRIEDRICH NIETZSCHE, *Thus Spoke Zarathustra*

European Nihilism

KARL LÖWITH is one of the most significant figures of twentieth-century German philosophy. In the English-speaking world, he is perhaps best known for his landmark studies of modern historical consciousness. Two of his works have attained the status of minor classics: *From Hegel to Nietzsche*, an erudite account of the decline and fragmentation of German classical philosophy, and *Meaning in History*, a controversial reading of the relationship between modern philosophies of history and their theological predecessors. When one combines these works with the more recent translation of his pathbreaking study of *Max Weber and Karl Marx* (first written in 1932), one gains a sense of the impressively original *oeuvre* that Löwith was able to assemble over the course of an extraordinarily prolific philosophical life.[1]

The dislocations and upheavals of modern historical life were the point of departure for Löwith's thought. In the tradition of *Geistesgeschichte*, his inquiries centered on the cultural and intellectual preconditions for the European catastrophe. In Löwith's view, the European crisis was in the first instance a *spiritual* crisis. The fatal die had already been cast by the mid-nineteenth century, as the educated elite decisively turned their backs on the classicism of Goethe and Hegel. Increasingly, they grew impatient with values that were "timeless" or that transcended the finitude of human temporal existence. Nature and the heavens ceased to be the touchstone for value and meaning. Instead, "man" became the measure. A sense of disorientation became pervasive. As Löwith observes, "Since the middle of the nineteenth century, European historians no longer follow the pattern of progress, but that of decay."[2]

Europe's poets and literati sensed the dislocations most acutely. In a 1825 letter to Zelter, the elderly Goethe proffered the following observations concerning impending European decline:

No one knows himself any longer, no one understands the element in which he moves and works, or the subject which he is treating. Pure simplicity is out of the question; of simpletons we have enough. Young people are excited much too early and then carried away in the whirl of the times. Wealth and rapidity are what the world admires and what everyone strives to attain. Railways, quick mails, steamships, and every possible kind of rapid communications are what the educated world has in view so that it over-educates itself and thereby continues in a state of mediocrity. . . . This is a century for men with heads on their shoulders, for practical men of quick perceptions who, because they possess a certain adroitness, feel their superiority above the multitude, even though they themselves may not be gifted in the highest degree. . . . We and perhaps a few others will be the last of an epoch which will not soon return.[3]

In *Bouvard and Pecuchet*, Flaubert satirized the philistinism of the bourgeois-European mind. His eponymous protagonists present inane disquisitions on learned matters of every sort, about which they know nothing. They busy themselves by mindlessly copying passages out of weighty books, as if this rote exercise will somehow make the knowledge sink in.

At about the same time, Baudelaire composed a series of portentously titled prose fragments, "The End of the World." After the failure of the revolutions of 1848, his sense of European decline exceeded that of Goethe and Flaubert.

> The world is drawing to a close. Only for one reason can it last longer: just because it happens to exist. . . . Suppose it should continue materially, would that be an existence worthy of its name and of the historical dictionary? . . . We shall furnish a new example of the inexorability of the spiritual and moral laws and shall be their new victims: *we shall perish by the very thing by which we fancy that we live.* Technocracy will Americanize us; progress will starve our spirituality so far that nothing of the bloodthirsty, frivolous or unnatural dreams of the utopists will be comparable to these positive facts. . . . Universal ruin will manifest itself not solely or particularly in political institutions or general progress or whatever else might be a proper name for it; it will be seen, above all, in the baseness of hearts.[4]

Only in "artificial paradise" could Baudelaire find solace and consolation for this distressing train of events.

In Löwith's view, Europe's descent into nihilism was a trend that culminated in Marx's veneration of the proletariat and Nietzsche's celebration of the "superman." For Löwith, this pattern signified a fatal anthropocentric misstep. It meant that there no longer existed any effective limitations or constraints upon the sovereignty of the human will. Marx endorsed the imperatives of proletarian violence—for example, in his famous characterization of revolutions as "the locomotive of history"—as an essential element of the philosophy of history he outlined in the *Communist Manifesto* and other works. Nietzsche's later philosophy celebrated the amoral excesses of "the will to power." As he remarks in the notes collected in *The Will to Power*: "A declaration of war on the masses by *higher men* is needed! . . . A doctrine is needed powerful enough to act as a breeding agent: strengthening the strong, paralyzing and destructive for the world-weary . . . A dominating race can grow up only out of terrible and violent beginnings. Problem: *where are the barbarians of the twentieth century?*"[5]

For Löwith, the removal of all traditional ontological constraints, along with the triumph of radical historicism, loosened the floodgates of European nihilism. Today he remains the unsurpassed chronicler of this trend.

In Löwith's estimation, those who wish to exempt the Christian tradition from being implicated in the European crisis have not thought the situation through deeply enough. Löwith embraced the so-called "secularization" thesis, according to which the fundamental categories of modern historical consciousness were merely secularized versions of theological positions.[6] Christian eschatology, with its conception of man as *imago dei*, sanctioned a radical anthropomorphization of experience and meaning that anticipated "modern" developments. The idea of redemption, which plays a central role in the foundational narratives of the Judeo-Christian tradition, is merely secularized in modern theories of history, claims Löwith. "Marx's historical materialism," he observes, "which seeks to change the world programmatically through a critique of existing reality, is only the most extreme atheistic consequence of the Biblical idea of creative will."[7] Whereas antiquity embraced a cyclical view of history, the historical consciousness of the post-traditional West is radically oriented toward the *eschaton* or end state.

Europe's descent into barbarism constitutes the background and subtext to Löwith's emphatic rejection of philosophies of history. As he remarks in the Preface to *Meaning in History*: "To the critical mind, neither a providential design nor a natural law of progressive development is discernible in the tragic human comedy of all times." "Nietzsche was right," Löwith continues, when he mocked the idea of regarding "nature as if it were a proof of the goodness and care of God [or] interpreting history as a constant testimony to a moral order and purpose." In the last analysis, man's "planning and guessing, his designs and decisions, far-reaching as they may be, have only a partial function in the wasteful economy of history which engulfs them, tosses them, and swallows them," observes Löwith, in a spirit of Stoic resignation.[8] In Löwith's view, *amor fati*, or acquiescence to fate, constitutes the better part of wisdom.

Nietzsche was among the first European philosophers to sense the impending catastrophe. Löwith, who during the 1930s labored concertedly on Nietzsche, regarded his work with a mixture of fascination and dread. In his view, Nietzsche was not only the most astute diagnostician of the European crisis, he was simultaneously its consummation and most acute representative. In *The Gay Science*, Nietzsche portentously announced the death of God. He viewed this proclamation as an exhortation toward "self-overcoming," the transcendence of "man" in the direction of the superman. But his summons fell on deaf ears. Zarathustra, who uttered a similar pronouncement, was greeted with the derisory laughter of the proverbial "last men"—"the most contemptible man . . . the man who can no longer despise himself," the man whom Nietzsche, in an earlier work, had disparaged as "human, all-too-human."[9] In relationship to the superman, the "last men" are an inferior breed; they are essentially "subhuman"—a classification that, in Löwith's view, was an ominous portent of things to come.[10]

Thus for Löwith, Nietzsche was Europe's foremost prophet of moral and intellectual nihilism. As a proponent of radical "will," of the virtues of self-assertion rephrased in the idiom of domination and conquest, Nietzsche's thought meshed seamlessly with modernity's Faustian self-understanding. In the half-century following his death, virtually all the events and catastrophes he had prophesied came true—in part, Löwith contends, because Nietzsche's own idiom of "active nihilism" helped to prepare the way.

Yet, there is another dimension of Nietzsche's thought that one must not lose sight of, for it expresses a kernel of ancient wisdom that has been neglected and repressed amid the frenetic busy-ness of modern civilization: the doctrine of eternal recurrence, to which Löwith dedicated a book-length study in 1934. As Löwith explains, Nietzsche was not only a soothsayer of catastrophe, but also:

> a true lover of wisdom, who as such sought the everlasting or eternal, and therefore wanted to overcome his time and temporality altogether. Nietzsche experienced the fullness of time, when to him the world became "perfect," in an ecstatic moment to which he gave the name "noon and eternity." An eternity at noon does not negate time . . . rather it means the eternity of time

itself in the world: the eternally recurring cycle of coming into being and passing away that is always the same, a cycle in which the permanence of "Being" and the change of "becoming" are one and the same."[11]

In Löwith's view, Nietzsche's theory of eternal recurrence represents a much-needed corrective to the discourse of European nihilism, including Nietzsche's own voluntarist fantasies as embodied in the "will to power" ideal.

World and Human World

In his later writings, Löwith, increasingly dissatisfied with the gamut of "modern" alternatives, actively embraced the standpoint of the ancients.[12] The Stoics, for example, viewed cosmos and nature as superior to the transient vagaries of human history. This perspective, argues Löwith, presents a much-needed corrective to the Cartesian desire to ontologically elevate the human world above the cycles of nature. Hans-Georg Gadamer felicitously characterized Löwith's perspective as follows: "We should look at the eternal cycle of nature in order to learn from it the equanimity that alone is appropriate to the minuteness of human life in the universe."[13]

One of the keys to understanding Löwith's mature thought concerns the distinction between "world" and "human world." For him, it was essential that all historicist attempts to subsume the concept of "world" by "human world" be kept at bay. As a number of commentators have pointed out, Löwith's stoicism has much in common with the "Oriental wisdom" he found so congenial during his five-year sojourn in Japan (1936–41), where he sought refuge from a Nazi-dominated Europe. This amalgamation of European and far-Eastern sensibilities emerges clearly in his claim that, "Once we have acceded to complete insight, then the mountain will simply become a mountain again and the river simply a river. In this final recognition of Being-so-and-not-otherwise, the world and man show what they are originally and ultimately."[14]

In Löwith's view, the West, to its own detriment, failed to heed such insights. Instead, it erroneously conflated "world" and "human world,"

resulting in modernity's unbridled anthropocentrism. Having been sub-
jected to the imperious nature of human design and planning, the integrity and simplicity of the world has been degraded and miscon-
strued. As Löwith observes:

> The supra-human world of heaven and earth, which are entirely
> independent and self-sustaining, infinitely surpasses the human
> world. World and human world are not equivalents. Whereas the
> physical world may be thought of without any reference what-
> soever to the existence of man, man cannot be thought of with-
> out the world. We come into the world and we separate from it.
> It does not belong to us; instead *we belong to it*.[15]

Taking his cue from Heidegger's influential critique of the modern
"world picture," Löwith shows how the ancient Greek concept of essence (*ousia*) transcended the machinations of subjectivity.[16] For the
Greeks, *nous* or Reason reflected a set of robust, divine, cosmological
ends. Conversely, in modern times, reason has been subjectively truncated. Max Weber's concept of "instrumental reason" best captures
spirit's fate in the modern world, where reason has been redefined as
the most efficient means of attaining a preestablished goal or end.
Thereby, the notion of "essence" has been subjectively debased, reduced to the idea of human ends or purposes. When all is said and
done, such human ends are the only ones that count.

Resolutely opposing such trends, Löwith insists that

> world and human world are not equivalents. . . . The world is not
> simply a cosmological "idea" (Kant) or a mere "total-horizon"
> (Husserl) or a world-"project" (Heidegger), but itself, absolutely
> independent: *id quod substat*. Only various world-pictures can be
> projected, *never the world itself*. . . . [The world] itself never ap-
> pears as an object like other objects; it encompasses everything,
> without itself being comprehensible. It is what is greatest and
> richest, and at the same time as empty as a frame without a
> picture.[17]

Even Heidegger's phenomenological concept of "world" remains too
anthropocentric for Löwith: "Since Heidegger's *Being and Time* one often speaks of Dasein as Being-in-the-world; but the world of Dasein is

not the ordered cosmos, but our . . . co-world and environing world [*Mitwelt und Umwelt*], whose order is determined by the care and solicitude of man."[18] Conversely, the sublimity of the "world" in Löwith's sense lies in the fact that, like the aforementioned mountain and river, it is without a goal and without a purpose.

The Stoic standpoint venerated by Löwith has been overwhelmed by modern intellectual tendencies. Foremost among these, in Löwith's estimation, is existentialism—a worldview ideally suited to the contingencies of modern life. For the Greeks, the structure of the world was eternal; for Christianity, it was created by God. Modernity, as an ideology of radical immanence, brusquely dismisses both standpoints and finds itself, unsurprisingly, destitute and disoriented, lacking a permanent "ground." Existentialism is thus an intellectual perspective ideally suited to the "groundless" character of modern existence, to the experiential flux that defines of modern life. As Löwith concedes, traditional ethical and philosophical orientations inevitably appear outmoded in light of the challenges and disruptions of modernity—hence, the "timeliness" of the philosophies of Nietzsche and Heidegger, both of which make their peace (albeit, in different ways) with the standpoint of modern nihilism.

Yet, despite Löwith's concerted attempt to distance himself from a Heideggerian philosophical mode, one wonders how successful his efforts were in the end. Were not his criticisms of Heidegger's residual anthropocentrism merely attempts to outflank the Master's own self-criticism of his early work as too beholden to the paradigm of the modern "subject"? In the last analysis, didn't Löwith essentially share Heidegger's own marked generational (and, as we shall see, confessional) prejudices against the modern world and its predominant political forms: individualism, liberalism, constitutionalism, public opinion, and so forth? And with regard to ethical and political questions, didn't he ultimately share Heidegger's standpoint of "total" (as opposed to "immanent") critique, implying that the injustices of modernity could not be remedied via recourse to internal methods and approaches? Indeed, Löwith's ultimate defense of a "Stoic withdrawal" from the challenges and problems of modern "society" (an intrinsically pejorative designation) bears an uncanny resemblance to Heidegger's own final standpoint of "Gelassenheit," or "releasement," as embodied in the philosopher's

oft-cited admonition to "let beings be." Hence, despite his insightful-
ness as a historian of philosophy and critic of modern "spirit," it seems
that the distortions and biases of Heidegger's philosophical tempera-
ment resurface in the key dimensions of Löwith's own mature thought.

Philosophical Apprenticeship

Löwith was born to an assimilated German-Jewish family in Munich in
1897. His father, Wilhelm Löwith, a convert to Protestantism, was a
successful artist and stimulated his son's early interests in European
cultural life. After attending high school in Munich, Löwith volunteered for World War I and was seriously wounded in the Italian campaign of 1915. He spent the next three years in a prisoner of war camp
near Genoa, an experience that inspired a lifelong affection for the
Mediterranean sensibility. He was deeply impressed by the rather un-
German traits of his Italian captors—their spontaneity and warmth,
their ability to live for the moment, their acceptance of fate. Löwith
returned to Italy twice, as a student and during his initial years of exile
from the Nazi dictatorship (1935–36).

In 1919, Löwith was privileged to hear Max Weber's famous Munich
lecture "Science as a Vocation." The address was delivered during the
height of Germany's postwar revolutionary tumult. Weber's concluding
plea for an "ethic of responsibility"—he recommended that, rather
than chasing after false prophets, "We set to work and meet the 'demands of the day,' in human relations as well as in our vocation"—had
a marked impact on the development of Löwith's ethical vision.[19] It
served as an astute warning concerning the perils of turning the academic lectern into a political platform, as well as the dangers of political Messianism.

Following the war, Löwith moved to Freiburg to study philosophy
with the founder of the phenomenological movement, Edmund Husserl. However, instead of continuing his studies with Husserl, Löwith
found himself seduced by the phenomenologist's brilliant young assistant, Martin Heidegger, whom he followed to Marburg in 1924. According to Löwith, "the palpable intensity and impenetrable profundity
of Heidegger's spiritual drive caused everything else to pale and made

Husserl's naive belief in an ultimate philosophical method seem irrelevant."[20] In Heidegger, Löwith, like so many others, found a challenging alternative to the sterile academicism of the reigning German school-philosophies.

In 1928, Löwith defended his habilitation study, *Das Individuum in der Rolle des Mitmenschen*, which was written under Heidegger's direction. Subtitled "A Contribution to the Anthropological Foundation of Ethical Problems," this "Jugendschrift" represented a polemical response to Heidegger's interpretation of "Being-with" (*Mitsein*) in *Being and Time*.

In *Being and Time*, the hallmark of "authenticity" (*Eigentlichkeit*) was a Self radically enclosed in its own Selfhood or "ownness" (*Jemeinigkeit*); a being—Dasein—that displayed all the traits of a Kierkegaardian, existential loneliness, culminating in the irreducible singularity of his or her confrontation with death. However, Heidegger's Kierkegaardianism was emphatically "post-theological": having internalized Nietzsche's adage concerning the "death of God," his understanding of Kierkegaard was correspondingly disillusioned. In Heideggerian *Angst*, one finds a de-theologized version of Kierkegaard's "fear and trembling." For Kierkegaard's "knight of faith," the prospect of salvation was, if never certain, always a possibility. Correspondingly, existential decision meant a wager on the prospect of an omniscient and benevolent deity. However, with Dasein—Heidegger's "modern knight of faith"—prospects for transcendence were blocked: consigned, as it were, to a pre-Nietzschean sphere of metaphysical delusion. Dasein's predominant "mood" (*Stimmung*) was one of forlorn existential abandonment. Moreover, insofar as Heidegger had bracketed off the realm of "everydayness"—which had been colonized by the "they"—as "inauthentic," possibilities for meaningful social choice were correspondingly restricted.

In fundamental ontology, the majority of "Selves"—*das Man*—systematically avoid the demands of authenticity via the ruses of social conformity: "busy-ness," "idle talk," "curiosity," and "publicness." As such, their Dasein remained ontologically mired in the nether sphere of inauthenticity. One consequence of this characterization is that, in Heidegger's framework, the sphere of "Being-with-others" or *Mitsein* seems a priori devalued. Thus, in *Being and Time*, prospects for meaningful human intersubjectivity seemed to be either negligible or nonexistent.

It is this dilemma of failed intersubjectivity that Löwith seeks to address in his youthful treatise on philosophical anthropology—a work that the philosopher Dieter Henrich characterized as an "as yet unsurpassed" exemplar of the genre.[21] Löwith takes aim at all claims concerning the ontological primacy of transcendental subjectivity, Heidegger's included. As such, his démarche displays marked commonalities with the dialogical thought of Martin Buber as well as the "symbolic interactionism" of Alfred Schütz and George Herbert Mead. All of these approaches emphasize that identity or the formation of the self is a product of intersubjective relatedness. As Löwith argues, the meaning of a Self is essentially defined by a network of social relationships: family, friends, associates, community, and acquaintances. In lieu of such relatedness, the very concept of selfhood ceases to be sociologically intelligible or philosophically meaningful. Thus Löwith claims that the "I" is primarily formed and shaped by a world of human intimacy, the "thou." As Gadamer has remarked: "If one may put into an abbreviated form what Löwith's book sought to bring into philosophical discussion at this time, it was to shed light on what the 'thou' in its radical particularity signifies for mankind."[22]

Before it is "my world," the human world is a "Mitwelt," a "co-world." Identity formation occurs nonsolipsistically, via a complex process of "reflection": by the individual seeing herself in the other and by the other seeing himself in her. Taking this insight a step further, Löwith goes on to claim that never—not even in the Heideggerian ultimate instance of Being-toward-death—does the individual stand in an immediate or non-reflected relation to Self. Instead, as a phenomenological construct, the Self is always mediated by preexisting structures of intersubjectivity:

> Man returns to himself, not primarily from objects, but from subjects, i.e., from Beings who are like him; for the "world" to which he principally turns is the co-world [*Mitwelt*] that corresponds to him. From the outset and without his doing, his own world is ever and always determined through the Dasein of Others, such that it would not be there at all or in this way without the having-been-there of determinate Others. . . . When we inquire about the Other or the co-world, this question implies inquiring about

one's own Self, for whom others are "Other" and a "world"—i.e., one is making inquiries about Being-with-others [*Miteinandersein*].[23]

In the annals of transcendental philosophy, the notion of a "mediated self" stressed by Löwith has received scant attention. If one scrutinizes its leading representatives—from Descartes to Kant to Husserl—all proceed from a "more or less abstractly conceived self-consciousness," observes Löwith. Much of Löwith's critical inspiration derived from Ludwig Feuerbach's anthropological humanism. As Feuerbach claims in the opening paragraphs of *Principles of a Philosophy of the Future*, "The true dialectic is never a monologue of the solitary thinker with himself; it is a dialogue between I and thou."[24] By the same token, for an insight to be "true," it must not be true for me alone. Instead, being true expresses a dimension of *universality*: the claim must be true for a plurality of others as well. Feuerbach gives voice to this idea when he remarks that, "Certainty about the objective reality of other things outside of me is for me mediated by the certainty of the reality of another person outside of me."[25]

In *Being and Time*, Heidegger questioned the adequacy of transcendental subjectivity as a basis for rigorous philosophical questioning. In his view, it was a standpoint that remained existentially impoverished, insofar as it falsely assumed the primacy of a theoretical standpoint (the Cartesian "I think") in trying to understand a being—Dasein—that was essentially defined by a series of more primordial, ontological world-involvements: "mood," "care," "solicitude," as well as the practical significance of objects for use, such as tools. Nevertheless, in Löwith's eyes the Master's philosophy had not gone far enough.

Revolution from the Right

Following Heidegger's triumphant enlistment in Germany's National Revolution, his contingent of talented Jewish students was faced with the conundrum of trying to reconcile their devotion to him with his new political faith. Often, their attempts to "account for the unaccountable" complemented one another. As trained philosophers and as eyewitnesses to the political tumult of 1929–1933, they shared a privileged perspective that enabled them to perceive the elective affinities between Heidegger's early philosophy and the politics propagated by the new regime. That there were elements of Heideggerian *Existenzphilosophie* that made it susceptible to a "national revolutionary" or proto-fascist reading was a point on which all would agree.

How might one account for the paradoxical fact that Heidegger, whom Husserl had accused of growing anti-Semitism in the years prior to 1933, had so many gifted Jewish students?[26] The explanation lies in the fact that, for the most part, these students did not regard themselves as Jewish, nor did Heidegger so regard them. Instead, they viewed themselves as fully assimilated Germans. Heidegger never shared the Nazis' version of biological anti-Semitism. Rather, his distaste for Jews was of the traditional cultural order—a mentality that, as a rule, was accepting of acculturated or baptized Jews. With the advent of the April 1933 Law for the Reconstitution of the German Civil Service, which banned Jews from civil service professions (including university teaching), Heidegger's Jewish students experienced a rude awakening. For many Jews who stemmed from the milieu of Germany's well-assimilated *Bildungsbürgertum*, it was the first time they felt themselves to be Jewish—a fact to which Löwith eloquently attests in his autobiography.

Löwith set forth his views on the problem of Heidegger and politics in his autobiography.[27] Written during Löwith's Japanese exile on the occasion of a fellowship competition for German émigrés sponsored by Harvard University, the work is a masterpiece of intellectual concision and insightful portraiture. Löwith devotes perceptive aperçus not only to Heidegger's milieu, but also to the Stefan George *Kreis*, Nietzsche's heirs, Spengler, the theologian Karl Barth, and Husserl. A type of *Bildungsroman* in reverse, Löwith's text is also a fascinating chronicle of the way Germany's most gifted philosophers and intellectuals were seduced by the promises of political redemption offered by Nazism.

For those who are interested in exploring the spiritual preconditions of the "German Revolution," there are few better sources than Löwith's account. He shows, for example, how the aristocratic pretensions of the George Kreis gradually became diffused throughout German society as a whole:

The ideals of this exclusive elite soon became generally accepted commonplaces, and it is hardly an accident if the [Nazi] minister and journalist, Goebbels, the mouthpiece of National Socialism, studied with the Jew [Friedrich] Gundolf. For these men, the entire bourgeois Christian world was already dead long before Hitler. They loathed the "bloodless intellect" and distinguished between "cultural" and "primal experiences," as well as propagating the hierarchical distinction between nobles and commoners against the universality of human rights.[28]

After Spengler's *Decline of the West*, the idea of "decline" was so pervasive among the German intelligentsia that even the most varied right-wing groups could agree that a program of radical dismantling or "destruction" was, for Germany (and, by extension, Europe), the preferred course: "In general, long before Hitler, the fact and consciousness of collapse had flourished to a point where it could transform itself into the idea of radical change"—at which point National Socialism stepped into the breach to give the will to destroy positive content and meaning.[29]

In general, Heideggerians have been at a loss to explain Heidegger's partisanship for Hitler. Part of this explanatory incapacity is undoubtedly defensive-psychological in nature: an innate human propensity to rationalize troublesome or inconvenient facts. But there is also a substantive dimension to such interpretive myopia, which suggests the perils of an exclusively textual approach to the understanding of philosophical works. In Heidegger's case in particular, a narrowly hermeneutic approach risks bypassing or misconstruing the historical-ideological dimensions of his thought that struck so many of his contemporaries.

Löwith's understanding of the entwinement of philosophy and politics in Heidegger's work is particularly illuminating. Because he was a philosophically informed contemporary, his critique stands as an indispensable counterweight to the commonplace ahistorical approaches to Heidegger's thought. Löwith's meditations on the philosopher's "Fall" (which in German means both "case" and "fall") provide us with an insightful account of the way in which Heidegger's own life and thought succumbed to the vicissitudes of the "historicity."

One of the common reactions to Heidegger's Nazism is the contention that his support for Hitler had nothing to do with his philosophy. Nazism, it is claimed, was too base and vulgar a phenomenon for there

to have been meaningful linkages between it and Heideggerian "fundamental ontology." Such reservations fail to acknowledge the way
Heidegger himself understood the demands of Germany's political situation circa 1933. In many respects, his case was paradigmatic for a
great number of right-wing intellectuals who were convinced that liberalism and democracy were, in essence, un-German and that a "national authoritarian" solution was required if Germany were to surmount the crises of the Weimar years and aspire to the "great politics"
(Nietzsche) of authentic German traditions.[30]

Heidegger, moreover, always understood himself as a radical nonconformist among the German mandarins.[31] Given his humble background, he always felt ill at ease among the largely upper-class professorate. Consequently, as someone who always felt out of step with
the dominant intellectual trends—be they positivism, neo-Kantianism,
or the sociology of knowledge—Heidegger adopted the persona of an
"anti-intellectual intellectual." This self-understanding as an outsider
goes far toward explaining his attraction to philosophical and political
radicalism. Following the precedents of Nietzsche, Spengler, and Jünger, in his view European traditions had so far decayed that only a
wholesale break with the complacency and corruption of the bourgeois
world seemed to offer a legitimate way out. As Löwith observes: "By
birth a simple sexton's son, by profession Heidegger became the pathetic representative of a [professorial] estate that he despised. . . . The
destructive radicalism of the [Nazi] movement and the petty bourgeois
character of all its 'strength-through-joy' institutions failed to make an
impression on him because he himself was a radical petty bourgeois."[32]
And to those who claim that Heidegger "compromised" fundamental
ontology by allowing its categories to serve as ideological window-
dressing for National Socialism, Löwith rejoins that, because his was a
philosophy of human existence, it makes perfect sense that the philosopher would seek to actualize his doctrines in temporal-historical fashion in the sphere of the "everyday":

Given the significant attachment of the philosopher to the climate
and intellectual mood of National Socialism, it would be inappropriate to criticize or exonerate his political decision in isolation
from the very principles of Heideggerian philosophy itself. It is

not Heidegger, who, in opting for Hitler, "misunderstood himself"; instead, those who cannot understand why he acted this way have failed to understand him. A Swiss professor regretted that Heidegger consented to compromise himself with the "everyday," as if a philosophy that explains Being from the standpoint of time and the everyday would not stand in relation to the daily historical realities that govern its origins and effects. The possibility of a Heideggerian political philosophy was not born as a result of a regrettable "miscue," but from the very conception of existence that simultaneously combats and absorbs the *Zeitgeist*.[33]

What, then, were the precepts of Heidegger's thought that bore such profound affinities with "the climate and intellectual mood of National Socialism"? Löwith's explanation centers on the philosopher's response to the problem of European nihilism.

According to Löwith, nihilism was the cultural predicament to which Heidegger sought to respond via the method of radical questioning he developed following World War I. The Freiburg sage was as much influenced by the cultural and religious standpoint of Luther, Pascal, Kierkegaard, Van Gogh, Rilke, and Dostoevsky as he was by the leading representatives of Western metaphysics. Hence, from the beginning, Heidegger's conception of "first philosophy" was inseparable from his self-understanding as *Zivilisationskritiker*—a critic of the moribund value structure of the modern West. By the war's end, Heidegger had fully internalized the nineteenth century's negative verdict on the totality of inherited values. In *Being and Time*, he celebrated the nihilistic resolve of "authentic decision" (*Entschlossenheit*) in face of the "Nothing" (*das Nichts*), the groundless "abyss" of human Being-in-the-world. As he wrote in a 1920 letter to Löwith: "I do only what I must and what I consider to be necessary, and I do this as I am able to—I do not slant my philosophical work toward cultural tasks for a universal present. . . . I work form out of my 'I am' and my spiritual, indeed factical heritage. With this facticity, existence *rages!*"[34]

Löwith perceived more than a passing affinity between National Socialism's animating spirit of revolutionary nihilism and the existential radicalism of Heidegger's philosophy.[35] In the early 1930s, Heidegger effortlessly transposed the essential concepts of *Being and Time*—authenticity, resolve, fate, potentiality-for-Being-a-Self, Being-toward-death, and *Jemeinigkeit* ("ownness")—from the individual "Self" to the Dasein of the German Volk. Moreover, the transition from an individual to a collective understanding of authenticity required less of a ideational leap than one might suspect. The conceptual structure of *Being and Time* Division II—which has been strangely neglected in the secondary literature—lays the groundwork for the transition from an individual to a collective standpoint. Categories such as *Gemeinschaft*, "destiny," "historicity," "choosing-one's-hero," and "das Volk" provide warrant for translating the individualistic standpoint of Division I into collective-political terms.[36] A historical and political reading of *Being and Time*, therefore, is hardly alien to the spirit of Heidegger's enterprise. In many respects, such a reading is in fact demanded. As the political biographies of Heidegger by Ott and Farias have shown, many of Löwith's suppositions concerning the affinities between Heidegger's philosophy and the Nazi movement have become a matter of historical record.

Heidegger and National Socialism shared an existential radicalism that responded in a "nihilating" manner toward traditions and values deemed unserviceable for the ends of historical greatness. Philosophically, Heidegger sought to promote the "Destruktion" of the traditional categories of Western metaphysics, just as the radical political movements of his day sought to eliminate those aspects of the past that were deemed unserviceable for the ends of "total mobilization" (Jünger). In Löwith's pithy characterization: "Instead of giving oneself over to the universal enterprise of education, as if one had been given the mission of 'saving the culture,' according to Heidegger one must engage in a 'radical dismantling and rebuilding' or a 'destruction' . . . without concerning oneself with the idle talk and the bustle of those sensible and enterprising people who reckon time with clocks."[37]

Löwith's most detailed assessment of Heidegger's case, "The Political Implications of Heidegger's Existentialism," appeared in Jean-Paul Sartre's *Les Temps Modernes* at a tenuous point in Heidegger's professional life. A Freiburg University denazification commission found Heidegger guilty of "having placed the prestige of his scholarly reputation . . . in the service of the National Socialist Revolution and thereby contributing to the legitimation of this Revolution in the eyes of educated Germans."[38]

According to Hannah Arendt, in fall 1945 Heidegger sought to ingratiate himself with the French occupation authorities, offering his services for purposes of politically reeducating the German people.[39] Since Baden's political future was in the hands of the French occupiers, the philosopher desperately sought out contact with French intellectuals who might help him plead his case. He first tried contacting Sorbonne philosophy professor Emile Bréhier, but Bréhier refused to respond: in his opinion, Heidegger's letter had come five years too late.

Next, Heidegger tried contacting Sartre himself. In a fulsome letter, Heidegger stressed the profound affinities he detected between *Being and Nothingness* and his own work. Here, remarked Heidegger, "I encounter for the first time an independent thinker who has fundamentally experienced the realm out of which I myself think. Your work is dominated by an immediate understanding of my philosophy the likes of which I have not previously encountered." Heidegger continued by distancing himself from the categorial framework of *Being and Time* (especially the concepts of "Being-with" and "Being-toward-death," which Sartre had criticized). He proposed a "philosophical ski trip" through his native Schwarzwald and urged an immediate German translation of Sartre's work.[40]

Yet the admiration Heidegger expressed for Sartre's philosophy on this occasion dovetails poorly with other accounts. Gadamer, for example, reports that upon receiving *Being and Nothingness*, Heidegger "cut" merely the first forty pages of the book before bequeathing it to his former student.[41] Moreover, a year later, as it became clear that Heidegger's profession of interest in Sartre's work remained unreciprocated, the German philosopher was moved to characterize Sartre's version of existentialism in less charitable terms. In the "Letter on Humanism," written in the fall of 1946, Heidegger pillories Sartre's philosophy for remaining imprisoned in the categories of Western metaphysics: "Sartre expresses the basic tenet of existentialism in this way: Existence precedes essence. . . . But the reversal of a metaphysical statement remains a metaphysical statement." In his programmatic postwar lecture, "The Humanism of Existentialism," Sartre had famously attempted to reconcile humanism and existentialism. "We are precisely in a situation," he declared, "where there are only *human beings*."[42] In the "Letter," Heidegger responded ungraciously by invoking the basic tenets of "philosophical antihumanism": "We are precisely in a situation where principally there is *Being*."[43]

The Critique of Carl Schmitt

In a landmark essay on the Nazi jurist Carl Schmitt, first published in 1936, Löwith pursued the important parallels between Heidegger's existential decisionism and Schmitt's political decisionism. Schmitt was one of Germany's leading legal theorists during the Weimar Republic. Like Heidegger, in 1933 he became a vigorous supporter of National Socialism. Heidegger and Schmitt were the two most celebrated academics to lend their support to the new regime. Acknowledging their mutual intellectual and political affinities, in August 1933 Heidegger wrote to Schmitt urging that the two make common cause on behalf of the German "Awakening." "The gathering of the spiritual forces, which should bring about what is to come, is becoming more urgent every-day," insisted Heidegger.[44]

According to Schmitt, in the modern world the traditional concepts of political obligation have been delegitimated and, consequently, have lost their power and influence. "Sovereignty," "king," "state," "majesty," "divine right"—even the concept of "the political" itself—have forfeited their authority in the wake of the *antipolitical* energies of liberalism. State authority, once majestic and robust, has progressively deteriorated, reaching a nadir with the "night watchman state" of the liberal era. (Schmitt treats the age of absolutism as a historical benchmark.) Traditional, *étatiste*-oriented genres of political discourse have thereby been deprived of their very ground. Along with his fellow conservative revolutionaries, Schmitt attempted to forge new concepts of political authority in order to counter the fateful "eclipse of the political." In his view, liberalism's ascendancy was primarily responsible for this eclipse. Under political liberalism, socioeconomic "interests" usurped the autonomous prerogatives of political rule.[45]

Though rich and informative in many respects, Schmitt's uncharitable depiction of modern politics compelled him to regard political authoritarianism as a desirable remedy. His 1920 book on the concept of "dictatorship" endorsed autocracy as a method of keeping at bay forces and interests that threatened to deplete the substance of political sovereignty. In *Political Theology* (1922), he contested the legitimacy of political modernity by claiming that its concepts were merely secularized variants of theological motifs. His influential study of "parliamentarism" concluded with an encomium to Mussolini's march on Rome:

> Until now the democracy of mankind and parliamentarism has only once been contemptuously pushed aside through the conscious appeal to myth, and that was an example of the irrational power of the national myth. In his famous speech of October 1922 in Naples before the March on Rome, Mussolini said, "We have created a myth, this myth is a belief, a noble enthusiasm; it does not need to be a reality, it is a striving and a hope, belief and courage. Our myth is the nation, the great nation which we want to make into a concrete reality for ourselves." . . . The theory of myth is the most powerful symptom of the decline of the relative rationalism of parliamentary thought.

Schmitt punctuates these claims with a suggestive comparison between Mussolini and Machiavelli.[46] In his view, Italian fascism's glorification of authority and myth was necessary in order to restore the lost primacy of the political.

In the Weimar Republic's waning years, the fascist elements of Schmitt's work came unambiguously to the fore. In his most influential book, *The Concept of the Political*, Schmitt, inspired by Nietzsche's musings on the importance of "having enemies," coined the infamous "friend-enemy" distinction to define the essence of the political: "The pinnacle of great politics," observes Schmitt, "is the moment in which the enemy comes into view in concrete clarity as the enemy."[47] According to Schmitt, in war—the "ultima ratio" of politics—one does not kill the enemy for aesthetic, moral, or for other nonpolitical reasons. Instead, in a classical justification of political existentialism, Schmitt argues that the enemy should be killed on strictly "existential" or "ontological" (*seinsmässige*) grounds.

As Löwith's essay demonstrates, in *The Concept of the Political*, Schmitt vigorously endorsed the notion of "homogeneity" (*Artgleichheit*)—an idea with unmistakable racial overtones—as essential to the modern state's self-preservation. Moreover, as a logical corollary of the "friend-enemy" distinction—and as an eerie portent of Nazi policy and practice—he stressed the importance of rooting out and annihilating the "domestic enemy": communists, Jews, social democrats, and other undesirables. Needless to say, in a historical era whose signature feature was concentration camps whose barracks were reserved for political and racial "enemies," such hypothetical prescriptions quickly lose their innocence.

An admirer of Jünger and the Soviet experiment in modernization from above, in the early 1930s Schmitt flirted with the notion of the "total state," according to which all domestic concerns must be subordinated to the primacy of foreign policy and, ultimately, preparation for war. The step from his authoritarian political doctrines of the 1920s to his support of Hitler's dictatorship in the early 1930s was, to be sure, a short one.[47] In addition to his books and articles endorsing the new regime, in 1933 Schmitt co-authored *Gleichschaltung* legislation.[48]

In Löwith's view, the intellectual affinities between Heidegger's philosophical existentialism and Schmitt's political existentialism are important and revealing. As he argues in "European Nihilism":

> It is no accident if Heidegger's existential ontology corresponds to a political "decisionism" in Carl Schmitt, a decisionism that shifts the "capacity-for-Being-a-whole" of Dasein which is always on its own, to the "totality" of the state which is always one's own. To the self-assertion of political existence and to "freedom towards death" corresponds the "sacrifice of life" in the political exigency of war. In both cases the principle is the same, namely "facticity," i.e., what remains of life when one does away with all life-content.[49]

The more one heeds Löwith's illuminating account of Germany's reigning spiritual mood during in the 1920s—a mood of existential nihilism, in which the pathos of resolute decision appeared as an obligatory standpoint—the more one appreciates the symptomatic profundity of the generational phenomenon at issue.

Heidegger's Retreat from Logos

Löwith's most enduring contribution to understanding Heidegger's philosophical legacy is the monograph, "Heidegger: Thinker in a Destitute Time," which has enjoyed the status of a minor classic since it first appeared in 1951.⁵⁰ The essay addresses the change of perspective or "epistemological break" between the early and later Heidegger—the *Kehre*, or "turn," in Heidegger's thinking. Perhaps nowhere is this shift of focus more evident than in the conceptual antitheses Heidegger used to describe his philosophical enterprise: whereas he characterizes *Being and Time* as a study in "existential ontology," his later philosophy seeks to fathom the "history of Being."

More than a few terminological subtleties are at stake in this momentous theoretical transmutation. As Löwith was perhaps the first to discern, at issue in the "turn" is fundamental ontology's viability as a mode of public discourse. Circa 1935, as Heidegger's political radicalism began to wane, his philosophical approach underwent a profound and lasting radicalization. Whereas in his early work Heidegger had engaged in a constant and productive dialogue with the major representatives of the tradition (a fact to which the lecture courses during the 1920s, recently published in the *Gesamtausgabe*, testify), from this point hence, he began to regard the tradition in its entirety as a "Verfallsphänomen": as a manifestation of decline.

According to this new understanding of the history of philosophy, Heidegger ceased to regard Platonism as the generative basis of Western metaphysics; he viewed it instead as the tradition's despoiler. According to Heidegger, with Plato there emerged the fateful ontological distinction between "sensible" and "supersensible" realms, from which our historical understanding of Being has never fully recovered. Thereafter, the truth of Being would be conceived as "Idea" or "representation"—as something subjective or proper to the *subjectum*. In Heidegger's view, Plato's misstep foreshadowed the post-Cartesian degeneration of philosophy to the terms of "calculative thinking." For Heidegger, "calculative thinking" and "reasoning" were the intellectual corollaries of the will to technological mastery characteristic of the modern "world-picture." According to this "picture" (*Bild*), Being—and beings—become grist for the mill of scientific manipulation *simpliciter*.⁵¹

Heidegger's sweeping repudiation of Western thought prefigures Derrida's disparagement of Western philosophy as "logocentric." This bold and totalizing maneuver had a debilitating effect on the communicative capacities of Heidegger's philosophy. Reconceptualized in the quasi-mystical idiom of the "destining of Being" (*Seinsgeschick*), Heidegger's thought forfeited its dialogical and argumentational character. Insofar as he was convinced that the entire philosophical tradition was contaminated by a progressively degenerative "abandonment by Being" (*Seinsverlassenheit*), there was little sense in engaging it in immanent or reasoned criticism. In fact, in his later work, he openly disavowed the standpoint of "philosophy" in favor of "thought" or "Denken." The etymological proximity between "thinking" and "thanking (*denken und danken*) becomes a recurrent leitmotif. "Thinking is thanking" (*Denken ist danken*) is an adage repeated ad nauseum.

According to this new interpretation of Western thought, philosophy experienced a brief efflorescence with the pre-Socratics—Heraclitus, Parmenides, and Anaximander, on whom Heidegger labors and lectures during the 1940s—whose philosophical fragments maintain a fragile sense of the truth of Being as "unconcealment" (*aletheia*). But, according to Heidegger, the pre-Socratic breakthrough was quickly covered up or re-concealed by post-Platonic "onto-theology." However, as Löwith points out: "The other side of Heidegger's endeavor toward a reappropriation of the originary thinking and discourse of the Greeks is the disparagement and the elimination of the entire philosophical language and conceptual apparatus of the modern age."[52]

In his reassessment of Western thought, Heidegger concluded that, owing to the causal relationship between metaphysics and the world-picture of modern technology (*das Gestell*), philosophy had forfeited its traditional cultural centrality. Today, *poets* rather than philosophers have proved most faithful to the oblique manner in which Being "comes to presence." Thus, in the 1930s and 1940s, Heidegger offered several lecture courses on Hölderlin, in which poetry's paramount role in the "setting-to-work of truth" received pride of place. Unsurprisingly, his conception of the essence of poetry was radically opposed to modernism's emphasis on formal experimentation or the aestheticism of art for art's sake. Nor was it entirely free of ideological taint. For Heidegger, the task of the poet is to ground the historical existence of a people or Volk. It is in this spirit that he proclaims Hölderlin to be both the poet of "German destiny" and the "voice of the Volk."[53]

Neologisms and terminological difficulties notwithstanding, the philosophical perspective Heidegger articulated in *Being and Time* was worldly and practical. Even though in Heidegger's eyes it remained a partial success (for example, the announced Part II on "Time and Being" was never written), it was a work that went far toward accomplishing the goal of reconciling the requirements of philosophical inquiry with the demands of human practical life. *Being and Time* repudiated transcendental philosophy's traditional point of departure— the monological self-enclosedness of the "thinking subject"—in favor of a rich plethora of "world-relations." At issue for Heidegger was Dasein's open-ended Being-in-the-world, rather than the self-referential insularity of "consciousness."

However—and herein lies the basis for Löwith's incisive and powerful critique—in Heidegger's later thought, such worldly concerns become, at best, a dim and distant memory. He no longer speaks from the engaged standpoint of Dasein's practical involvements or "worldliness." Instead, his discourse proceeds from the hermetic standpoint of Being itself. It attempts to give voice to the mysterious "destinings of Being," and he philosophizes from the standpoint of Being qua "fate" (*Seins-geschick*). Heidegger's later philosophy seeks to articulate the ineffable, which defies the habitudes and terms of public discourse. The history of Being is a story that can be told only via insinuation and evocation. Thus, in the "Letter on Humanism," in response to the question, "What is Being?", Heidegger can only offer the feeble rejoinder: "It is It itself," "*transcendens* pure and simple"—a self-identical, primordial substratum that resists the "logos," the philosophical method of providing coherent, intelligible accounts.[54] Instead, with the later Heidegger, we are confronted with mandates and claims that function as ex cathedra pronouncements, with positions that often defy the norms of intersubjective accountability. As Löwith observes, "Heidegger's claim concerning the necessity of his thinking will only convince those who along with him believe that his thinking has itself been sent by Being, a 'destining of Being' [*Seinsgeschick*] that expresses a 'decree concerning the truth of Being.'"[55] Heidegger's "farewell to reason" is epitomized by his conviction that, "Thinking begins only when we have come to know that reason, glorified for centuries, is *the most stiff-necked adversary of thought.*"[56]

As Löwith points out, the difficulty in evaluating the merits of Heidegger's later approach "lies in following a thinking that fundamentally disapproves of arguments and a 'logical' development. . . . Instead of proof on the basis of demonstration and evidence, there are only cryptic 'gestures' and hints."[57] Whereas Hegel's philosophy still moved comfortably within the orbit and terminology of Western metaphysics, "Heidegger's language dissociates itself from this very rationality. As an 'overcoming' [*Überwindung*] of onto-theology, it does not merely seek to avoid all conceptual determinacy but rather passes over into a 'saying Non-saying' [*ein sagendes Nicht-sagen*]." In Heidegger's quasi-apocalyptical worldview, continues Löwith: "Human beings are not 'rational animals' but instead ecstatic 'shepherds of Being'; all theoretical representing and technological producing, in which scientific thinking is grounded, is a degeneration of subjectivity to objectivity and a decline to unconditional objectification."[58]

Heideggerian "thinking" intentionally flirts with a prophetic-oracular rhetorical mode—to wit, the oft-cited claim from the 1966 *Der Spiegel* interview that "only a god can save us."[59] His later philosophy tends to provoke either fascination or repulsion; rarely does it elicit the type of sober and measured evaluation conducive to appraising its genuine intellectual worth. As Löwith points out, the danger of a discursive mode like Heidegger's is that, insofar as it claims for itself privileged access to a "kind of Being that not only surpasses all beings (including humans) but, like an unknown God, lingers and 'essences' in its own truth," it risks assuming the character of an impenetrable, hieratic doctrine. By seeking to articulate events that defy "experience," Heidegger risks forsaking the "bounds of sense," the intelligible limits of the phenomenal world. As Kant demonstrated in the *Critique of Pure Reason*, the distinction between sense and non-sense remains meaningful only in the case of judgments that respect the limits of experience—judgments that fall this side of the phenomenal/noumenal tandem. Conversely, Heidegger was fond of citing a portentous (and potentially anti-intellectual) Kierkegaard maxim: "The time of distinctions is past."

To inquire after the cogency of Heidegger's later thought means that ethical and political issues are never far removed. Although the doctrine of the "history of Being" studiously avoids the bustle of current events, it nevertheless scrutinizes modern politics under a harsh and unforgiving *metapolitical optic*. The later Heidegger remains a philosopher of "time" and "historicity"; as such, he is also a philosopher *of* his time, whose reflections on technology, politics, and society derive from his own historical situatedness. To the end, however, his summary pronouncements on postwar life (e.g., his claim in the aforementioned *Spiegel* interview that "modern literature [is] predominantly destructive")[60] expressed both insight and extreme judgmental myopia. As Löwith observes with reference to the later Heidegger's tendency to collapse history into "Being" qua *physis* or nature: "Is Heidegger's artful linguistic structure really able to illuminate the essence or nonessence of history, if history, with respect to Being as such, coincides with nature as *physis*? . . . History, which for Heidegger was at issue from the beginning, loses all definite and demonstrable meaning if, like *physis*, it is a ubiquitous emergence into the open and a retreat into what is closed off."[61] The rarefied metapolitical standpoint from which Heidegger's pontifications concerning politics and history proceed often acts as a hindrance to an immanent and fair-minded consideration of events in the world.

Needless to say, it would be erroneous to conclude as a result of such criticisms that one should no longer read Heidegger. Instead, one should no longer read him naively—that is, without careful attention to those aspects of his thought and intellectual habitus that facilitated his alliance with the Nazis in the early 1930s. Yet, as Löwith's arguments suggest, even Heidegger's postwar thought is hardly above taint. Years after the war ended, Heidegger continued to wax lyrical about the "inner truth and greatness of the National Socialism."[62]

Löwith's criticisms and observations remain timely. As a Heidegger student and intimate, his reflections present a unique vantage point from which to judge the complexities of Heidegger's case. Without malice or prejudice, he was able to expose those aspects of Heidegger's thought that evolved out of the *Zeitgeist* of the interwar period. Löwith disputes not Heidegger's greatness as a thinker, but the uses to which Heidegger allowed that greatness to be put. Heidegger's was an ambiguous greatness, one that was convinced of the need for a "total critique" of the modern world. In his view, the demands of total critique—a Spenglerian legacy of the 1920s—justified the adoption of any and every means in order to hasten the redemption of a degenerate historical present. But as Löwith inquires appropriately: "Is such a totalizing claim the result of historical knowledge and philosophical thinking or is it instead the translation of the doctrine of original sin into the perdition of the world of beings?"[63] With Heidegger's case, we are offered a parable concerning the perils of redemptory metapolitics. Few better understood the implications and import of this parable than Löwith.

Löwith's Retreat from History

The substance and tone of Löwith's critique incensed Heidegger. In a letter to a friend written shortly after the publication of "Thinker in a Destitute Time," Heidegger reacted as follows:

> I am not surprised that a fifty-five year-old man who, from 1919 on, took my courses and seminars for nine whole years and almost every other day in Marburg dashed into our house in order to squeeze something out of me can report on some things and thereby *appear* to many uninformed people to be in the know. The same author, while an immigrant in the United States, spread the most outrageous lies about me. . . . In 1929, when Löwith was the reddest Marxist (today he has turned Christian and occupies the chair at the University of Heidelberg), he wrote about *Being and Time* saying it was a "concealed theology." Later on he changed that to "atheism"—as one uses that term.[64]

Ironically, the pointed nature of Löwith's criticisms masked his own continued philosophical indebtedness to Heidegger. After all, Löwith had studied with Heidegger for nearly a decade and had written a habilitation study under his supervision. His approach to the history of philosophy and understanding of philosophical method were profoundly beholden to Heidegger. Unsurprisingly, such formative intellectual influences continued to play a major role in Löwith's mature thought.

Whereas Heidegger criticized the degeneracy of the modern world from the superordinate perspective of "Being," Löwith perfected an analogous critique of modernity proceeding from a "cosmological" standpoint. In "Thinker in a Destitute Time," Löwith objected to Heidegger's metaphilosophical standpoint of the "history of Being," which he claimed played the role of a first "unmoved mover," fundamentally inaccessible to human experience. However, much the same can be said with reference to Löwith's notion of the "cosmos." The uncritical celebration of "origins" (*das Ursprüngliche*), moreover, is quintessentially Heideggerian. As one critic has astutely observed: "The beginning that is supposed to count as the 'first' is declared to be beyond the continuity of historical development and is legitimated in the end through the sheer aura of an immemorial primordiality."[65]

Of course, by "cosmos," Löwith does not mean the heavens as an object of astronomical study. Instead, his standpoint is phenomenological. He seeks to convey the Stoic idea of the paltriness of human concerns when viewed against the backdrop of the universe as something eternal. The risks and uncertainties of modern historical consciousness—in essence, the problem of nihilism that occupied center stage in the thought of Nietzsche and Heidegger—compel Löwith to return to a purely "theoretical" standpoint: the classical ideal of the *bios theoretikos*. The virtue of "contemplation" is that it stands apart from the busy-ness and folly of worldly involvements.[66]

It was this attitude of Stoic detachment, he claimed, that allowed him to avoid succumbing to the Faustian temptations of modern political extremism. But the idea that one must reject historical consciousness entirely is itself an extreme measure. It sanctions the abandonment of history as a realm of senseless contingency. It is to confuse the *excesses* of modern historical consciousness—the crimes of totalitarian states—with the entirely legitimate emergence of democratic freedoms coincident with the revolutionary era.[67] To his discredit, Löwith refuses to recognize the moral legitimacy of the modern age: the fact that acts of democratic self-determination are able to compensate for and offset historical contingency. Even Marxism, as a variety of modern historical consciousness, is not, as Löwith claims in *From Hegel to Nietzsche*, a nihilistic abandonment of German classical philosophy. Instead, it is a critique (in the Kantian sense) of an approach to philosophy—Idealism—that displays a principled indifference to the demands of historical change.

Stoic detachment can too readily be deployed as a pretext for simply avoiding taking a stand. As such, it threatens to become ideological, a strategy of complacency vis-à-vis the "human world" and its problems. When philosophers, as the self-appointed guardians of eternal value and meaning, shelter "nature" and "cosmos" from the real-world demands of history, the distinctiveness of the human world—forged in labor, language, and political practice—disappears. When one views the world of human affairs with cosmological detachment, one courts the risks of anachronism, of succumbing to an interpretive antiquarianism and judgmental irrelevance. Tellingly, in one of the few instances where Löwith deigned to comment on contemporary affairs—a radio series on the problem of death in the modern world—his thoughts turned predictably to the Stoic ideal of suicide, which he endorsed enthusiastically as an exemplary moral choice. He gave not a thought to the problem of industrialized mass murder, the risks of nuclear annihilation, or the immorality of capital punishment. Instead, Löwith remained satisfied with a Third Century B.C.E. credo, whose modern exponents were Goethe, Hegel, and Burckhardt.[68]

Heidegger referred to his later standpoint as "releasement" or *Gelassenheit*. In stark contrast to his earlier *Existenzphilosophie*, which emphasized the importance of authenticity, resolve, and Dasein's potentiality to be a "Self," his later thought justified a quiescent adaptation to the mysterious dispensations of Being: "No mere [human] action will change the state of the world," observes Heidegger, "because Being as effectiveness and effecting closes all beings off in the face of the Event."[69] One would be perfectly justified in inquiring whether Löwith's perspective of Stoic detachment—his Nietzschean *amor fati* and complacent endorsement of "the worldhood of the world"—does not in fact surreptitiously ape Heidegger's own later approach, aptly summarized in Heidegger's injunction to "let beings be."

Both Löwith and Heidegger insist on the fecklessness of "action" or practical reason. They contend that the modern project of human self-assertion, beginning with the scientific revolution and the age of European expansion, has reaped nothing but disaster. But their understanding of the consequences and potential of the modern age remains limited and one-sided. In truth, the project of modernity is multidimensional. There are various logics or normative potentials at stake in each of modernity's various spheres.[70]

Both Heidegger and Löwith interpret modernity under the sign of "instrumental reason." They steadfastly ignore the aspects of modernity that are irreducible to these terms. They hastily write off advances in universalistic morality that are coincident with the expansion of democracy and social egalitarianism: the progression from civil to political to social and cultural rights.[71] Over the course of two centuries, the distinction between active and passive citizenship has largely been eliminated, culminating in the reality of universal suffrage. The claims of previously disenfranchised groups—women as well as various cultural and ethnic minorities—have also been acknowledged. Such sweeping social and political transformations, far from being "epiphenomenal," have gone a long way toward approximating the ideals of political democracy: self-determination and popular sovereignty. Even institutionalized science, despite its self-proclaimed aims of "world-mastery," possesses a reflexive dimension. With the disturbance of the balance of nature and other unintended consequences of untrammeled technological growth, concerned scientists have often organized themselves in a politically effective manner with the public interest in view. Yet, all such incremental transformations remain imperceptible from the "cosmological" perspective endorsed by Löwith and Heidegger.

Hans Jonas:

The Philosopher of Life

Being As Fate

ON APRIL 9, 1964, an intellectual event of international magnitude took place. The occasion was a Drew University conference on the relevance of Martin Heidegger's thought to Protestant theology. Originally, Heidegger himself had been scheduled to give the inaugural lecture, but a few months before the event he withdrew for reasons of health. In his stead, the conference organizers invited New School for Social Research philosophy professor Hans Jonas to give the opening address. The choice of Jonas as a replacement seemed a logical one. For four years during the 1920s, Jonas had studied philosophy under Heidegger at the University of Marburg. Under the guidance of Heidegger and the Protestant theologian Rudolf Bultmann, Jonas wrote a brilliant dissertation on the varieties of Gnostic religion in late antiquity. In 1934, the first volume of Jonas's study appeared in Germany. But by then Jonas had long fled his native land. Hitler's Law for the Reconstitution of the German Civil Service had effectively barred Jews from university posts. In 1933, Jonas sought refuge in London. Two years later, he emigrated to Palestine.

By the time of the Drew University gathering, the "Heidegger and theology" vogue had reached its pinnacle. The later Heidegger's celebration of an ineffable and primordial "Being," whose "call" humankind was supposed reverently to heed, was surely an oblique way of talking about God. In his 1947 "Letter on Humanism," whose title was

Fig. 3. Hans Jonas, Mönchengladbach, c. 1932. Photo by his cousin, Lisl Haas.

suggestive of an apostolic epistle, Heidegger characterized Being in neoscholastic terms as a type of first unmoved mover. Its mysterious "destinings" had nothing to do with "man" or "humanity," Heidegger claimed: "Man does not decide whether and how beings appear, whether and how God and the gods or history and nature come forward into the lighting of Being. . . . *The advent of beings lies in the destiny of Being.*"[1] In a celebrated 1966 interview with the German news magazine *Der Spiegel*, Heidegger boldly proclaimed that so forlorn and misguided had modern humanity become that "only a god can save us"—which seemed to clinch matters indeed. After his apostasy in the 1920s as proponent of a "existentialist humanism," Heidegger, the lapsed Catholic and the world's greatest living philosopher, had surely returned to the fold. Theologians everywhere could barely conceal their glee.

Few were prepared for the unyielding, yet sober, polemic that Jonas delivered from the podium that afternoon. Theologians had been seduced, he claimed, by the pseudo-religious implications of Heidegger's notion of the "fate-laden" character of thinking. Yet true Christian faith, explained Jonas, meant that the believer would be *delivered from* the arbitrariness of fate. Redemption, moreover, and the belief that inspired it, were not events of this world and thus were far from predestined or "fated." Instead, Christianity had always depended on a spiritual dignity that transcended mundane temporality and the injustices of fate. Lastly, God's biblical injunctions—to Adam, to Cain, to Abraham—were all *ethical commandments*, not summonses to blind ontological obedience. And in the event the audience had any doubts as to where Heidegger's own "obedience to fate" had led during the 1930s, Jonas took it upon himself to refresh their memories:

> As for Heidegger's Being, it is an occurrence of unveiling, a fate-laden happening upon thought: so was the Führer and the call of German destiny under him: an unveiling of something indeed, a call of Being all right, fate-laden in every sense: neither then nor now did Heidegger's thought provide a norm by which to decide how to answer such calls. . . . Heidegger's own answer is, to the shame of philosophy, on record and, I hope,

not forgotten: "Let not doctrines and 'ideas' be the rules of your Being. The Führer himself and alone is the present and future German reality and its law. Learn ever deeper to know: that from now on each and everything demands decision, and every action, responsibility. Heil Hitler!"[2]

Jonas's astute critique of the ethical deficits besetting "fundamental ontology" had a marked impact on subsequent Heidegger scholarship. Although the Drew University conference had been conceived and staged as a "pro-Heidegger" event, Jonas's moral eloquence and humanity ultimately held sway: as he finished speaking, the audience rose to give him a standing ovation. The Heideggerian faithful proffered their rebuttals. Yet, by daring to confront Heidegger's Nazism directly and—what was at the time even more controversial—by seeking to tie the philosopher's political *lapsus* directly to the deficiencies of his thought, Jonas displayed the unwavering moral integrity that would become the hallmark of his life and work.

Untimely Meditations

Hans Jonas was born in 1903 in Mönchengladbach, Germany. Though his philosophical studies began in 1921, for the next three years he was also a student at Berlin's University for the Science of Judaism. An interest in Jewish theology remained an abiding concern until the end of his life. As émigrés, Löwith, Jonas, and Hannah Arendt would, in succession, assume positions in the philosophy department of the New School for Social Research. Jonas's tenure there began in 1955 and ended with his retirement in 1976.

With the exception of Jonas, for whom Judaism had always been a living concern, the rest of this group came from highly assimilated backgrounds. In the late 1920s, like most acculturated Jews, they labored under the delusion that German nationality was largely a question of language and culture, not one of race. Circa 1933, the scales abruptly fell from their eyes. In *My Life in Germany Before and After 1933*, Löwith provides eloquent testimony concerning the shock of recognition experienced by assimilated Jewry at the outset of the Nazi years.

Speaking of fellow-Heidegger student Oskar Becker, Löwith observes: "The same person who in our Freiburg student days had studied mathematics, music and philosophy, read Dostoevsky and Kierkegaard, and whose best friends had been a Jewish girl and I, had not the least scruple about showing complete indifference to the universal fate of the Jews."[3]

In a lecture delivered at a memorial tribute to Rudolf Bultmann following the theologian's death in 1976, Jonas recounts a more heartening experience from the same dark hour of German-Jewish history:

> It was the summer of 1933, here in Marburg. We sat around the dinner table with [Bultmann's] lovely, so richly emotional wife and their three schoolgirl daughters, and I related what I had just read in the newspaper, but he not yet, namely, that the German Association of the Blind had expelled its Jewish members. My horror carried me into eloquence: In the face of eternal night (so I exclaimed) the most unifying tie there can be among suffering men, this betrayal of the solidarity of a common fate—and I stopped, for my eye fell on Bultmann and I saw that a deathly pallor had spread over his face, and in his eyes was such agony that the words died in my mouth. In that moment I knew that in matters of elementary humanity one could simply rely on Bultmann, that words, explanations, arguments, most of all rhetoric, were out of place, that no insanity of the time could dim the steadiness of his inner light.[4]

Upon emigrating to Jerusalem, Jonas supported himself by teaching and part-time publishing work. With the onset of the war, he promptly enlisted in the British Army's Jewish Brigade, bypassing a position in military intelligence to serve on the front lines. He fought for five years—the Italian campaign of 1943 proved particularly brutal—and in 1945, still wearing a British uniform, he participated in the liberation of his native Germany, thereby fulfilling a vow of twelve years earlier to return to German soil only as the soldier of a conquering army. Only upon returning to Jerusalem in 1945 did he receive the crushing news that, in 1942, his mother had been murdered at Auschwitz.

In 1948, he once again donned a uniform, this time assigned to an artillery unit during the Israeli war of independence. Following demobilization, he emigrated to Canada, where for six years he taught at McGill and Carleton Universities before settling permanently in New York. Jonas always maintained that his combat experience permanently altered his philosophical views. One of the noticeable gaps of his professional training in Germany during the 1920s had been a lack of focus on both the body and nature. In the course of Heidegger's seminars, for example, there was never much discussion of either theme. For Jonas, conversely, the body and nature represented fundamental aspects of what it meant to be human. Hunger and mortality—two fundamental instances of our indebtedness to the natural world—were irreducible components of human experience, no matter how much post-Cartesian philosophy had sought to minimize or deny them. As Jonas explains in a brilliant and moving essay, "Science as Personal Experience," the opportunity for reflections on the somatic dimensions of human existence

> came with [my] years as a soldier during the Second World War, when I was forced to abandon historical research for what one can reflect upon without books and libraries, since it is always at one's disposal. Perhaps the sheer fact of physical exposure, in which the body's fate thrust itself to the fore, and in which its mutilation became a primary fear, helped facilitate this new way of thinking. In any event, at this point I fully rejected the idealist prejudices of the philosophical tradition. I saw its hidden dualism, a thousand-year legacy, refuted by the *organism*, whose existential attributes we share with all living things. An ontological appreciation of the organism would close the gap that separates the self-awareness of the soul from the knowledge of physics.[5]

In this way, Jonas sought to broaden the methods of existential analysis he had learned during his apprenticeship with Heidegger in Marburg. By appreciating those aspects of being we share with nonhuman life, humanity is not thereby degraded; instead, the prospect of a new cosmic harmony appears. In Jonas's philosophy of nature, possibilities for a genuinely symbiotic relationship between man and nature—suppressed for centuries as a result of the technological domination of nature—reemerge. Thus, amid the agonies and deprivations of battle, Jonas had put his training as a phenomenologist to good use. The essential precariousness of human existence made clear to him our irreducible existential proximity to the rest of organic nature.

Jonas's philosophical output was modest by conventional standards. He had three major books and several volumes of essays to his credit. Nevertheless, there is little doubt that his was one of the more original and important philosophical minds of the twentieth century. Sadly, it seems that his philosophy never really caught on in North America. Although his work was certainly admired and appreciated by *cognoscenti*, it never received the broad attention it truly merited. German literary critic Walter Benjamin always feared that, were he to emigrate to the United States, he would be put on public display as "the last intellectual." So integrally bound were his ideas and persona to a European cultural context that they were predestined to be misunderstood in a civilization in which *Geld* was of greater import than *Geist*.

Jonas, who made few compromises with the dominant intellectual trends of his adoptive homeland, seems to have suffered a fate roughly analogous to the one Benjamin feared. The reigning schools of American philosophy—logical positivism, linguistic analysis, and pragmatism—had little use for the incurably European metaphysical habitudes that were the mainstays of his approach. For most of his professional life, Jonas remained preoccupied with "eternal" philosophical questions—humanity's place in the cosmological scheme of things; the meaning of God after Auschwitz; the ontological basis of ethics—that American philosophy, with its hard-nosed empirical bent, had long condemned to the realm of intellectual irrelevancy. Such concerns were officially belittled as "pseudo-problems." They proved refractory to the sober and painstaking methods of philosophical analysis. As such they should be left to the fantasies of poets, theologians, and *Luftmenschen*.

Ironically, it was in his native Germany—the land Jonas was forced to flee upon pain of death in 1933—that his intellectual legacy received its proper due. Jonas wrote his major philosophical work, *The Imperative of Responsibility*, in German. Published in 1979, five years before it appeared in English, this breathtaking meditation on the ethical implications of modern technology catapulted him to international renown. To date, the German edition alone has sold an astounding 200,000 copies: a figure that is especially remarkable, since, of all his books, it is the most philosophically recondite. But with this insightful meditation on the unprecedented moral challenges posed by an age of nuclear fission and environmental devastation, Jonas's philosophical instincts proved, for once, perfectly in tune with the *Zeitgeist*. Scholarly conferences were devoted to his work. Captains of German industry vied to appear alongside him in public discussions. German news magazines eagerly sought him out for interviews and professional counsel. *The Imperative of Responsibility* (*Das Prinzip Verantwortung*) became something of a shibboleth among the German Greens and their sympathizers. Allusions to Jonas and his work became *de rigeur* at almost any discussion or forum where environmental ethics were at issue. Rival philosophical schools set out to refute him. In 1987, at the age of 84, Jonas was awarded the prestigious Peace Prize of the German Booksellers' Association. That same year, he received the Federal Republic of Germany's Distinguished Service Cross. Most of this acclaim took place during the ninth and final decade of his life. On February 5, 1993, the eighty-nine-year-old Jonas died at his home in New Rochelle, New York.

Nihilism and Gnosis

Jonas achieved intellectual maturity amid the turmoil and uncertainties of Germany's short-lived Weimar Republic. The 1920s remains one of the defining decades of the twentieth century, in part because of the profound problems of political and cultural instability it posed. In many respects, it represented the high-water mark of aesthetic modernism. While stationed in provincial Marburg, Jonas personally had little direct contact with the modernist spirit. Yet the intellectual disorientation and perplexity that were its signatures left a profound imprint on his thought, in ways both subliminal and manifest.

Jonas's inaugural study of Gnostic religion, written under the tutelage of Heidegger and Bultmann, was a resolutely antiquarian undertaking.[6] Gnosticism—from the Greek word for "knowledge"—was a religious orientation peculiar to early Christianity. As a doctrine, Gnosticism's signature is a radical dualism between God and the world. Gnosticism begins by positing a primordial condition of divine integrity. This original unity is subsequently disrupted, accounting for the emergence of the world and the demonic powers controlling it. "Man" becomes the crucial pawn in this eschatological pageant, with the restoration of cosmological wholeness contingent upon his salvation. The cleft between heaven and earth is one of Manichean intensity. God is alleged to be entirely supramundane, even acosmic. Only by purifying itself of all mundane attributes—symptomatic of the purgatory of earthly existence—and associating itself exclusively with the transcendent divine *pneuma*, or spirit, can humanity attain salvation. Gnostic doctrine is to provide the secret "knowledge" leading to redemption and a restoration of cosmic unity. As Jonas describes this process:

> The human constitution is comparable to an onion with many layers, on the model of the cosmos itself but with the order reversed; what is outermost and uppermost in the cosmos is innermost in man, and the innermost or nethermost stratum of the cosmic order, the earth, is the outer bodily garment of man. Only the innermost or pneumatic man is the true man, and he is not of this world, as his original in the total order, the deity, is external to the cosmos as a whole. In its unredeemed state the spirit, so far from its source and immersed in soul and flesh, is unconscious of itself, benumbed, asleep, or intoxicated by the poison of the world—in brief, it is ignorant. Its awakening and liberation are effected through knowledge. . . . Revelation, or the "call," is already a part of salvation. Its bringer is a messenger from the world of Light who penetrates the barriers of the spheres, outwits the archons, awakens the spirit from its earthly slumber, and imports to it the saving knowledge from without.[7]

Jonas described the fundamental Gnostic dualism between God and world as deriving from specific sociohistorical conditions: "the immanent experience of the disunion of man and world [which] reflects a human condition of alienation."[8] In the early 1930s, Jonas believed he had uncovered an analogous dualism, a parallel "human condition of alienation," in the modern period. He concluded that existentialism expressed the same pronounced man-world dualism, the same heightened sense of human alienation from the world. This realization caused him to reassess his entire scholarly focus. He gradually relinquished his antiquarian concerns; instead, his work became relentlessly present-oriented. In direct response to the agonizing historical catastrophes that Jonas had witnessed firsthand—the rise of Nazism, two world wars, and the Holocaust—he set himself an enormous intellectual task: to uncover the philosophical origins of the crisis of Western civilization, and thereby to suggest, however tentatively, a new, positive orientation for humanity.

The key to Jonas's probing diagnosis of the modern age and its failings lay with the idea of nihilism. Modern nihilism was preponderantly an outgrowth of modern science. Science had been so successful in challenging and unmasking every variety of superstition and ungrounded belief that, in the end, it left men and women with nothing left in which to believe.

For Jonas, the parallels between modern science and the worldview of Gnosticism were undeniable. Both eras suffered from a radical crisis of meaning that led to a profound sense of homelessness. Worldly existence was wholly scorned or devalued. All that remained was humanity's self-inflated belief in its own subjectivity as a key to restoring the immanence of meaning. Yet this made for a volatile situation that was paradoxically capable of encouraging a frenetic voluntarism as humanity desperately sought to reestablish the lost connection between existence and meaning. In the case of Gnosticism, acosmic sentiments, in alliance with the precepts of negative theology, could easily lead to an antinomian attitude of untrammeled licentiousness: since law applied only to the *profane* sphere of worldly existence, transgressions were viewed positively insofar as they might point the way to redemption. As Jonas explains: "there is a positive duty to perform every kind of action, to leave no deed undone, no possibility of freedom unrealized, in order to render nature its due and exhaust its powers; only in this way can final release from the cycle of reincarnations be obtained."[9] Political Messianism arose in response to nihilism in order to restore, via secular means, the condition of integrity that had been lost amid the lacerations and divisions of modern society. Political Messianism—communism, fascism, varieties of integral nationalism—also displays antinomian traits insofar as it sanctions unethical means to further the ends of political salvation.

Science and Existential Homelessness

In "Gnosticism, Existentialism, and Nihilism," which appeared as part of *The Phenomenon of Life*, Jonas traced nihilism's origins back to the scientific revolution. According to the cosmologies of classical antiquity and Christianity, there was as yet no ontological abyss separating humanity from the natural world. For the ancient Greeks, who were denied an afterlife, virtue was primarily oriented toward worldly achievement. Greek religion, moreover, was naturalist and nondualistic. With Christianity, a fissure between humanity and the world began to emerge. Humanity's higher self was spiritual, and the earth was a vale of tears. Yet (fallen) nature, too, was ultimately God's creation, and with the Second Coming, the original harmony between humanity and nature would be restored.

But with the emergence of modern science, prospects for reconciling humanity and nature were abruptly suspended. Nature was viewed primarily through the lens of instrumental reason: as an object to be controlled, exploited, and manipulated. In the words of Francis Bacon, "the sovereignty of man lieth hid in knowledge. . . . Now we govern nature in opinions, but we are thrall unto her in necessity: but if we would be led by her invention, we should command her by action."[10] And so the hunt began. By the time of Descartes, the final traces of nature's ensoulment, of all prospects for maintaining a fraternal bond between humanity and nature, had been extirpated. Instead, nature was degraded to the status of *res extensa* or "extended substance." "Man," conversely, was redefined as *res cogitans* or "thinking substance." The ontological chasm between these two types of being—one of the hallmarks modern thought—became essentially unbridgeable.

A moment of delectable absurdity arose when the question of how to classify animals—which appeared to fit neatly into neither category—arose. Descartes's solution to this Hobson's choice was to claim that animals were "inanimate" and thus to subsume them under the *res extensa* side of the ledger. The folly of such reductive and dichotomous schemes culminated in the high Enlightenment, when *philosophe* Julien de La Mettrie decided the world would be better off if humans, too, were understood in exclusively physicalist terms. The consequences of this ingenious deduction were well-expressed in the title of his 1748 work, *L'Homme machine* ("Man a Machine"). Between the extremes of mind and the physical world, a third term, organic nature, had been inexplicably left out of the picture.

In "Gnosticism, Existentialism, and Nihilism," Jonas expressed the basic paradox of Descartes's philosophical legacy as follows: "That by which man is superior to all nature, his unique distinction, mind, no longer results in a higher integration of his being into the totality of being, but on the contrary marks the unbridgeable gulf between himself and the rest of existence."[11] With this insight, the reasons subtending humanity's "existential homelessness" first become intelligible. Once the universe is so thoroughly divested of intrinsic meaning—Galileo thought of the moon as little more than a big rock—values forfeit their ultimate ontological basis, and the isolated human self is confronted with the daunting prospect of having to generate meaning entirely from within itself, solipsistically. According to the cosmology of the Middle Ages, all created being is separated into existence and essence, and God alone exists perfectly or essentially. Once the perfection of the creator is eliminated, both humans and world are catapulted into unbounded existential flux. As Jonas observes:

> modern nihilism [is] infinitely more radical and more desperate than gnostic nihilism ever could be for all its terror of the world and its defiant contempt of its laws. That nature does not care, one way or the other, is the true abyss. That only man cares, in his finitude facing nothing but death, alone with his contingency and the objective meaninglessness of his projecting meanings, is a truly unprecedented situation.[12]

The *coup de grâce* for our understanding of the natural world as inherently meaningful occurred with Darwinism. According to the traditional view, nature functioned teleologically. As such, it was interpreted as a repository of prior causes or ends that were predestined to come to fruition. All such assurances were cancelled in the aftermath of Darwin's theory of evolution. Instead, it became clear that the course of organic life failed to conform to any preconceived pattern. The watchwords of the post-Darwinian understanding of nature became: chance, natural selection, and diversity. At a later point, the durability of heredity was undermined by the notion of mutation as a driving force behind evolutionary "progress." As Jonas affirms in *The Phenomenon of Life*: "The Darwinian theory of evolution, with its combination of chance variation and natural selection, completed the extrusion of teleology from nature. Having become redundant even in the story of life, purpose retired wholly into subjectivity." In this way, the doctrine of evolution "completes the liquidation of immutable essences, and thus signifies the final victory of nominalism over realism, which had its last bulwark in the idea of natural species."[13]

Nietzsche once remarked that, "Since Copernicus, man has been rolling from the center to point *X*."[14] Darwinism delivered an additional traumatic blow to human narcissism. Humanity ceased to be the crown of creation. Instead, its undignified simian origins unmasked, humans, like all other species, were reduced to the status of a biological accident.

The Imperative of Life

From the recesses of modern nihilism, Jonas painstakingly began to reconstruct a philosophical program capable of raising questions concerning the ultimate ends of human existence. His undertaking was unfashionable, even anachronistic in crucial respects. Yet the conclusions he reached were no less remarkable for that reason. Unlike many of his contemporaries interested in similar problems, Jonas refused to regress behind the empirical standards that had been established by modern science. Instead, he attempted to utilize them as the basis for a new philosophy of nature. Yet, whereas modern physics and biology had come to the conclusion that the universe and life on earth were essentially devoid of intrinsic meaning, Jonas boldly took it upon himself to provide a restoration of purpose and meaning. To this end, Jonas sought to reestablish the fact that organic life, insofar as it is governed by purposes or ends, is meaningful; and that humanity's place in the cosmological scheme of things, when viewed against the background of purposive nature, is similarly replete with purpose.

We know that life is governed by certain necessities and regularities: the imperatives of nourishment, procreation, and mortality. But what sense does it make to describe life—not just human life, but the totality of organic life—as intrinsically meaningful? For Jonas, life is meaningful insofar as all of organic life may be said to display purposes, strivings, even—in however rudimentary a form—"subjectivity." Ultimately, Jonas would take this controversial argument a step further, claiming that all life manifests an inclination toward freedom. As he remarks in *The Phenomenon of Life*: "it is in the dark stirrings of primeval organic substance that a principle of freedom shines forth for the first time within the vast necessity of the physical universe—a principle foreign to suns, planets, and atoms."[15] With the emergence of life, the existential distinction between being and non-being first becomes meaningful: perennially threatened by the prospect of its negation, life must tenaciously maintain itself in being; it must undertake a series of elaborate and resourceful acts of self-preservation if it is to avoid succumbing to its diabolical contrary, death. In this way the drama of life, momentarily suspended between non-being and negation, initiates the idea of existential purpose in a manner that is entirely foreign to the realm of inorganic nature. Thereby, the concepts of "concern" and "meaning" enter into being for the first time. As Jonas expresses it:

> Not-being made its appearance in the world as an alternative embodied in being itself; and thereby being itself first assumes an emphatic sense: intrinsically qualified by the threat of its negative it must affirm itself, and existence affirmed is existence as *concern*. So constitutive for life is the possibility of not-being that its very being is essentially a hovering over this abyss, a skirting of its brink: thus being itself has become a constant possibility rather than a given state, ever anew to be laid hold of in opposition to its ever-present contrary, not-being, which will inevitably engulf it in the end.[16]

The "existential paradox" of life may be summarized as follows: the fact that life carries its own negation within itself is what provides it with the ultimate incentive for self-affirmation (self-preservation). The imminent prospect of non-being—life's ultimate existential precariousness—is what drives it on to maintain itself in being.

In Jonas's view, an understanding of the "unity of life" allows us to surmount the dualisms of modern thought—mind and body, subject and object, idealism and materialism—in the direction of a holistic naturalism. He accomplishes this not by downgrading or relativizing humanity's singularity, but instead by arguing that nature itself—like man, though on a more humble scale—manifests traces of subjectivity. To be sure, this contention is one of the more controversial aspects of Jonas's philosophy. One of the keys to his argument is a brilliant, if highly speculative, understanding of the teleological implications of "metabolism."

Jonas concurs with modern science that metabolism is something that distinguishes organic from inorganic life. However, he views this claim as being replete with metaphysical significance. For Jonas, metabolism suggests a capacity for existential autonomy that distinguishes organic life from the rest of the physical world. The organism's capacity for freedom—the defining expression of its "subjectivity"—lies in its formal independence vis-à-vis the material world. At one point, Jonas goes so far as to speak of the emergence of life as marking an "ontological revolution in the history of matter."[17] Whereas matter remains self-identical, life is self-mediating and self-transformative. Life's formal independence versus inorganic nature manifests itself in the internal identity of the organism above and beyond all metabolic transformations it might undergo.

Because of this capacity to maintain their identities, Jonas attributes "selfhood" to the entities of organic nature. The understanding of life that emerges is quasi-Hobbesian: "An identity which from moment to moment reasserts itself, achieves itself, and defies the equalizing forces of physical sameness all around is truly pitted against the rest of things. . . . The challenge of selfhood qualifies all [that is] beyond the boundaries of the organism as foreign and somehow opposite: as 'world,' in which, by which, and against which it is committed to maintain itself."[18]

Jonas terms the freedom, or selfhood, of organic nature "dialectical"; the capacity for metabolism is both a sign of independence and a mark of biological necessity—hence dependency, for life cannot cease to metabolize without ceasing to be. Jonas phrases the problem succinctly: "its liberty itself is its peculiar necessity."[19]

Jonas's metaphysical reinterpretation of the workings of organic nature discerns subjectivity, freedom, and selfhood where one might least expect to find them. In life's struggle for self-preservation, its efforts to maintain its boundaries vis-à-vis the inorganic world, Jonas sees anticipations of "mind." In his view, even the lowest forms of sentient life anticipate inwardness or spirit, however faintly. As Jonas explains: "Whether we call this inwardness feeling, sensitivity and response to stimulus, appetition or nisus—in some (even if infinitesimal) degree of 'awareness' it harbors the supreme concern of organism with its own being and continuation in being. . . . With the first dawn of subjective reflex, the most germinal 'experience' of touching, a crack as it were opens in the opacity of divided being, unlocking . . . the dimension of *inwardness*."[20]

Speculative theses such as those attributed by Jonas to organic life can be neither wholly proved nor disproved. Instead, they require that we suspend our customary, objectivating attitude toward nature—the attitude predominant among the natural sciences—and take time to marvel at the wonder of life.

The Technological Threat and the Heuristics of Fear

When Jonas was born in 1903, the horse-drawn carriage was still a leading mode of transportation. By the end of his life, nuclear fission had been discovered, jet travel had become routine, and "moonwalks" were commonplace. An ambitious scientific study was underway to discover and map human genetic makeup in its entirety. The ethical repercussions of this undertaking—the so-called Human Genome Project—the seemingly unlimited prospects it provided for biological engineering, gave pause to many. In human history, the period spanning the invention of tools to the advent of modern technology was an eternity. On the scale of evolutionary history, it represented the blink of an eye.

During the twentieth century, the balance between humankind and the natural world has been radically and permanently altered, largely due to humanity's technological inventiveness. Such changes have unleashed a wholesale transformation of the parameters of human experience. Its familiarity and predictability can no longer be presupposed in view of the drastic rate and scope of scientific change. As Georg Simmel observed in "The Metropolis and Mental Life": "The psychological foundation upon which [modern] individuality is erected is the intensification of emotional life due to the swift and continuous shift of external and internal stimuli: rapid telescoping of changing images, pronounced differences within what is grasped at a single glance, and the unexpectedness of violent stimuli." Whereas traditional forms of life placed an emphasis on the personality as a whole, the modern division of labor militates against wholeness. Instead, the individual is reduced to a "negligible quantity": "a single cog as over against the vast overwhelming organization of things and forces which gradually take out of his hands everything connected with progress, spirituality and value."[21]

In *The Imperative of Responsibility*, Jonas sought to confront the moral implications of humanity's unprecedented technological reach. When the work appeared, Hannah Arendt reportedly exclaimed, "Hans, that is the book that God had in mind when he created you!"[22] In Jonas's view, so formidable and potent have the new technologies at humanity's disposal become that they have rendered obsolete 2,500 years of ethical discourse. Heretofore, humankind's interventions in the natural world were limited in scope, and their consequences were readily foreseeable. For this reason, the balance between humanity and nature was never fundamentally in doubt. No such assurances can be provided concerning the impact of modern technology, which, contrary to all precedents, has already permanently altered the earth's biosphere in numerous respects and which continues to do so in ways whose consequences have yet to be fully determined.

The breathtaking pace of technological change not only affects the interchange between humanity and nature; it precipitates a rash of existential doubt, a crisis in human self-understanding. Ironically, humanity's enhanced mastery of external nature has often left it feeling more vulnerable, more exposed to unanticipated side effects and risks. Who is controlling the process? Who is dictating the rate of technological change? No one knows for sure. Human ingenuity has engendered a giant mechanism, and no one can tell what its ultimate repercussions might be. As Jonas puts it: "Outshining in prestige and starving in resources whatever else belongs to the fullness of man, the expansion of his power is accompanied by a contraction of his self-conception and being."[23]

Traditional approaches to ethics—Aristotle's "phronesis," Kant's "categorical imperative"—were accustomed to dealing with human action that fell within well-defined and familiar parameters. Such doctrines were based on seemingly immutable historical and biological regularities. Under the radically changed situation inaugurated by technological modernity, however, ethical prescriptions that are merely oriented toward "the good" (Aristotle), or that rest content to treat persons as "ends in themselves" (Kant), might well prove defenseless in the face of the worst-case scenario of ecological catastrophe. Under such conditions, argues Jonas, a fundamental reevaluation of humanity's relation to the natural world has itself become an ethical imperative.

One of the features that makes Jonas's approach to environmental ethics appealing and that distinguishes it from various trendy eco-fundamentalisms is that his strategy is both rationalist and anthropocentric. According to Jonas, one ought to approach nature with a measure of ethical forbearance not because the earth represents something sacred (as "Gaiaists" would have it), nor because all living species are of equal worth; instead, it behooves us to act responsibly toward nature insofar as the survival of humankind itself is at stake. In this respect, Jonas unfashionably wears his indebtedness to the Western tradition on his sleeve. He has no doubt that humans are the noblest creatures that the evolutionary process has yielded. He readily owns up to the fact that the philosophy of nature adumbrated in *The Phenomenon of Life* is anthropocentric, insofar as it attributes human purposes (mind, subjectivity, and freedom) to subhuman organic life. Lastly, there is nothing remotely anti-intellectual about Jonas's approach. He does not seek to explain the current ecological threat, for example, by claiming that the culprit is a surfeit of human reason. To be sure, the one-sidedness of human rationality—its instrumentalist biases—plays an important role in his account. But Jonas firmly believes that only the hand that has inflicted the wound—in the case at issue, human ingenuity itself—can cure the disease.

In keeping with this avowedly anthropocentric orientation, Jonas defines the "imperative of responsibility" as follows: "Act so that the effects of your action are compatible with the permanence of genuine human life." Expressed negatively, it reads: "Act so that the effects of your action are not destructive of the future possibility of such life." Thus formulated, the imperative of responsibility seeks to respond to the fact that, for traditional ethics, the scope of human action has always been strictly limited. Never before has ethical theory been forced to confront the prospect that technology could place life as a whole at risk.

One of the controversial features of Jonas's attempt to provide an ethics appropriate to the age of modern technology is that his efforts fly in the face of the philosophical injunction against deriving "ought" from "is," the adage that value judgments cannot be based on statements of fact. The "fact/value" distinction suggests that merely because things exist in a certain way does not mean that this was the way they were *meant* to be or that they should necessarily continue to be that way. Instead, "ought" or "right" are the province of human reason; they are not constants inscribed in the laws of nature.

Part of the reason Jonas feels compelled to transgress this hallowed philosophical precept pertains to the dire nature of the present crisis: when the fate of life itself hangs in the balance, moral foundations must be forceful and unarguable, even if this means grounding them ontologically—in Being as such. Thus, by referring to "life" as an inherent value and claiming that we have a duty to ensure its future viability, Jonas implicitly relies on the metaphysics of nature he sketched in *The Phenomenon of Life*. The preservation of life is not merely something that we owe to ourselves qua humans. It is an imperative that is incumbent upon us as part of a greater living whole for which we, as nature's most potent creation, bear special responsibility.

By seeking to ground ethics in life, Jonas seeks to provide morality with an objective basis, in contrast to the merely subjective, hence nonbinding, character of most modern ethical systems. As Jonas succinctly phrases matters: "*Being, in the testimony it gives of itself, informs us not only about what it is but also about what we owe it.*"[24] Were Being deprived of the richness and variety proper to organic life, it would become faceless and mute, devoid of purpose, ontologically impoverished to an extreme. Like the later Heidegger, Jonas believed that the "remembrance of Being" should become a spur to the ethical betterment of humanity in the here and how. As Jonas concludes: "Only from the objectivity of value could an objective 'ought-to-be' in itself be derived, and hence for us a binding *obligation* to the guarding of being, that is, a responsibility toward it."[25]

The urgent demands of the contemporary historical hour suggest the need for what Jonas calls a "heuristics of fear." Since humanity's hypertrophic technological capacities have placed the future of life as such in jeopardy, the threshold for experimentation or risk-taking must be reduced to an absolute minimum, he argues. Motivated by a sense of imminent catastrophe, the "heuristics of fear" suggests that our technological interventions must be tempered and guided by a "comparative futurology" that places a premium on the elaboration of worst-case scenarios. With stakes of such magnitude, to proceed other than with the greatest circumspection and vigilance would be to succumb to the temptations of irresponsibility. It would be tantamount to flirting with collective self-annihilation; a course that, in view of the sanctity of life, is ethically impermissible. According to Jonas, therefore, we need the "*threat* to the image of man to assure ourselves of his true image by the very recoil from these threats."²⁶ Too often, long-term environmental risks—whose realities are often matters of conjecture—exist at such a temporal remove from the historical present that they are very difficult to factor into the horizon of our short-term ethical purview. A heuristics of fear is needed, argues Jonas, as an urgent reminder of the unprecedented nature of our new technological reach.

But also at stake in the use-value of this concept is a crucial insight into the workings of human psychology. According to Jonas, once again agreeing with Hobbes, it is an empirical fact that humans are often more readily motivated by fear than by an appreciation of the good. "This is the way we are made," he contends: "the perception of the *malum* is infinitely easier to us than the perception of the *bonum*; it is more direct, more compelling, less given to differences of opinion or taste. . . . An evil forces its perception on us by its mere presence, whereas the beneficial can be present unobtrusively and remain unperceived, unless we reflect on it."²⁷ Developing an attitude of existential "openness" toward the prospects of this *malum* is, therefore, one of the primary duties of the ethic of responsibility that Jonas favors.

Perils of Political Guardianship

While the dynamism and scope of Jonas's metaphysical vision are undeniably powerful, that vision, like all claims to knowledge, is hardly above criticism. The strategy of his philosophy of life, which insists vitalistically upon attributing "mind" and "subjectivity" to all manifestations of organic nature, down to the cellular level, entails intellectual and ethical risks. By humanizing nature and naturalizing humanity, we in effect strip humankind of its specifically human capacities. Is it meaningful to speak of the "freedom" of organic molecular life, when, as Jonas himself points out, such freedom, in the form of metabolism, is governed by an overriding necessity? In truth, organisms have no choice: they must metabolize or die. By metabolizing, they gain a measure of formal independence vis-à-vis the dead matter of inorganic nature; but does it make sense to equate such limited independence with "freedom"? By virtue of such comparisons, do we not risk remaining satisfied with a seriously truncated definition of freedom? Viewed historically, freedom connotes a hard-won achievement, a condition that is the result of struggle and courage. To suggest affinities between freedom and metabolism implies that we should rest content with a subhuman notion of freedom's entailments.

Another risk entailed by Jonas's insistence on life as an absolute value is that our conception of the human good is devalued. Instead of setting our sights high and aiming at a notion of the good in which individuals are encouraged to flourish—where they are allowed to realize or fulfill their capacities—Jonas's metaphysical vitalism tends to privilege "mere life" or survival over the "good life." If we accord normative priority to aspects of life we share in common with the rest of organic nature, those features of human life that are peculiarly *human*— cultural excellence, friendship, productive communal ties; in sum, all the characteristics of human life that *separate* us from the animal world— suffer. Thus, the price one pays for reintegrating humankind with the natural world is a diminution of human distinctiveness.

Many of the aforementioned difficulties crystallize in those aspects of Jonas's thought that one might describe as Hobbesian. Like the author of *Leviathan*, Jonas's conception of human life is predicated on a pessimistic philosophical anthropology. For both Hobbes and Jonas, the state of nature is anything but benevolent. Hobbes describes human interaction there as a *bellum omnium contra omnes*—a war of all against all—in which life is "violent, poor, nasty, brutish, and short." The motivations compelling individuals to abandon this state and form a social compact are anything but noble or exalted. Instead, the primary incentive to establish society is *fear*—fear of a violent death. Jonas's proximity to Hobbes (not to mention Darwin) becomes clear in his characterization of life as essentially a competitive struggle for survival. By taking nature and biology as his normative points of departure rather than, say, life in civil society, Jonas is led to anticipate the worst from humanity, rather than to expect the best.

The element of resignation implicit in Jonas's metaphysical vision cannot help but affect his approach to ethics. For example, in *The Imperative of Responsibility*, Jonas contends that the parent-child relationship is the archetype or primal instance of human responsibility. For Jonas, one will recall, compelling ethical claims cannot be a matter of arbitrary subjective preference. Instead, in order to be truly persuasive, they must be rooted in the nature of things or in "Being." This is one reason why the parent-child relationship suggests itself to him as the paradigmatic case of responsibility. It is in principle something nearly all humans have experienced, either as parents or as children themselves. In Jonas's view, the fundamental intensity of this bond, though it might be dishonored in individual cases, is so indubitable that he considers it to be universal. As Jonas observes: "When asked for a single instance where that coincidence of 'is' and 'ought' occurs, we can point at the most familiar sight: the newborn, whose mere breathing uncontradictably addresses an ought to the world around, namely, to take care of him."[28]

But the problems involved in trying to establish values on the basis of facts haunt Jonas's analysis. It is not the fact that there are many historical and empirical exceptions to the parent-child bond that undermines its plausibility (hence, its universality) as a model. Instead, the problems pertain to the lack of generalizability of the model itself. The very uniqueness of the rapport between parent and child interferes with the prospect of transposing it to extra-familial settings. Its exclusive nature poses serious obstacles to extending it to other human relationships, let alone to humanity in general. One could easily turn the tables on Jonas and avow that it would be *impossible* to feel a degree of commitment toward fellow men and women, qua strangers, comparable to what a parent feels for a child. Instead, it may be more productive to own up to the fact that the social bond will inevitably prove thinner than familial ties and proceed from there to construct a theory of human solidarity.

When Jonas extends the results of his ethical reflections to the realm of politics, the conclusions are similarly flawed. Once again setting the parent-child bond as the archetype of human responsibility, he contends that one can perceive a kindred ethical imperative in the duty of a statesman to care for his citizens. The paternalistic, antidemocratic implications of such an approach to politics are patent. The idea of citizens as political "charges" whose welfare the statesman must cultivate follows logically from Jonas's pessimistic conception of human nature. It is, moreover, of a piece with premodern theories of political guardianship, whose *locus classicus* is Plato's notion of the philosopher-king. According to this theory, since the majority of men and women are incapable of leading virtuous lives, the next best thing would be for them to follow the directives of a sapient elite who comprehend the good and are capable of instructing their intellectual inferiors accordingly. As Jonas remarks:

> There is a natural element also within the artificially created *officium* of the statesman, when he—stepping out of the equality of siblings and citizens—assumes for all of them a role which is parent-like in its responsibilities. . . . The "statesman" in the term's full sense has, for the duration of his office or his power, responsibility for the total life of the community. . . . It extends from physical existence to the highest interests, from security to abundance of life, from good conduct to happiness.[29]

The Advantages of Tyranny

Jonas's prophecies of impending ecological catastrophe are empirically uninformed. Remarkably, he takes into consideration none of the relevant scientific debates concerning the extent and gravity of environmental devastation. Instead, his depiction has the character of a *transcendental deduction*; his findings are merely assumed rather than demonstrated or argued for. Like his mentor Heidegger—whose name is curiously nowhere to be found in *The Imperative of Responsibility*—

Jonas's discussion of modern technology and its effects proceeds on an a priori basis. The devastation of the earth, as it were, *inheres in the very concept of technology*. There is little room for ambiguity, for nuanced discussion of alternative positions. The tone of his writings remains an apocalyptic one. From a performative standpoint, such categorical postulates compel compliance instead of fostering dialogue and debate.

Similarly, Jonas's recourse to vitalism (or, to use the German term of art, *Lebensphilosophie*) suggests a number of troubling questions. As in Heidegger's case, it raises concerns about an existential grounding of ethics: basing ethics on the way things are—on Being—rather than on principle. In Jonas's case, the foundations of ethics are avowedly naturalistic, even quasi-Darwinian. As he remarks in *The Imperative of Responsibility*: "encroaching on other life is *eo ipso* given with belonging to the kingdom of life. . . . In simple words: *to eat and be eaten is the principle of existence*."[30] Of course, Jonas ultimately seeks to use Darwin against Darwin: his ethics employ a Darwinian point of departure against social Darwinism ("survival of the fittest") and in favor of a vitalist sanctification of "life" as an ultimate good.

But in German *Geistesgeschichte*, vitalism has an ambiguous legacy. Historically, it has been employed as an intellectual weapon in the struggle against the (Western) idea of "reason." Vitalism originated as a challenge to the scientific biology of Darwin. In opposition to the mechanistic implications of the doctrine of natural selection, vitalism claimed that life could not be explained in exclusively causal terms. Taking a page from Goethe's philosophy of nature, it preferred to view organic life as ensouled. At a later point, "life" connoted a dimension of "experiential immediacy" that was purportedly superior to the intellect's more abstract musings. In the German context, the ideological thrust of this standpoint is unmistakable. As Herbert Schnädelbach has remarked: "If the later history of life-philosophy is so little known . . . this is chiefly because life-philosophy is branded with the stigma of irrationalism and of being a precursor of fascism. It is certainly undeniable that the 'heroic realism' of Bäumler, Krieck and Rosenberg, which was considered to be the official philosophy of National Socialism, was 'inspired' by the traditions of life-philosophy after Nietzsche and above all by Oswald Spengler."[31] The subterranean affinities of

Jonas's position with the "German Ideology" in its vitalist phase are indeed troubling.

The questions and doubts that arise with regard to Jonas's resolutely antimodern epistemological orientation are heightened when one examines his explicit political recommendations. The second half of *The Imperative of Responsibility* consists of a dialogue with the traditions of Marxism and state socialism. Strangely, in the secondary literature on his work, this dimension of his study remains entirely neglected. In the "political" chapters of *The Imperative of Responsibility*, Jonas adopts a position on the "decline of the West" that differs only by degree from the standpoint espoused by Spengler and Heidegger. Like Germany's national revolutionaries, Jonas assumes that liberal democracy is without a future. Culturally and historically, it remains inextricably entwined with the scientific and industrial revolutions. Liberalism is therefore inseparable from the age of technology and the "planetary devastation" it has wrought. Consequently, for Jonas, the search for an alternative to liberal democracy became a political imperative correlative to his search for contemporary ethical renewal.

It is easy to see how, in an American political context, Jonas's reflections on the virtues of economic planning would fall on deaf ears. However, in the Germany of the 1970s, an entirely different political constellation was operative. The Social Democrats, who had not yet renounced planning in favor of the market, were in power. *Ostpolitik*—a policy of rapprochement and conciliation vis-à-vis the German Democratic Republic—was still in vogue. Hence, from a German standpoint, *The Imperative of Responsibility* assumed an immediate and far-reaching political relevance. Moreover, Jonas's implicit critique of anthropocentrism—his denigration of humanity's preeminence in the natural hierarchy—found great resonance with the German peace movement. Thus, his claim that "Nature could not have incurred a greater hazard than to produce man" could have served as the credo of the movement's fundamentalist wing.[32]

The "state of emergency" precipitated by the global environmental crisis informs the horizon of Jonas's political thought. The crisis has gone so far, argues Jonas, as to impact necessarily all aspects of collective human decision-making. In view of the impending ecological catastrophe, questions of "the good" or the "best life" have become irrelevant: "In the total danger of the world-historical Now we find ourselves thrown back from the ever-open *question, what* man ought to be . . . to the first *commandment* tacitly always underlying it, but never before in need of enunciation: *that* he should be." The authoritarian overtones of Jonas's political prescriptions echo clearly in his claim that *"only a maximum of politically imposed social discipline can ensure the subordination of present advantage to the long-term exigencies of the future."*[33]

In Jonas's view, the idea that contemporary capitalism is incapable of reforming itself is treated as an established fact. Postwar transformations in the direction of the "social welfare state"—"capitalism with a human face"—fail to make an impression on him.[34] Such palliatives serve system-stabilizing purposes and thus help perpetuate conditions that are in need of more fundamental and sweeping modification. Conversely, state socialism has staked a historical claim to surmounting the "anarchy of production" characteristic of capitalism, and Jonas considers this an option well worth exploring:

> only the Marxist program, which integrates the naïve Baconian idea of dominating nature with that of reshaping society and from that expects the definitive man, can be seriously regarded today as the source of an ethic which aims action predominantly at the future and thence imposes norms on the present. One can say that it proposes to bring the fruits of the Baconian revolution under the rule of the best interests of man and thereby to redeem its original promise of an elevated mankind. . . . To an economy governed by the profit motive, socialism can oppose the promise of a greater *rationality* in the management of the Baconian heritage.[35]

The gist of Jonas's political philosophy is contained in an ominously titled section of *The Imperative of Responsibility*, "The Advantage of Total Governmental Power." His indebtedness to the antidemocratic prejudices of Plato's doctrine of the philosopher-king—prejudices that also seduced Heidegger in the early 1930s—is palpable. Jonas openly praises the advantages of autocracy—for example, the fact that "the decisions from the top, which can be made without prior assent from below, meet with no resistance . . . in the social body." In this way, total governmental power can circumvent the base instincts of the *hoi polloi*, who are, it seems, incapable of the virtues of *sophrosyne* or self-limitation. Jonas admits that his political views sanction the "governmental advantages of . . . tyranny"—albeit "a well-intentioned, well-informed tyranny possessed of the right insights." But, given the proportions of the impending global catastrophe, he believes that an abrogation of basic democratic liberties has become unavoidable.[36]

Since the advent of autocracy is inevitable, the only question that remains is whether a dictatorship of "right" or "left" would be preferable. According to Jonas, left-wing dictatorship wins hands down: "in techniques of power [communist tyranny] appears superior, for our uncomfortable purposes, to the capabilities of the capitalist-liberal-democratic complex." One of the distinct advantages of communism is the degree of moral commitment it demands (which conveniently obviates the need for governmentally enforced commitment, or "terror"), as well as the ascetic traits of "socialist discipline," which are to be preferred to the administered hedonism of capitalist consumer society. As Jonas observes: "Now a great asset of Marxism is the emphatic 'moralism' with which it pervades the society formed and ruled by it. . . . To live 'for the whole' and to 'do without' for its sake is a credo of public morality."[37]

Conversely, one of the primary drawbacks of the communist credo is its utopianism—an ethos that, in Jonas's view, exists in symbiotic proximity to the Faustian aspirations of the industrial and scientific revolutions. Thus, whereas in the short run the ascetic traits of socialist discipline represent a distinct advantage, ultimately they run the risk of raising social expectations excessively; after all, the renunciations of socialism are supposed to be a temporary prelude to the advent of a classless society. To defuse this potential source of conflict, Jonas relies on another disputed Platonic legacy, the "noble lie" of *Republic* Book III. In order to ensure that the citizens of the ideal state will passively bear its regimentation and inequities, Plato's guardians purvey the "myth of the metals." The dissemination of lies is justified for the sake of preserving a greater truth.

Jonas hints that an analogous recourse to deception might be necessary for the success of his own authoritarian political construct (in passing, he notes the irony of the fact that whereas, heretofore, Marxism was predicated on the unmasking of "false consciousness," in his scenario, it would become the *purveyor* of false consciousness for the sake of the *true*). Specifically, the guardians of Jonas's ecological dictatorship may have to conceal the fact that, in light of current environmental limits, the renunciations demanded of its subjects are permanent rather than transitory in nature. Thus, the utopia in whose name sacrifice is demanded will never arrive. "I do not stand aghast at the thought [of institutionalized political deception]," admits Jonas. "Perhaps this dangerous game of mass deception (Plato's 'noble lie') is all that politics will eventually have to offer: to give effect to the principle of fear under the mask of the principle of hope. . . . In special circumstances, *the useful opinion may be the false one*; meaning that if the truth is too hard to bear, then the good lie must do service."[38]

That Jonas's fascination with the lures of political autocracy was more than a passing fancy is documented in an interview he gave to the German news magazine *Der Spiegel* toward the end of his life. Seeking to refute optimistic prognoses concerning the triumph of liberalism following communism's collapse, he vigorously restates the despairing diagnosis of the times formulated in *The Imperative of Responsibility*. If anything, the catastrophic outlook developed in his 1979 *chef d'oeuvre* remains even more relevant, argues Jonas. He fears the "tragic collapse of higher civilization as we know it, its decline into a new stage of primitivism . . . mass poverty, mass death and mass murder, the loss of all treasures that spirit has produced beyond the exploitation of nature."[39] To counteract such tendencies politically, Jonas engages in a thought experiment analogous to the one he undertook in *The Imperative of Responsibility*: he entertains the idea of a "world government," "a dictatorship of the saviors of humanity." Correspondingly, he views a curtailment of individual freedom as a "self-evident" requirement of the current ecological predicament. His verdict is driven by the suspicion that democracy as it now functions, with its narrow-minded orientation toward short-term consequences, is an "unsuitable form of government."[40]

Ultimately, Jonas admits that the state socialist approach, too, must be rejected. In the last analysis, Marxism remains overly enamored of the ethos of modern productivism. Its promethean orientation and utopian telos suggest that the interests of nature would fare little better under Marxist jurisdiction than under capitalism. Marx himself never concealed the fact that he viewed communism as a rational consummation of the modern industrial system. In all likelihood, under a Marxist regime the exploitation of nature would merely proliferate exponentially. Nor, of course, does the environmental track record of the "really existing" socialist states inspire confidence. Jonas finds fault with these states for engaging in a type of rapacious "national egoism," whereby unrealistic state production quotas are substituted for the profit motive of capitalism.

Nevertheless, Jonas's willingness to contemplate seriously the merits of political autocracy is disconcerting, as is the alacrity with which he is willing to dismiss the virtues of political liberalism. In the aforementioned *Der Spiegel* interview, he engages in yet another nightmarish thought experiment. Could it be, he suggests pessimistically, that modernity as a whole might be a false path: "Was modernity perhaps an error that must be rectified? Is this path a correct one—the combination of scientific-technical progress along with the enhancement of individual freedom? Was the modern age in certain respects a false path that should no longer be pursued?"[41] In his manner of posing questions, which craftily predetermines the parameters of possible response, one detects the return of a disconsolate, Spenglerian sensibility that was widespread in Germany during the 1920s on both the left and right sides of the political spectrum.

Post-Holocaust Theology

Jonas's contributions to post-Holocaust theology are among his most important writings, yet they represent the aspect of his work that is probably least known and understood. For obvious reasons, the Holocaust poses grave problems for Jewish religious thought. According to the classical texts of Jewish theology, the God of the Old Testament is both perfect and omnipotent, creator and redeemer. As lawgiver to the people of Israel, He is a benevolent God, but also one who is not averse to dispensing severe punishment for violations of His law. This traditional understanding of God is thrown into radical doubt in the aftermath of the Holocaust, where, unlike previous historical catastrophes, there seems to be no discernible correlation between the massive extent of Jewish suffering and religious transgressions of His people. The evils of the Holocaust are so extreme that they transcend considerations of theodicy. Even the concepts of martyrdom or bearing witness to God (*Kiddush-hashem* or "sanctification of the Name"), which were so important amid the persecutions of medieval Jewry, were rendered obsolete by virtue of the ignominious deaths the Jews endured at the hands of the Nazis.

Theological responses to the Holocaust span a wide spectrum. One of the first, entirely natural reactions to the catastrophe was simply to claim that Auschwitz proved the nonexistence of God, for if an omnipotent God did exist, He certainly would never have permitted the horrors of Auschwitz to come to pass. Even if by some strange reckoning the bestialities of Nazism could be construed as a form of divine punishment for Jewish impiety or misdeeds, the deaths of a million innocent Jewish children fall entirely outside of the calculus.

Other theologians argued that to interpret the destruction of the European Jews as evidence for God's nonexistence would be to accord Hitler a posthumous and total victory over the Jewish people. Having deprived two-thirds of European Jewry of their lives, he would succeed in wresting from the surviving remnant their faith. One of the foremost representatives of this standpoint has been the philosopher Emil Fackenheim. Fackenheim argues that instead of an abandonment of Judaism, what is needed is a post-Holocaust theology; that is, a religious renewal that takes the caesuras of Jewish life and faith after Auschwitz into account. The theological task of "mending the world"— the ingathering of scattered fragments of divine substance—must continue.

Jonas opts for a via media between the two aforementioned positions. He denies that the Holocaust provides definitive evidence of God's nonexistence. Yet he also argues that it would have been impossible for the benevolent and omnipotent God of the Old Testament to have presided in silence over the gruesome events of the Holocaust.

Instead, Jonas pursues a different theological tack—one that is highly speculative, just as all theology must deal with claims that are largely conjectural. According to Jonas, there is a further theological possibility that neither of the approaches just described has been adequately explored: the prospect that God exists but was powerless to intervene. Thus, for reasons unknown to us, God may have ceased to be omnipotent. It is possible that divine energies were exhausted in the act of creation. Another hypothesis suggests that, after creating the world, God engaged in an act of self-limitation in order to make room for free will. This theory is consistent with the Kabbalistic doctrine of *tzimtzum*, the self-contraction of God following the creation of the universe. To be sure, this relativizes our traditional notion of an omnipotent God. Yet, by virtue having "temporalized" Himself via the act of creation, and by allowing Himself to be affected by human suffering, His all-powerfulness had already undergone a diminution. As Jonas points out, the presumption of divine omnipotence makes for a theological pageant that is devoid of drama and interest. Under such circumstances, moreover, the concept of free will would be deprived of all meaning. As Jonas explains: "Absolute power, in its solitude, has no object on which to act. But as objectless power it is a powerless power, canceling itself out: 'all' equals 'zero' here. . . . Power meeting no *resistance* in its relatum is equal to no power at all: power is exercised only in relation to something that itself has power."[42]

The only way to render the concept of God meaningful after Auschwitz is to avow that His goodness is compatible with the existence of evil. But to admit this fact is to recognize that God is not omnipotent. As Jonas puts it: "Having [in the act of creation] given Himself whole to the becoming world, God has no more to give: it is man's now to give to Him."[43]

Looking Back at Heidegger

Toward the end of his life, Jonas returned to the question of Heidegger's impact and influence in the course of an interview broadcast on Swiss radio. Echoing the testimonies of other observers, Jonas remarked that, to a considerable extent, the philosopher's capacity to mesmerize derived from the "impenetrable" nature of his discourse. Thus, students had the feeling that, despite their incomprehension, behind Heidegger's words there lay "something worth understanding." Jonas confirmed that, in informal settings, Heidegger betrayed an orientation toward German nationalism; nevertheless, the philosopher's demonstrative embrace of Nazism in 1933 took him genuinely by surprise. This was not the case, however, for his fellow students, who, he recalls, retorted: "Why are you so astonished? They [Heidegger's political affinities] were always there, you could tell by the style of his thinking."[44] On further reflection, Jonas was forced to admit that such compromising stylistic traits had indeed been present; for whatever reasons, he had merely failed to register them.

When pressed by his interlocutor to articulate what it may have been about Heidegger's philosophical habitudes that may have pushed him in the direction of Hitler, Jonas suggested that the concept of existential "resolve" or "decisiveness" (*Entschlossenheit*) played a key role. According to Jonas, the problem with this concept was its contentlessness. It remained normatively vacuous, offering no intrinsic measure to distinguish ethical from unethical political commitments. Instead, the determinants of "resolve" were purely formal or (to highlight the parallels with Carl Schmitt) "decisionistic": its effectiveness should be judged by the sheer quantum or degree of engagement on behalf of a given cause, regardless of ends.

According to Jonas, the "contentless" nature of resolve is crucial to understanding Heidegger's political choice. It suggests that, in order to provide resolve with meaning and direction, one is both at the mercy of contemporary history and powerless to defend oneself against it. As Jonas explains:

> As the hour of January 1933 struck, history offered the opportunity for decisiveness. . . . It was at this time that the enormous dubiousness of the Heideggerian outlook in its entirety became clear to me. Whereas he accused idealist philosophy of a certain idealism—it claimed to study the forms of thought, the categories, according to which the world is ordered, and thus [did] everything at a certain remove [from the world]—one could accuse him of something much more serious: the absolute formalism of his decisionism, where decision as such becomes the highest virtue.[45]

With his reflections on life, ethics, and theology, Jonas presents us, to borrow Nietzsche's phrase, with a series of "thoughts out of season." There remains a distinctly Sisyphean quality to his philosophical labors: in an era dominated by thoughtlessness and technological frenzy, Jonas refused to let the so-called "ultimate questions" of Western metaphysics disappear without a trace. His thought, which never shied away from taking risks, stands as a forceful indictment of the shortsightedness of contemporary humanity and the paltriness of its concerns. For Jonas, a humankind that refused to contemplate its own *raison d'être* remained impoverished and disoriented, fundamentally bereft. The American society that offered him refuge from a war-ravaged Europe was certainly preferable to the one he had fled. Yet, at times, he must have fretted for the condition of its soul. An often ruthless possessive individualism had replaced the traditional virtues that had once made the country an object of universal envy: piety, self-reliance, public-spiritedness, civic engagement, and rooted communities. Of late, such broader concerns have been almost wholly supplanted by a self-interestedness that is insular and smug. What makes Jonas's thought an enduring achievement is that he was able to bring a keen sense of philosophical wonder to so many areas of human and cosmological concern.

FIG. 4. Herbert Marcuse, mid-1970s. Photo courtesy of Herbert Marcuse-Archive, Stadt- und Universitätsbibliothek, Frankfurt am Main.

Herbert Marcuse:

From Existential Marxism to Left

Heideggerianism

The Crisis of Marxism

HERBERT MARCUSE achieved renown as a Marxist philosopher and intellectual prophet of the New Left, but from 1928 to 1932, he studied philosophy with Heidegger in Freiburg, and traces of Heidegger's influence would imprint his mature thought in subtle and unanticipated ways. In the estimates of some, even the later Marcuse remained at base a "Heideggerian Marxist."[1] But here the terms of Marcuse's appropriation of Heideggerian concepts must be carefully defined. Unlike the other philosophers we have considered, even in his youth, Marcuse was never a convinced Heideggerian. Instead, his interest in Heidegger's thought was always moderated by an enduring commitment to Marxism. Marcuse's foundational political experience occurred during the stillborn German Revolution of 1918–19. As a young infantryman, he was elected as a Social Democratic deputy to one of the soldier's councils that mushroomed throughout Germany at the close of World War I. The brutal crushing of the 1919 Spartacus uprising by Gustav Noske's Freikorps, culminating in the summary executions of Rosa Luxemburg and Karl Liebknecht—events that were sanctioned and encouraged by the ruling Social Democratic government—forever alienated Marcuse from the Social Democratic path and entrenched his lifelong commitment to Marxism as a doctrine of revolutionary social transformation.[2]

Following the war, Marcuse wrote a dissertation on the German artist-novel, worked in Berlin, and compiled a bibliography on the poet Friedrich Schiller. In 1927, seemingly out of nowhere, Heidegger's *Being and Time* appeared: a work that, by self-consciously breaking with the stale academicism of the reigning *Kathederphilosophie*, seemed to open up unprecedented and rich possibilities for philosophical inquiry. Whereas the dominant modes of *Schulphilosophie*—neo-Kantianism, logical positivism, and so forth—systematically ignored the disorientation of the historical moment, Heidegger's philosophy explicitly embraced the mood of crisis as a valid "ontic" point of departure for ontological inquiry. As Marcuse described his path to Freiburg:

> The failure of the German Revolution—which my friends and I actually experienced in 1921, if not earlier, with Karl's and Rosa's murder—was decisive. There didn't seem to be anything with which we could identify. Then Heidegger came along, *Being and Time* appeared in 1927. . . . What happens when the revolution fails? A decisive question for us. Philosophy was certainly taught at the time, the academic scene was dominated by neo-Kantianism and neo-Hegelianism, and then suddenly *Being and Time* appeared as a really concrete philosophy. One spoke of "life" (*Dasein*), "existence" (*Existenz*), the "they" (*das Man*), "death" (*Tod*), "care" (*Sorge*). That seemed to speak to us.[3]

Marcuse attempted to synthesize the concerns of Marx and Heidegger in a number of early essays. Yet he never became a full-blooded Heideggerian. Heidegger's existentialism, he believed, might be serviceable for Marxist ends, rarely the other way around. As Marcuse observed in his first published essay: "The historicity of existence demands a correction of phenomenology in accordance with the dialectical method, which reveals itself as *the proper approach to all historical subject matter*."[4] The emancipatory ends of Marxism—putting an end to the degradation of the working class at the hands of a commodity-producing society—always remained Marcuse's normative benchmark. In retrospect, however, he conceded that these early efforts to combine

Marxism and existentialism ultimately ended in failure. As he observed in a 1971 interview:

> I . . . believed there could be some combination between existentialism and Marxism, precisely because of their insistence on concrete analysis of the actual human existence, human beings and their world. But I soon realized that Heidegger's concreteness was to a great extent a phony, a false concreteness, and that in fact his philosophy was just as abstract and just as removed from reality, even avoiding reality, as the philosophies which at that time had dominated German universities.[5]

The story of Marcuse's youthful encounter with Heidegger is a fascinating one, not least of all insofar as it foreshadowed subsequent attempts to fuse Marxism and existentialism by the likes of Jean-Paul Sartre, Maurice Merleau-Ponty, the Czech philosopher Karel Kosik, and the Italian phenomenologist Enzo Paci. Such efforts, which sought to lay the philosophical foundations for a "Marxism with a human face," came to naught when Warsaw Pact troops crushed the Prague Spring in August 1968. Thereafter, the European left realized that all hopes of reforming Marxism from within were illusory. Eastern European communism could no longer be explained as merely a historical "deformation" of Marxism; instead, it revealed something about the essence of Marxism itself.

That in the late 1920s Marcuse thought it plausible and desirable to bring together Marx and Heidegger bespeaks the "crisis of Marxism." Talk of a crisis of Marxism emerged around the turn of the century in conjunction with the so-called revisionism debate. The German Social Democratic theorist Eduard Bernstein decreed that the transition to socialism would occur "organically" and that, consequently, the idiom of revolution had become superfluous. Bernstein had in many respects accurately described the current state of the European working class movement, in which workers had, on the whole, been extremely successful in having their demands for higher wages and better working conditions met. Why should they be interested in seizing political power when their economic concerns were being met within the context of the capitalist system itself? Bernstein's fellow socialists treated his views (for example, his slogan: "the goal is nothing, the movement everything") as heretical; but, in the end, it was difficult to deny that he had identified a crucial gap in Marxist doctrine. Workers were indeed becoming less revolutionary, less political, and increasingly content with their lot under capitalism, which meant that Marx's prognostications concerning the advent of socialism were fatally flawed.[6]

Another crisis, and one that Marcuse himself would witness, emerged following World War I. The European powers had been morally discredited by the war. In Germany and elsewhere, economic conditions were abysmal. Yet revolution took place only in the backwater of Tsarist Russia; those that occurred in central Europe (e.g., the Bavarian and Hungarian soviet republics) proved fleeting and inconsequential. This scenario, too, contravened the expectations of Marxist orthodoxy. Moreover, although the Social Democrats became Germany's ruling party after the war, it was under their auspices that the revolutionary uprisings in Berlin and Munich had been crushed. Henceforth, there could be no doubt about Social Democracy's antirevolutionary nature.

From the standpoint of European Marxism, the Bolshevik Revolution seemed to create as many problems as it solved. Communist parties throughout Europe found themselves forced to assume a posture of obsequious servility vis-à-vis Moscow's dictates and decrees. The Bolsheviks' lack of theoretical sophistication (e.g., Bukharin's primer, *The ABC's of Communism*) was notorious. Traditionally, Marxism claimed that it would replace the formal equality of bourgeois society with genuine equality. As a philosophy of history, it had inherited the utopian aspirations of the Enlightenment. The philosophical writings of the early Marx had incorporated romantic claims to individual wholeness and restored community. With the crisis of Marxism, all of these hopes seemed to subsist at an infinite remove from the degraded historical present.

What possible relationship could exist between the crisis of Marxism and the philosophy of Heidegger? Though the linkages may seem implausible, upon closer scrutiny they are not as far-fetched as they may at first appear. The crisis of Marxism was also a crisis of Marxist doctrine; it assumed the form of an *epistemological crisis* that affected the integrity of Marxist theory, its status as a doctrine of revolutionary social change. Under the tutelage of the later Engels, German Social

Democracy had reconceived Marxism as a variant of scientism: just as Darwin had set forth the evolutionary laws governing the natural world, in *Das Kapital* Marx had established those governing human societies. According to this view, Marxism had realized the high Enlightenment dream of a "science of society," thereby complementing the empirical achievements of the natural sciences.

Yet, as philosophically-trained Marxists knew, from a political standpoint the idea of Marxism as a mode of scientific determinism was potentially fatal. If all the proletariat needed to do was wait for the purported laws of capitalist development to work themselves out, then political activism was superfluous. Workers need only await the final crisis of the capitalist system and then step into the breach. Ultimately, scientific Marxism proved a recipe for organizational passivity and working class inaction. Yet, as recent events had shown, the crisis assumed neither the pattern nor the proportions prophesied by Marxist theory. It was in response to these developments that Lenin, in *What Is to Be Done?*, formulated his controversial doctrine of revolutionary vanguardism: a cadre of professional revolutionaries would lead the working class out of the morass of "trade union consciousness" and onto the promised terrain of political revolution. Formulated in the context of disputes internal to the Russian Social Democracy, Lenin's political voluntarism and reformulation of the role of the party had enormous consequences for the future of Marxist theory and practice.

German Social Democracy never reconciled the glaring contradiction between its political and theoretical standpoints. It organized, initiated political reforms, and made policy recommendations; yet, technically, all such preparations were "premature" in light of the anticipated final collapse of capitalism. On another level, however, Social Democracy's epistemological determinism was increasingly reflected in the growing bureaucratic sclerosis of party organization and management style. The party's bureaucratic paralysis became the subject of Robert Michel's important book, *Political Parties*, in which Michel articulated his famous thesis concerning the "iron law of oligarchy."

In the 1920s, the crisis of Marxism elicited a number of prominent theoretical responses. Georg Lukács and Karl Korsch formulated the best known and most influential explanations in 1923. Lukács' brilliant study, *History and Class Consciousness*, went on to become a subterranean classic, the *urtext* of the Hegelian Marxist renaissance. The critical theory of the Frankfurt School—Marcuse's new intellectual home during the 1930s—would be unthinkable without Lukács' innovative philosophical recasting of Marxist precepts. And in the post-World War II era, Lukács' forgotten masterpiece gained a new lease on life among intellectual dissidents and student revolutionaries on both sides of the iron curtain, despite the orthodox Marxist protestations of its author.

Steeped in the tradition of classical German philosophy, Lukács underwent a conversion to Marxism following the Bolshevik revolution. Transposing his earlier enthusiasm for Dostoevsky and Russian literature to Lenin and company, he wagered that the "Russian soul," in the guise of Bolshevism, would ultimately redeem the despiritualized and materialistic West. Four decades later, Lukács reconstructed his intellectual itinerary circa World War I in the following terms:

> When I tried at this time to put my emotional attitude into conscious terms, I arrived at more or less the following formulation: the Central Powers would probably defeat Russia; this might lead to the downfall of Tsarism; I had no objection to that. There was also some probability that the West would defeat Germany; if this led to the downfall of the Hohenzollerns and the Hapsburgs, I was once again in favor. But the question arose: *who was to save us from Western civilization?*[7]

With the Russian Revolution of 1917, the answer to Lukács' supplicatory appeal seemingly materialized overnight.

History and Class Consciousness was a landmark in the annals of Marxist thought. Lukács realized, as did few others at the time, that the central tenets of Marxism had grown out of a confrontation with Hegel and the legacy of classical German philosophy. Moreover, he contended that unless one took stock of Marxism's philosophical origins, Marx's doctrine was destined to remain unintelligible. The political implications of Lukács' argument represented a formidable challenge to Marxist orthodoxy: he insinuated that, in essence, it constituted a false path or dead end.

Perhaps his most damning argument against the reigning variants of orthodox Marxism was that, by viewing Marxism as a "science," they had adopted a standpoint that was fundamentally bourgeois. With its a priori interest in the domination of nature, science merely traced the "logic of the object," it mirrored the standpoint of "things" or "objectivity." In seeking to subject nature and society to the power of objective laws, science reified everything it touched; it was essentially a blueprint for domination. In contrast, Lukács argued that, as a mode of dialectical thought, Marxism was concerned with the *interaction* between subject and object. Marxism—and it alone—supplied the crucial element of *mediation*, thereby remedying the one-sidedness of both idealism and materialism.

Lukács' central contribution to Marxist thought lay in his appreciation of Marxism's Hegelian origins. Without access to Marx's "Paris Manuscripts," which were published nine years after *History and Class Consciousness* first appeared, Lukács was able to demonstrate that Marxism originated as an attempt to solve a problem bequeathed by classical German philosophy: the separation of (or alienation between) subject and object. This was a problem that had reached epic proportions under capitalism, a society characterized (in Marx's words) by "objective [*vergegenständlichte*] relations between persons and social relations between things."[8] In Marx's view, the proletariat represented a force capable of making a lacerated or reified social totality whole once again. As Marcuse observes, "The central point of the Marxist approach is the historical possibility of radical action which is to bring about a necessarily new reality that makes possible the total man."[9] Yet Marxism would accomplish this feat not because of the objective laws of capitalist development but by virtue of superior historical insight or "class consciousness." In a later essay, Marcuse expressed this insight as follows: "The objective relations [of society] can only become human and social if man himself is conscious of them *as such*, i.e. in his *knowledge* of both himself and the object."[10]

As a result of his remarkably prescient reconstruction of the early Marx's intellectual path, Lukács was able to show that Hegel's influence was not something that the mature Marx had casually jettisoned. Instead, as Marx himself acknowledged in his "Theses on Feuerbach" (1845), German idealism accounted for the "active side" of the dialectic, the side that mandated "revolutionary, practical-critical activity" or "praxis." As Marx explained:

The chief defect of all hitherto existing materialism—that of Feuerbach included—is that the thing, reality, sensuousness, is conceived only in the form of the object or of *contemplation*, but not as *human sensuous activity, practice*, not subjectively. Hence it happened that the *active* side, in contradistinction to materialism, was developed by idealism—but only abstractly, since, of course, idealism does not know real, sensuous activity as such.[11]

Unless materialism's "active side" were adequately appreciated, the dimension of human practical activity or "praxis" risked falling into eclipse—a condition that accurately described the methodological status of Marxism qua scientism during the 1920s.

Concrete Philosophy

It was the publication of *Being and Time* that attracted Marcuse to Freiburg. He viewed Heidegger's existentialism as an expression of "concrete philosophy." Contemporary academic philosophy shunned questions of human existence, dismissing the reigning mood of "crisis" and "decline" as beneath the dignity of serious intellectual discussion. Heidegger's thought, conversely, identified such questions as legitimate matters of philosophical reflection. As he observes in *Being and Time*, every ontology presupposes a determinate ontic standpoint.[12] In other words, in order to philosophize *about* the world, one must inevitably first be situated *in* the world. Any philosophy that sought to deny this basic ontological fact violated the fundamental terms of what it meant "to exist." *Existenz*, in Heidegger's view, is primordial. Before it can be treated as a metaphysical problem or theme, it simply *is*. To suppress the incontrovertible existential basis of human Being-in-the-world is to violate the basic terms of human practical situatedness. No other contemporary philosophy—including Marxism—seemed as willing to thoughtfully engage the fundamental questions of human practical life as did Heidegger's early philosophy of existence.

At the same time, from the very beginning, Marcuse was cognizant of the limitations of Heidegger's approach. One theme constantly recurs in Heidegger's early essays: unless the concerns of fundamental ontology are translated into concrete historical terms, they are destined to remain abstract and irrelevant; aspirations toward "philosophical concreteness" will evaporate into an airy "pseudo-concreteness."[13] In *Being and Time*, Heidegger adhered to a principled separation between ontological and ontic levels of inquiry. The latter dimension, which corresponds to the concerns of everyday "factical" life, supposedly transcended the scope of ontological inquiry. But, Marcuse argues, should fundamental ontology systematically ignore the historical character of existence, it risks becoming yet another "first philosophy" in the pejorative sense, its normative prescriptions no more effective than an abstract Kantian moral "ought." As Marcuse argues in "Contributions to a Phenomenology of Historical Materialism" (1928): any philosophy that "attempts to validate its logical consistency, universal coherence or its timeless cogency from any standpoint over and beyond Marxism . . . misses the point from the very beginning." Marxism's truths, claims Marcuse, are "not cognitive but actual." Marxism "comprehends all the knowledge derived from historicity from the character, structure, and movement of actual events."[14] Marcuse privileges Marxism insofar as he believes that, its methodological deficiencies notwithstanding, it provides the most sophisticated approach to understanding the contemporary crisis. By ignoring history, fundamental ontology, as a species of transcendental philosophy, risked promoting "dialectical illusion": conceptually brilliant, it remained factually and empirically impoverished.

Following Lukács, Marcuse did not wish to endorse Marxism as merely another particular ideology or worldview. Instead, he sought to justify it as a fallibilistic method of historical understanding. The advantages Marxism possessed over existential phenomenology concerned its superior capacities for historical discernment. Unlike fundamental ontology, its analytical scope was not restricted to the timeless and essential structures of human existence (Heidegger's *Existenzialen*). Instead, real historical content and struggles, which fundamental ontology had derogated to the level of the merely "ontic," suffused its theoretical framework.

The idea of "historicity" had been topical since the middle of the nineteenth century. Ironically, though, the predominant discussions of it remained profoundly ahistorical: historians and philosophers studiously avoided addressing its potential implications for the historical present. In his reinterpretation of Dilthey's concept of historicity in Division II of *Being and Time*, Heidegger claimed to avoid this trap.

Whereas Dilthey and others had acknowledged that human life took place *in* history, Heidegger sought to show that Dasein was itself *historical*—thereby adding a element of "self-constitution" missing in previous accounts. But, in Marcuse's view, Heidegger's discussion of historicity still remained too formal to incorporate the concerns of real history. Ultimately, fundamental ontology's claims about historicity proved pseudo-concrete.

At the same time, Marcuse was clearly fascinated by the similarities between the Marxist and Heideggerian accounts of historicity. If a potential for rapprochement between these two schools existed, then it lay above all in this parallelism. Moreover, important similarities also existed between Marx's notion of revolutionary "praxis"—the process whereby the working class rises up to make an inhuman world human again—and Heidegger's concept of authenticity. As Marcuse notes sympathetically, "What is important is the new philosophical direction of [Heidegger's] interpretations. The fundamental question of all living philosophy is raised in light of the awareness of its utmost necessity: *What is authentic existence, and how is it generally possible?*"[15]

A careful reading of *Being and Time* Division II illustrates that, in certain respects, Heidegger's concerns are not entirely foreign to those of the early Marx. Division I depicts Dasein in the modalities of "average everydayness"—Dasein as it succumbs to the blandishments of inauthentic existence: "publicness," "idle talk," "curiosity," and "indecision." Viewed formally, these expressions of inauthentic Being-in-the-world share a common feature: all resist or repress what Heidegger refers to as the active or "ecstatic" moment of human existence. Instead, inauthentic Dasein allows its Being-in-the-world to slacken to the point where it resembles the *Being of things*. By refusing to "temporalize" its Being-in-the-world—to project itself authentically toward the future—it degenerates to the point where it resembles something objective or merely "present-at-hand" (*Vorhandenheit*). In other words, inauthentic Dasein becomes *reified*, at which point the similarities with Marxism become palpable. Nor was Heidegger himself unaware of the cogency and import of these parallels. In *Being and Time*, he twice alludes to Lukács' theory of the "reification of consciousness." "The Thinghood itself which such reification implies," observes Heidegger, "must have its ontological origin demonstrated if we are to be in a position to ask what we are to understand positively when we think of unreified Being—of the subject, the soul, consciousness, spirit, the person."[16] On the basis of this revealing avowal, it would not be far-fetched to conclude that the central goal of fundamental ontology is the *overcoming of reification*, of Dasein's self-understanding qua "thing." Unarguably, this was one of the most important philosophical conclusions that Marcuse drew from his lengthy and intensive confrontation with *Being and Time*: "Knowledge of authentic historicity and consciously historical existence is possible only when existence *shatters reification*."[17]

Now the immense philosophical promise that the young Marcuse perceived in *Being and Time* becomes comprehensible. By virtue of the critique of inauthenticity in *Being and Time*, Marcuse felt justified in understanding Heidegger as a Marxist fellow traveler. Following Lukács, Marcuse understood Marxism primarily as a critique of reification: as the demystification of a social order in which individuals are systematically degraded to personifications of economic categories—in the lexicon of contemporary industrial relations theory, to the status of "human capital."

A cursory glance at "Contributions to a Phenomenology of Historical Materialism" indicates the profundity and extent of this youthful intellectual indebtedness. "From the very beginning," Marcuse observes, "the unity of the [existential] predicament leads directly into historicity." He continues by citing Marx, but it is clearly *Lukács'* Marx—the Marx of the as yet undiscovered Paris Manuscripts—that Marcuse invokes, as opposed to the scientific Marx currently in vogue:

> Everything is an endless sum of activities, one after the other, yet all are inextricably interconnected and determined. All these activities are divorced from the agent who is not part of them, but only deals with them, minds his own business, or—the ultimate absurdity—must undertake activities in order to live. It is "the metamorphosis of personal into material powers," which has left behind "abstract individuals, deprived of all true vitality," so that man's own activity confronts him as an alien power. This penetrates to the very *foundation* of capitalist society. It goes beneath the economic and ideological forms of the "reality of an inhuman existence." On the other hand, it confronts this with the reality of human existence demanding *radical action*.[18]

In "On Concrete Philosophy," an essay from the same period in which the theme of reification figures prominently, Marcuse offers a more historically precise account of the same phenomenon:

> The intoxication with power has caused people to overlook the fact that, in spite of the progressive technicization and rationalization of contemporary society, man's *human* power over nature and "things" has diminished rather than increased! Today, as "economic subjects and objects," men stand in the service of a commodity economy that has metamorphosed into an autonomous "thing" instead of serving as a suitable means of their existence. In the same way, their "tools"—machines, means of transport, light, and electricity—have become so extensive and immense that, from a human standpoint, men increasingly must organize their existence in accordance with them, stand in their service . . . in order to maintain them in their "functioning." This is only one aspect of the fact that in capitalist society all human values are lost or placed in the service of technical and rational "objectivity."[19]

A demand for "radical action" was a position that Marx and Heidegger shared. For Marx, it took the form of "praxis," "revolutionary, practical-critical activity." On the basis of authentic temporality, Dasein, too, demanded a radical practical response to the realities of alienated social existence: "Past, present, and future are existential characteristics, and thus render possible fundamental phenomena such as understanding, care, and resolve," observes Marcuse, endorsing a Heideggerian idiom. "This opens the way for the demonstration of historicity as a fundamental existential concept—which we regard as the decisive point in Heidegger's phenomenology."[20] For Heidegger, observes Marcuse, "action is grasped as *'existential,'* i.e., as an essential attitude of, and deriving from human existence."[21] Despite being an "undialectical thinker," Heidegger, like Hegel before him, demonstrated a profound appreciation for the "active side" of dialectics. Given the reified condition of contemporary Marxist theory, Heidegger's emphasis on the philosophical importance of this active side seemed extraordinarily timely. Hence, Marcuse's genuine enthusiasm concerning *Being and Time*'s ultimate philosophical promise: "*Being and Time* . . . seems to indicate a *turning point in the history of philosophy*: the point where bourgeois philosophy transcends itself from within and opens up the way to a new 'concrete' science." Hedging his bets slightly, Marcuse goes on to observe that "[Heidegger's] work remains 'true,' even though it contains a considerable amount of error."[22]

In a preface to the 1967 edition of *History and Class Consciousness*, Lukács, while careful to distance himself from the philosophical errors of his youth, proffered a remarkably frank avowal concerning the intellectual affinities between him and Heidegger, which turned on their shared interest in the problem of *alienation*:

> To assess the impact of the book [*History and Class Consciousness*] at that time, and also its relevance today, we must consider one problem that surpasses in its importance all questions of detail. This is *the question of alienation*, which, for the first time since Marx, is treated as central to the revolutionary critique of capitalism and which has its theoretical and methodological roots in the Hegelian dialectic. Of course the problem was in the air at the time. Some years later, following the publication of Heidegger's *Being and Time*, it moved into the center of philosophical debate. . . . The statement that the problem was in the air is perfectly adequate, particularly as it is not possible to discuss the reasons for this here and to lay bare the mixture of Marxist and Existentialist ideas that were so influential after World War II, especially in France. . . . What is important is that the alienation of man is a crucial problem of the age in which we live and is recognized as such by both bourgeois and proletarian thinkers, by commentators on both right and left.[23]

Thus, though Heidegger and Marx marched to different drummers, at times they seemed to be striving to reach a similar terminus. In Marcuse's view, both Heidegger and Marx strove to redirect the utopian energies latent in the Western philosophical tradition toward the practical goal of remedying the shortcomings of the human condition. In doing so, both abandoned the telos of the *bios theoretikos*, or the contemplative life, in favor of the demands of "worldliness" and "praxis," thereby reversing a time-honored hierarchy that had congealed into an article of faith, an immovable philosophical prejudice. Marx's attitude toward the tradition—and his basic philosophical radicalism—was well summarized by the eleventh of his "Theses on Feuer-bach": "Hitherto, philosophers have merely interpreted the world in various ways; the point, however, is to change it."[24] Seconding Marx, Marcuse observes that "historical necessity is realized *through men's activities*. Men can bypass this activity—recent history is full of such bun-gled revolutionary situations—and can degrade themselves from sub-jects to objects of history. The task of theory is to free praxis in light of the knowledge of necessity."[25]

Unlike Marx, however, in *Being and Time* Heidegger embraced the standpoint of a manifestly undemocratic "aristocratic radicalism." He firmly believed that the ends of "self-overcoming" (Nietzsche) or "au-thenticity" were accessible only to a chosen few, a spiritual elect. Mar-cuse was also concerned about the dangers of dissolving the concrete-ness of the current historical situation amid the resolutely ahistorical framework of fundamental ontology. By treating reification as a time-less feature of the human condition, existentialism ran the risk of diver-ting attention from its real social origins: a capitalist economy in which men and women are incorporated as factors of production or "variable capital."

In Marcuse's view, Heidegger's approach possessed both advantages and weaknesses. Both sides of the equation were evident in fundamen-tal ontology's methodological point of departure: the existing individ-ual or Dasein. Ideally, Heidegger's focus on the individual would be able to offset one of Marxism's major deficiencies: a neglect of the individual in favor of the standpoint of society or the "laws of history." In keeping with Hegelian Marxism's emphasis on the role of "con-sciousness," Marcuse argued that the advent of progressive historical change was necessarily tied to the individual's capacity for awareness and insight. The transformation of society must be a consciously willed process—a process of *self*-transformation—or else it is valueless. As Marcuse observes, "Only individuals exist, and society can never de-prive the individual of his authentic existence." To be sure, the individ-ual is not the "subject of history." And, ultimately, "Heidegger's solu-tion based on solitary existence rather than action must be rejected."[26] Yet, at the same time, Marcuse insists that although "the meaning of philosophy is not limited to the individual, it can only be realized through every individual and grounded in individual existence."[27]

Nevertheless, Marcuse questioned whether existentialism's methodological limitations would ultimately outweigh its positive contributions, for despite its resolute focus on everydayness, it seemed doubtful whether *Existenzphilosophie* could attain the requisite dimension of historical concreteness. Historicity is an ontological structure, a nonempirical mode of Dasein's temporal comportment, and in this respect it necessarily exists at a remove from the "ontic" sphere of real history. Ultimately, ontic or "real" history seems to be a matter of indifference to Dasein and the "formal indications" that structure it. For Marcuse, this point became the hinge on which all other matters turned. In his view, to appreciate the nature and depth of the contemporary crisis meant incorporating a level of historical concreteness that seemed alien to fundamental ontology's "structural" concerns. It meant understanding imperialism and monopoly capitalism in their full historical and phenomenal specificity. Yet, from a Heideggerian perspective, no matter what the social setting, the structural features and potentials of Dasein—the so-called *Existenzialien*—remained the same. In the last analysis, the success of Heidegger's enterprise depended on its ability to address "the material constitution of historicity—a breakthrough that Heidegger nowhere achieves or even mentions. . . . The analysis of an historical object grounded in historicity must take into consideration the concrete, historical situation, and its concrete, material condition. Therefore a phenomenology of human existence falls short of the necessary clarity and completeness if it bypasses the material condition of historical existence. As already indicated, this is the case with Heidegger."[28]

Moreover, as Marcuse emphasizes in "On Concrete Philosophy," unless the positions and "resolutions" of concrete philosophy enter the public sphere (*Öffentlichkeit*) as issues of debate and concern, its standpoint will prove ineffectual. Talk about the need for philosophy to become practical will remain idle talk. As Marcuse observes: "Only when [concrete philosophy] influences existence in the public sphere, in its daily being, in the sphere where it really exists, can it hasten the movement of this existence in the direction of truth. . . . At the end of every concrete philosophy stands the public act."[29] Although fundamental ontology makes much of its status as practical philosophy, it consistently devalues "publicness" as an expression of "inauthenticity." According to Heidegger, the public sphere has been a priori monopolized and colonized by the "they" (*das Man*). Those in search of authentic modes of comportment systematically avoid it. Understandably, Marcuse has considerable difficulty attempting to reconcile fundamental ontology's practical claims—its self-understanding as a philosophy of *existence*—with its unrelenting hostility to the values of "publicness."

In an insightful review of Marcuse's habilitation study, *Hegel's Ontology and the Theory of Historicity*, which was written under Heidegger's direction, Theodor Adorno observed that the opposition between historicity and real history in Heidegger's work remained so deeply entrenched that any possible reconciliation between Heidegger and Marx was consigned in advance to failure. In Adorno's view:

> With this thesis, Marcuse appears to depart decisively from Heidegger's public teaching, which he otherwise represents with the strictness of a disciple: he inclines from the "meaning of Being" toward the disclosure of beings; from fundamental ontology toward the philosophy of history; from historicity toward history. This is what makes the work significant as well as vulnerable to criticism. If Marcuse goes so far as not only to give an ontological exposition of the possibility of factual being but deduces the possibility of the exposition of factual being from the ontological structure itself, it would have been consistent to ask: why indeed should the "ontological" question precede that of the interpretation of real, historical facts, since Marcuse himself would like to bridge the gap between ontology and facticity?[30]

In other words: if it is ultimately the dimension of "real history" that interests Marcuse, and the concepts of fundamental ontology present themselves as an interference, why not dispense with ontology altogether and concentrate directly on history?

Ontology, Life, and Labor

Marx's *Economic and Philosophical Manuscripts* appeared in 1932. Marcuse viewed their publication as "a crucial event in the history of Marxist studies," one that was destined to place "the discussion about the origins and original meaning of historical materialism . . . on a new footing."[31] The same year, Marcuse penned a magisterial review essay affirming their fundamental importance. The manuscripts revealed a profoundly philosophical Marx, still partly under the spell of Hegel, a Marx heretofore unknown outside of the (relatively circumscribed) circles of Hegelian Marxism. Marcuse insisted on viewing their arguments and claims as ultimately compatible with the aspects of Heidegger's work he prized.[32]

Marcuse viewed the Paris Manuscripts as a ringing confirmation of the theoretical perspective he had developed in "Contributions to a Phenomenology of Historical Materialism" and "On Concrete Philosophy." Marx's early writings made it clear that, from its inception, Marxism was concerned with philosophical themes that went to the very heart of the concerns of the Western intellectual tradition. The Paris manuscripts sought to address two fundamental questions: (1) what constitutes the "essence of man"; and (2) under what historical conditions might that essence be realized? When viewed from this vantage point, Marxism did not represent a scientific *break* with the philosophical tradition. It represented instead its consummation or—in Hegelian terms—its dialectical supersession. When Marx, who began as a young Hegelian, characterized his project as a *"critique* of political economy," he employed the word "critique" in a Kantian-philosophical sense: he sought to demonstrate the "limits" of political economy as a method of social reasoning. As a theoretical approach, political economy was in essence a *discourse of reification*. It served as a rhetoric of legitimation for an inverted social world—a world of "alienation," in which "things" (in the form of commodities) had become the prime movers and people were degraded to the status of objects. In the Paris Manuscripts, Marx describes this situation in the following terms:

> The worker is related to the product of his labor as to an alien object. For on this premise it is clear that the more the worker spends himself, the more powerful the alien objective world becomes which he creates over-against himself. . . . The alienation of the worker in his product means not only that his labor becomes an object, an external existence, but that it exists outside him, independently, as something alien to him, and that it be-

comes a power of its own confronting him; it means that the life which he has conferred on the object confronts him as something hostile and alien.[33]

But what was the normative basis for Marx's notion of critique? It was a philosophically derived notion of human essence or "species-being," a concept that remained implicit in Marx's later writings on political economy. For the early Marx, political economy's major flaw was that it justified and promoted a distortion of human essence. According to Marx, the essence of labor was human self-enrichment: not only do individuals fulfill themselves through their work; through labor they succeed in reclaiming and humanizing brute nature. Yet, under capitalism, the opposite occurred: the more individuals produced, the more they furthered their own impoverishment and self-degradation. Human labor was distinguished from that of animals by the fact that it was universal and free. Whereas for animals labor was a means to life and nothing more—hence, a function of necessity—for humankind, labor was an essential means of self-realization: extending beyond the realm of necessity, labor helped fashion a social environment that was durable and aesthetically pleasing. Through labor, men and women created a world that conformed to the sublimity of higher human ends: a world in which they could feel at home and which they could ultimately recognize as their own. Capitalism, however, placed all of these potentials at risk. It created a world in which human ends were sacrificed to rigid, heteronomous economic laws. It thereby replaced the laws of nature with a new, artificial necessity, a "second nature."

Marcuse believed that the Paris Manuscripts confirmed the compatibility between Marxism and fundamental ontology. There, Marx himself twice invokes "ontology" in a positive sense. According to Marx, it is "through the medium of private property [that] the *ontological* essence of human passion comes into being." In a related passage, he avows that "man's feelings, passions [are] truly *ontological* affirmations of being."[34] Consequently, if at stake for the early Marx was a philosophical validation of the concept of human essence, then the projects of Marxism and fundamental ontology, rather than operating at cross purposes, were emphatically complementary. Marcuse summarizes the gist of Marx's position as follows:

As the result of an idea about the essence of man and its realization evolved by Marx in his dispute with Hegel, a simple economic fact appears as the perversion of human essence and the
loss of human reality. . . . Bourgeois political economy has to be
basically transformed in the critique for this very reason: it never
gets to see man who is its real subject. It disregards the essence of
man and his history and is thus in the profoundest sense not a
'science of people' but of non-people and of an inhuman world of
objects and commodities. . . . The fact that capitalist society calls
into question not only economic facts and objects but the entire
'existence' [*Existenz*] of man and 'human reality' [*Dasein*] is for
Marx the decisive justification for the proletarian revolution as a
total and radical revolution, unconditionally excluding any partial
upheaval or 'evolution.'[35]

Even before the Paris Manuscripts appeared, Marcuse was already
fascinated by the notion of an "ontological vocation of labor." In his
1932 habilitation study, labor plays a key role although, in marked contrast with his other essays of this period, Marx's name is never mentioned. Of course, this omission was largely strategic: Marcuse sub-
mitted *Hegel's Ontology* as part of a (highly formalized) process of
professional qualification. In an academic study, questions of political
commitment had little place. Moreover, he was submitting the work to
Martin Heidegger, whose political sympathies certainly did not lie with
the Left.[36]

Despite the lack of explicit reference to Marx, the Heidegger-Marx
synthesis that preoccupied Marcuse during this period remained its un-
stated central theme in *Hegel's Ontology*. As Marcuse remarked at the
time in a revealing missive to Karl Löwith:

A longer work of mine on Hegel will appear this fall: it is an
interpretation of the *Logic* and the *Phenomenology of Spirit* as the
foundations for a theory of historicity. The Hegel-Marx question is
not explicitly addressed, although I hope that this interpretation
will throw some new light on this connection. Neither does this
work contain a critical discussion of Heidegger nor is it intended
to do so. Rather, the whole is a necessary preparation for articu-
lating the fundamental nature of historical happening.[37]

The origins of this historical turn in German thought could be traced to the philosophy of Hegel. In Marcuse's view, Hegel's concept of life as "motility" (*Bewegtheit*) contains the seeds of this important intellectual shift. In both the *Phenomenology* and the *Science of Logic*, "life" plays a crucial role. It signifies the moment when spirit emerges from its immersion in Being or externality and reaches the plane of subjectivity. If the goal of Hegel's philosophy is accurately captured by his well-known dictum, "Substance must be comprehended as subject," the concept of life stands as a crucial anticipation of this development.

Marcuse elected to focus on the concept of life because he believed it would help clarify what Marx meant in the "Theses on Feuerbach" when he praised German idealism for having developed the "active side" of the dialectic. The transformation of contemplative philosophy into a historically oriented theory of praxis was made possible on "ground prepared by Hegel and by holding onto tendencies intrinsic to Hegelian philosophy."[38] Moreover, the idea of life suggested an immediate practical dimension that Marcuse found lacking in pre-Hegelian philosophy. Life stressed an *active* component that was missing from traditional systematic philosophy because of its contemplative biases. Insofar as it embodied the virtues of "motility," life displayed a capacity for self-constitution that was shared by no other entity. In this respect, the parallels between Hegelian "life" and Heideggerian "Existenz" seemed compelling.[39] Once questions of "existence," "motility," and "self-constitution" surface, issues of historical meaning soon arise.

In *Hegel's Ontology*, Marcuse's discussion of life remained abstruse, confined to the rarefied philosophical terrain of Hegel exegesis. But his discussion of "work" breaks out of this mold. From it, one can better appreciate the intellectual motives that led him to undertake such a study.

Hegel's best-known discussion of work occurs in the master-slave section of the *Phenomenology of Spirit*. Interestingly, Marcuse elected *not* to focus on this celebrated episode. In his view, it remained wedded to the standpoint of individual "self-consciousness" and hence was insufficiently attentive to the questions of historicity. Instead, Marcuse chose to concentrate on a later section of the *Phenomenology*, in which Hegel discusses the collective life of a people. In retrospect, this section represents a remarkable anticipation of the doctrine of historicity in *Being and Time*, where questions of "fate," "generation" and the "historical life of a people" (*Volk*) are to the fore. Early in the *Phenomenology*, Hegel announced that *"action is the becoming of Spirit as self-consciousness."*[40] But in Marcuse's view, this discussion remained underdeveloped. Only in the "Spirit" chapter did his treatment of the theme begin to address questions of authentic historical existence or "historicity."

Here, the concept of work plays a key role. According to Hegel, insofar as the products of work exist not merely for the individual but for all, work possesses an "element of universality." As such, work exists for "universal consciousness." The element of universality in work expresses the fact that self-consciousness need not feel tied to things in the world as such. Instead, it recognizes them as inherently malleable, as materials suitable for transformation in accordance with the needs and designs of consciousness. As Marcuse observes, action, in the form of work, "occurs because it constitutes the Being of life which generates and discloses all reality with its own act. . . . Being true is an aspect of the fact of the thing itself (of the *pragma*); it is intrinsically dependent on being affected by a consciousness which makes certain that it is the truth and which proceeds to actualize it."[41] The mutability of beings attests to the universality of self-consciousness, whose essence lies in the fact that it can never be identical with any of its individual acts of self-objectification. It finds expression in them, yet it transcends them. As Hegel observes, as a result of work, "the originally *determinate* nature of the individual has lost its positive meaning of being *in-itself* the element and purpose of its activity; it is merely a superseded moment and the individual is a *self* in the form of a universal self."[42] With the transition from the "individual" to the "universal" self, the stage is set for the movement to history proper.

Marcuse stresses the fact that Hegel, unlike Kant, sees truth as neither merely subjective nor confined to an ineffectual noumenal realm. Since Hegelian self-consciousness is "active," truth must become "actual." Thus, it is clear that in his mind the self-actualizing character of Hegelian "spirit" foreshadows Marxism as a form of practical philosophy or a philosophy of the "deed." As Marcuse observes in a key passage:

> The first ontological determination of Life has been from the beginning *activity*. This fact alone suffices to indicate the distance between the fundamental ontological framework of Hegelian phi-

losophy and every other form of logicism and rationalism as well as Kantian transcendentalism. Nowhere in Western philosophy since the Greeks have Life and its activity and the world of Life as work and *pragma* been placed at the center of things. . . . Decisive here is its character as *deed*.[43]

From Marx to Schiller

Marx's conception of labor as praxis and Heidegger's notion of Dasein's practical situatedness (along with the related notions of authenticity, resolve, and historicity) helped to provide Marcuse with a philosophically cogent ontological definition of labor. The problem, however, was that this ontological ideal had little bearing on the current situation of labor. Instead, that understanding was prejudicially determined by the discipline of political economy. Thus, in the factical context at hand, the conception of labor as a mode of human self-realization was entirely absent. Instead, the function of labor was exclusively viewed in crude economic terms: as a factor of production, "variable capital," an object of administrative control to be managed by Taylorites and efficiency experts.

Marcuse believed that philosophy was a form of practical criticism whose primary aim was the defetishization of false consciousness. Moreover, if the present crisis could accurately be described as a crisis of "subjectivity"—of the reification of consciousness—then the tasks of philosophical enlightenment, far from being "theoreticist deviations," remained absolutely central. Whereas vulgar Marxism decreed that social being determined social consciousness, Marcuse, faithful to his training as an Hegelian, believed that such methodological fatalism condemned the proletariat to mirror the current state of social decomposition. Thus, an adequate philosophical grounding of labor as a form of "species-being" might be an important first step toward reversing the defeats suffered by the European labor movement.

Marcuse addressed this task in his final attempt at a Heidegger-Marx synthesis, "On the Philosophical Foundation of the Concept of Labor in Economics." Published in 1933, this resolutely Heideggerian essay (their break would occur shortly following its publication) is noteworthy because it foreshadows the utopian framework of *Eros and Civilization* and other works.

Insofar as the "everyday" concept of labor had been prejudicially determined by the discourse of political economy, one needed a phenomenological "reduction" that would bracket this everyday meaning in order to arrive at labor's ontological essence. Thus, Marcuse made it clear that he was searching for a definition of "labor [as] an *ontological concept of human existence as such*."[44] In *Being and Time*, Heidegger claimed that he had uncovered the basic ontological structures of human Being-in-the-world. But there was no reason to assume that Heidegger's list was definitive. Moreover, from the standpoint of an interest in historicity informed by a concern for social justice, the inclusion of labor was an entirely plausible addition.

Marcuse describes the phenomenological essence of labor in terms reminiscent of his earlier Heideggerian-Marxist standpoint. As a modality of praxis, labor is an essential component of human self-realization.

> Labor is that in which every single activity is founded and to which they again return: a *doing* [*Tun*]. And it is precisely the doing of human beings as the mode of one's being in the world: it is that through which one first becomes "for oneself" what one is, comes to one's self, acquires the form of one's Dasein, winning one's "permanence" and at the same time making the world "one's own." . . . In labor something happens with man and with the objectification in such a manner that the "result" is an essential unity of man and the objectification: man "objectifies" himself and the object becomes "his," it becomes a *human object*."[45]

In contrast with the discourse of political economy, here labor is determined not by a series of external standards and goals, but according to the requirements of human existence (*Existenz*). Ironically, however, the essay's moment of genuine conceptual innovation concerns not the notion of labor but the idea of "play."

The concept of play figures prominently in Schiller's *Letters on the Aesthetic Education of Man* (1795). In letter fifteen, Schiller sets forth his radical proposition: "Man plays only when he is in the full sense of the word a man, and *he is only wholly Man when he is playing*."[46] Marcuse took Schiller's maxim to heart. It became one of the signature ideas of

his mature work. His discussion of play, while brief, indicates his growing dissatisfaction with the unphilosophical, productivist conception of
labor in the discourse of orthodox Marxism. (Late in life, Adorno
opined that Marx wanted to turn the world into a giant sweatshop.)[47]
Marcuse sensed that a fully human world—the "humanization of nature and the naturalization of man," to cite Marx's early definition—
must ultimately transcend a narrowly utilitarian understanding of labor. Increasingly, Marcuse came to view labor as a realm of necessity;
not through labor but *beyond* it lay the realm of freedom. At stake was
a revision of Marxism that surpassed the terms of Marxist orthodoxy
and that anticipated the libidinal politics of the 1960s.

Given Marcuse's understanding of Marxism as a critique of reification, Schiller's *Letters on the Aesthetic Education of Man* represented a rich
critical resource. The *Letters* were a classic example of the romantic
protest against the distortions of bourgeois society. Under modern conditions, "the more intricate machinery of states made necessary a more
rigorous dissociation of ranks and occupations," lamented Schiller. As a
result, "the essential bond of human nature was torn apart, and a ru-
inous conflict set its harmonious powers at variance."[48] Schiller criticized bourgeois society's lack of wholeness, as illustrated by the fact
that intellectual and emotional faculties operated at cross-purposes.
The intellect sought to produce a world that was logical and coherent,
but was impervious to the laws of the heart. Consequently, in the
modern era, principle and feeling had become disjointed. As Schiller
observes, "Today, necessity is master, and bends a degraded humanity
beneath its yoke. *Utility* is the great idol of the age, to which all powers
must do service and talents swear allegiance. In these clumsy scales the
spiritual service of art has no weight."[49]

With the arguments of Kant's recently published *Third Critique* fresh
in mind, Schiller introduced his idea of the "play impulse." In the aesthetic sphere, the laws of beauty serve freedom rather than necessity.
As Schiller contends:

> Reason demands, on transcendental grounds, that there shall be a
> partnership between the formal and the material impulse, that is
> to say a *play impulse*, because it is only the union of reality with
> form, of contingency with necessity, of passivity with freedom,

that fulfils the conception of humanity. . . . Man is only serious with the agreeable, the good, the perfect; but with Beauty *he plays*.[50]

Schiller's aesthetics, which, following Kant, emphasized the benefits of "disinterested pleasure" or "play," represented an ideal foil to Marxism's traditional glorification of instrumental reason qua labor. Following the Paris manuscripts, the romantic-utopian dimension of Marxism—Marx's original concern with a restoration of human wholeness—had, to historical materialism's discredit, fallen out of account. In the words of utopian Marxism's leading representative, Ernst Bloch, the "cold current" of Marxism had triumphed over its "warm current."

Marcuse sensed that Marxism, as a metaphysics of labor, embodied the consummation of political economy, instead of transcending it. The early Marx upheld a broad definition of labor as an expression of human self-realization—a definition that had more in common with Aristotle's notion of praxis than with Locke's Puritanical conception of "the sweat of our brow and the blood of our hands." For the later Marx, however, labor became tantamount to "instrumental reason." The philosophical ideal of human fulfillment—the ideal of self-formation or *Bildung* that the young Marx had inherited from German idealism—no longer stood at the center of Marxism. Instead, Marxism's sole concern seemed to be the rational mastery of nature.

In "The Philosophical Foundations of the Concept of Labor in Economics," Marcuse openly vented his intellectual misgivings about the centrality of labor in the Marxist tradition. His argument stressed the "burdensome character of labor" (*Lastcharakter der Arbeit*), the fact that, as an expression of need, labor seeks to compensate for human "lack." Moreover, since labor always stands in the service of "lack," it can never be entirely free as a form of human activity. Instead, it always remains in thrall to the being-in-itself of the object, the laws of necessity:

Whether explicitly or not, willingly or not, in labor what is at stake is always the thing itself. In laboring, the laborer is always "with the thing": whether one stands by a machine, draws technical plans, is concerned with organizational measures, researches scientific problems, instructs people, etc. In his activity he allows himself to be directed by the thing, subjects himself and obeys its laws, even when he dominates his object, directs it, guides it, and lets it go its own way. In each case he is not "with himself," does not passively stand by his own existence.[51]

The Greek notion of autonomy understood freedom in terms of the ideal of self-legislation: following laws of one's own creation. Marcuse argued that since labor as a form of praxis necessarily followed the contours and laws of *the object*, in the true ontological sense it could never be free. As Marcuse explained, "Since one's becoming human in the world is first and foremost 'self-activity'—the process of determining one's own existence or in being-oneself in every existence—and since, on the other hand, this self-being is only made possible by rendering objectivity passive as a being-with-others and for others, laboring upon objectivity is *essentially burdensome*."[52]

In ancient philosophy, activities pursued for their own sake were of greater ontological value than those whose ends lay outside themselves. The former types of activity possessed a degree of self-sufficiency absent in activities of the latter variety. As Aristotle remarked with regard to happiness or *eudaemonia*: "Activities desirable in themselves are those from which we seek to derive nothing beyond the actual exercise of the activity."[53] With this characterization, Aristotle defined "virtue." Acting virtuously is not something we do for the sake of extrinsic ends; unlike labor, which is still chained to the realm of necessity, and whose ends are therefore extrinsic, acting virtuously is something we do exclusively for its own sake. It is an *intrinsic good* and end in itself. In Marcuse's view, one of the tragedies of bourgeois society was that praxis—which, in the *Nichomachean Ethics*, Aristotle defined as "action in accordance with virtue"—had degenerated to labor qua necessity or "burden." Alternative forms of praxis consistent with the higher Greek ideal of "self-activity" had either disappeared or, like so many other features of social and cultural life under capitalism, had been commodified. One of the reasons that play and the "aesthetic dimension" came to occupy a privileged niche in Marcuse's ontology of value was that these precepts openly flaunted the laws of necessity. As Marcuse observes in a remarkably lyrical passage:

In play the "objectivity" of objects and their effects, and the actuality of the objective world with which one is usually forced constantly to deal, thus learning to respect it, are temporarily suspended. For once, one does entirely as one pleases with objects; one places oneself beyond them and becomes "free" from them. This is what is decisive: in this self-positing transcendence of objectivity one comes precisely to oneself, in a dimension of freedom denied in labor. *In a single toss of a ball, the player achieves an infinitely greater triumph of human freedom over objectification than in the most powerful accomplishment of technical labor.*[54]

Marcuse's encomium to the virtues of play follows Marx's discussion of the relationship between freedom and necessity in *Capital*, Volume 3. In contrast to the romantic-utopian conception of labor developed in the Paris Manuscripts, in *Capital* Marx equates social labor simply with the realm of necessity. Following Aristotle, he argues that the realm of freedom—which, returning to the Hegelian language of his youth, he defines as "the development of human powers as ends in themselves"—can only transpire *beyond* the realm of necessity, during leisure or "free-time."

Like Marx, Marcuse oscillated between these two competing visions of the philosophical meaning of labor. In *Eros and Civilization*, following the early Marx, he argued for an "expressive" notion of labor: labor as an essential form of human self-realization. Yet in other writings he downplayed this prospect in favor of the ideal of a cybernetic utopia in which enhanced conditions of technological proficiency would essentially render labor obsolete. According to this scenario, the extension of leisure or "free-time" meant that the time available for human self-realization would be significantly augmented. As Marcuse speculates in *One-Dimensional Man*:

Advanced industrial society is approaching the stage where continued progress would demand the radical subversion of the prevailing direction and organization of progress. This stage would be reached when material production . . . becomes automated to the extent that all vital needs can be satisfied while necessary labor time is reduced to marginal time. From this point on, technical progress would transcend the realm of necessity. . . . Technology would become subject to the free play of faculties in the struggle for the pacification of nature and society. Such a state is envisioned in Marx's notion of the "abolition of labor."[55]

Heidegger's Betrayal of Philosophy

A month after Marcuse's departure from Freiburg in December 1932, Hitler was appointed Germany's chancellor. Within two months, he skillfully manipulated the Weimar constitution in order to destroy the last vestiges of democratic rule. Thereafter, all questions of academic advancement for Jews and leftists (let alone Jewish leftists) became moot. Marcuse, who, through the intercession of Husserl, had established contact with the Institute for Social Research in Frankfurt, soon followed his new colleagues into exile. In May 1933, Heidegger, in his new guise as Freiburg University's first Nazi rector, emphatically declared his loyalties to the new regime. In retrospect, it seems plausible that political circumstances played an important, if indirect, role in Marcuse's and Heidegger's intellectual parting of ways. During his philosophical apprenticeship to Heidegger, Marcuse contributed regularly to a leading Social Democratic journal, *Die Gesellschaft*. It is inconceivable that Heidegger was unaware of his young admirer's left-wing political convictions. Heidegger was undoubtedly cognizant of the Marxist-existentialist synthesis that formed the core of Marcuse's philosophical worldview; and, given his resolute anticommunist standpoint, it is hard to imagine that he viewed such dalliances sympathetically. It seems safe to conclude that, despite Marcuse's circumspect omission in *Hegel's Ontology* of all matters pertaining to Marx and Marxism, Heidegger sensed the direction of Marcuse's work and disapproved.[56] Ultimately, however, we are confronted with conflicting evidence: there is no documentation to indicate that Heidegger ever expressly rejected the direction of Marcuse's research. Yet we know that in December 1930, Marcuse's efforts to habilitate abruptly met with failure.

Certainly, Heidegger's demonstrative support for the "German Revolution" effectively sealed the breach between them. Thereafter, Marcuse's public references to his former mentor were sparing but critical. When queried in a 1974 interview about whether he or his fellow students had sensed Heidegger's impending political turn, he responded as follows:

> Now, from personal experience I can tell you that neither in his lectures, nor in his seminars, nor personally, was there ever any

hint of [Heidegger's] sympathies for Nazism. . . . So his openly declared Nazism came as a complete surprise to us. From that point on, of course, we asked ourselves the question: did we overlook indications and anticipations in *Being and Time* and the related writings? And we made one interesting observation, *ex post* (and I want to stress that, *ex post*, it is easy to make this observation). If you look at his view of human existence, of Being-in-the-world, you will find a highly repressive, highly oppressive interpretation. I have just today gone through again the table of contents of *Being and Time* and had a look at the main categories in which he sees the essential characteristics of existence or Dasein. I can just read them to you and you will see what I mean: "Idle talk, curiosity, ambiguity, falling and Being-thrown, concern, Being-toward-death, anxiety, dread, boredom," and so on. Now this gives a picture which plays well on the fears and frustrations of men and women in a repressive society—a joyless existence: overshadowed by death and anxiety; human material for the authoritarian personality.[57]

One of the concepts from *Being and Time* that Marcuse viewed with suspicion was Being-toward-death. Although its importance has often been underplayed in the vast secondary literature on *Being and Time*, Being-toward-death proves a crucial way station on the road to authenticity. Whereas everyday Dasein (the "they") systematically shuns and avoids confronting the predicament of human finitude, authentic Dasein distinguishes itself by a willingness to confront the phenomenon of death unflinchingly. An awareness of death's inevitability sharpens Dasein's worldly involvements and commitments. Since *Existenz* is inherently finite (there is no salvation or eternal life), Dasein's commitment to temporality and worldliness must be radical and total.

Yet, as Marcuse notes, Heidegger's ontological characterization of death betrays a specific ontic context: the glorification of the "front experience" in Germany following World War I. For example, in Ernst Jünger's provocative battle chronicles, *In the Storm of Steel* and *War as Inner Experience*, the confrontation with death in war was elevated to the status of a supreme existential rite of passage. It is difficult to dissociate Heidegger's exaltation of Being-toward-death from this postwar

cultural context. Ultimately, this ethos, which emphasized the imperatives of "sacrifice" and the importance of Nietzsche's maxim, "Have the
courage to live dangerously," found a home in the martial ethos of
National Socialism. Heidegger's own political speeches on behalf of the
regime are suffused with the rhetorical bombast characteristic of this
idiom.[58]

As Heidegger's contemporary and an eyewitness to the historical
experiences in question, Marcuse was well situated to evaluate the political implications of such rhetoric. Decades later, while insisting on
the continued relevance of Heidegger's concept of authenticity ("I certainly wouldn't deny that authenticity . . . is becoming increasingly
difficult in the advanced industrial society of today"), Marcuse believed
that Heidegger's preoccupation with Being-toward-death

> served to justify the emphasis of fascism and Nazism on sacrifice
> as an end-in-itself. There is a famous phrase by Ernst Jünger, the
> Nazi writer, who speaks of the necessity of sacrifice "on the edge
> of the abyss, or on the edge of nothingness" [*am Rande des Nichts
> oder am Rande des Abgrunds*]. In other words a sacrifice that is
> good because it is a sacrifice, and because it is freely chosen . . .
> by the individual. Heidegger's notion [of Being-toward-death] re-
> calls the battle cry of the fascist Futurists: *Eviva la muerte*.[59]

In *Eros and Civilization*, Marcuse again emphasized the fundamentally repressive role played by Being-toward-death in Heidegger's existential ontology. Contemporary capitalism, he argued, systematically
suppresses eros or the "life instincts." Predicated on the requirements
of the "performance principle," it cultivates an ethos of instinctual renunciation in order to maintain a vast edifice of alienated social labor.
In Marcuse's view, *Existenzphilosophie*'s preoccupation with Being-toward-death is perfectly suited to the ideological needs of an instinc-
tually repressive social totality. As Marcuse observes:

> Theology and philosophy today compete with each other in cele-
> brating death as an existential category: perverting a biological
> fact into an ontological essence, they bestow transcendental bless-
> ing on the guilt of mankind which they hope to perpetuate—they
> betray the promise of utopia. . . . Whether death is feared as a

constant threat, or glorified as supreme sacrifice, or accepted as fate, the education for consent to death introduces an element of surrender into life from the beginning—surrender and submission. It stifles "utopian" efforts. The powers that be have a deep affinity to death; death is a token of unfreedom, of defeat.[60]

Despite such retrospective criticisms, elsewhere Marcuse insisted that Heidegger's "decision" for Nazism signified an act of intellectual self-betrayal rather than a logical extension of his philosophical framework. In his first published article following Nazism's triumph, in which he probes National Socialism's philosophical origins, Marcuse distinguishes between genuine Nazi thinkers, such as Carl Schmitt and Ernst Forsthoff, and someone like Heidegger whose support for the regime was at variance with his theoretical convictions. Marcuse wastes no time excoriating Heidegger's servile political conduct. But he insists that, ultimately, Heidegger's partisanship for Nazism signified a "radical denial" of his own philosophical standpoint:

Existentialism collapses the moment its political theory is realized. The total-authoritarian state for which it yearned gives the lie to all its truths. Existentialism accompanies its collapse with a self-abasement that is unique in intellectual history; it carries out its own history as a satyr-play to the end. It began philosophically as a great debate with Western rationalism and idealism, in order to redeem the historical concretion of individual existence for this intellectual heritage. And it ends philosophically with the radical denial of its own origins; the struggle against reason drives it blindly into the arms of the reigning powers. In their service and protection it betrays that great philosophy which it once celebrated as the pinnacle of Western thinking.[61]

Perhaps Marcuse's most insightful observation is that "the struggle against reason drives [existentialism] blindly into the arms of the reigning powers." Though Marcuse refrains from offering a more precise explanation of what he means, attention to his later philosophical course helps clarify the situation considerably. In his subsequent works, he became an implacable defender of the philosophical "reason" (Vernunft), especially as it had been articulated in the writings of German idealism (to wit, his 1940 study of Hegel, *Reason and Revolution*). Existentialism, notes Marcuse, had begun as a "debate with Western rationalism and idealism." In his view, however, the debate ended prematurely and on a false note. Instead of attempting to *realize* the ideals of reason in a meaningful and worldly fashion, existentialism rejected them. In ethical terms, *Existenzphilosophie* embraced a decisionism (*Entschlossenheit*) that flowed entirely from the demands of the concrete situation, unmediated by reason or higher moral norms. In *Being and Time*, Heidegger inquires, "On what basis does decisiveness decide? Only the decision itself can tell."[62] It seems that this is what Marcuse has in mind when he suggests that existentialism's "struggle against reason drives it blindly into the arms of the reigning powers." Bereft of higher norms in light of which he might judge Germany's Brown Revolution, Heidegger was left morally defenseless and capitulated to the demands of the situation at hand. In Hitler he had "chosen his hero" and cast his lot with German "destiny." Thus, Heidegger's decision for Nazism, far from being a contingent biographical choice, was in fact based on the requirements of authentic historical commitment or "historicity" as spelled out in *Being and Time*.[63]

Despite Marcuse's characterization of Heidegger's surrender to Nazism as an instance of self-betrayal, he maintained that "that is one of the errors a philosopher is not allowed to commit." In Marcuse's estimation, a commitment to Nazism was not merely a particular wrong or injustice. It constituted *"the betrayal of philosophy as such and of everything philosophy stands for."*[64]

In 1947, Marcuse, now in the employ of the State Department, visited Heidegger's Todtnauberg ski cabin. As Marcuse later recalled, their conversation, which centered on recent political events, was "far from pleasant." In their subsequent correspondence, Marcuse reiterated the betrayal-of-philosophy criticism, distinguishing between errors in judgment—from which no thinker is immune—and a conscious disavowal of the vocation of philosophy itself. He implored Heidegger, as the "man from whom I learned philosophy from 1928 to 1932," to express a public word of contrition, a word that would diminish the gruesome blemish on Heidegger's philosophical reputation. Marcuse articulates his position as follows:

I—and very many others—have admired you as a philosopher; from you we have learned an infinite amount. But we cannot make the separation between Heidegger the philosopher and Heidegger the man, for it contradicts your own philosophy. A philosopher can be deceived regarding political matters; in which case he will openly acknowledge his error. But he cannot be deceived about a regime that has killed millions of Jews—merely because they were Jews—that made terror into an everyday phenomenon, and that turned everything that pertains to the ideas of spirit, freedom, and truth into its bloody opposite. A regime that in every respect imaginable was the deadly caricature of the Western tradition that you yourself so forcefully explicated and justified. . . . Is this really the way you would like to be remembered in the history of ideas?[65]

Yet Heidegger proved unrepentant. He alleged that atrocities perpetrated by the Allies were equal to those of the Nazis; yet whereas the Nazis' crimes were kept a secret from the German public (which was, therefore, presumably innocent), those of the allies were not.[66] After a final reproach-filled missive from Marcuse, their correspondence broke off abruptly.

Left Heideggerianism

Marcuse broke with Heidegger in 1933 following Heidegger's vigorous declaration of support for the Nazi regime. Yet there was no denying the fact that Marcuse's early philosophical orientation had been decisively shaped by Heidegger. Consequently, it would be surprising were Heideggerian leanings and influences entirely absent from Marcuse's mature philosophical work.

In Marcuse's postwar writings, the Heideggerian dimension is muted but nevertheless traceable. It sits in uneasy juxtaposition with the predominant Marxist focus. For obvious reasons, Marxism's resolute historicism conflicts with philosophy's search for timeless first principles; in many ways, the two approaches operate at cross-purposes. Yet, perennially, and especially in times of revolutionary retreat, intellectuals have sought to provide Marxism with a rigorous philosophical grounding. When the proletariat's privileged role in the course of historical development seems in doubt, philosophical precepts provide necessary clarification and insight. Such was the strategy of the Austro-Marxists, who sought to buttress Marxism via recourse to Kant; Lukács pursued a similar strategy by relying on Hegel; and under Horkheimer's tutelage, the Frankfurt School pursued an approach known as "interdisciplinary materialism."[67]

Marcuse diagnosed the postwar industrial order as a "one-dimensional society." It was a world of *inauthenticity*—a mass society of blind conformity. For Marcuse, the problems that militated against the realization of an authentic existence were in the first instance social rather than ontological. Moreover, following Marx, he reasoned that were society to succeed in surmounting the *social* basis of alienation, many of the ontological causes of alienation would also be conquered. Thus, in *Eros and Civilization*, his most speculative work, he went so far as to suggest that labor could be "eroticized" and that death would no longer be experienced as a deprivation but as an "act of freedom."[68]

Traditionally, a potent working class movement had contested relations of domination under capitalism. But in advanced industrial society, such conflict potentials were all but muted. Instead, a newly affluent working class felt fully at home in its alienation. Class conflict had been pacified, not only by higher wages, but through consumer strategies in which human needs were ideologically manipulated and administered. Thus was born Marcuse's theory of "repressive desublimation." It described a process of mass regression whereby consumers came to identify libidinally with the commodities they purchased. The suffusing of life and work with Eros that Marcuse had prescribed in *Eros and Civilization* had failed to occur. Instead, potentially explosive libidinal energies were siphoned off and rechanneled via the consumer capitalist ethos of consumption for consumption's sake. "By virtue of the way it has organized the technological base, contemporary society is *totalitarian*," claimed Marcuse, unconsciously echoing Heidegger's claim that modern society represents a state of perfect nihilism.[69] Marcuse continues:

People recognize themselves in their commodities. They find their soul in their automobile, hi-fi set, split-level home, kitchen equipment. . . . The result is not adjustment but *mimesis*: an immediate identification of the individual with his society and, through it, with the society as a whole. . . . This identification . . . constitutes a more progressive stage of alienation. The latter has become entirely objective; the subject which is alienated is swallowed up by its alienated existence. There is only *one dimension*, and it is everywhere and in all forms.[70]

The historical dynamic leading to a classless society prophesied by Marx had reached a total standstill. The logic of repressive desublimation characteristic of late capitalism drove the reification of consciousness portrayed by Lukács to qualitatively new heights. The method of immanent critique, on which Marxism had traditionally relied to expose capitalism's developmental contradictions, appeared permanently foreclosed. By virtue of its unprecedented technological prowess, its capacity to deliver the goods and perpetually stimulate new—albeit false—consumption needs, the reigning social order seemed all but immune to the powers of critique.

Since the dialectic of history had apparently ground to a halt, it became necessary to explore new, nonhistorical sources of political contestation. Reprising a motif from *Eros and Civilization*, in the late 1960s Marcuse flirted with the idea of a "biological basis for socialism." Could there exist, conjectured Marcuse, an anthropological drive toward libidinal gratification; a drive capable of overturning late capitalism's sophisticated mechanisms of social-psychological adaptation and corresponding universe of false needs? For Heidegger, authenticity was ontologically rooted; it lay in the a priori capacity of a spiritual elite to heed the "call of conscience" and thereby surmount the pitfalls of "everydayness." Might there exist, wondered Marcuse, an analogous set of ontological capacities capable of propelling humanity beyond the performance principle of late capitalism and its attendant distortions? As Marcuse speculates in *An Essay on Liberation*:

Prior to all ethical behavior in accordance with specific social standards, prior to all ideological expression, morality is a disposition of the organism, perhaps rooted in the erotic drive to counter aggressiveness, to create and preserve "ever greater unities of life." We would then have, this side of all "values," an instinctual foundation for solidarity among human beings—a solidarity which has been effectively repressed in line with the requirements of a class society but which now appears as a precondition for liberation.

According to Marcuse, under conditions of late capitalism, the total reification of consciousness compels Marxism to tap into heretofore unexplored reservoirs of resistance, such as the *"biological dimension in which the vital, imperative needs and satisfactions of man assert themselves."*[71] Although Marcuse freely admitted the utopian character of such claims, he believed he had discerned their genuine outlines in the erotic sensibility of the 1960s counterculture. A slogan like "make love not war" captures the elemental sense of libidinal-cultural rebellion Marcuse sought to foster. In his view, given the hyper-rationalist excesses of advanced industrial society—environmental devastation, capacity for nuclear overkill, and the obscene disparity between private opulence and mass poverty—the maxim, "the more primitive the better," seemed to hold.

In many ways, Marcuse's later social theory reproduces the contours and content of a left Heideggerianism. He transposes the sweeping critique of "everydayness" set forth in *Being and Time* to the social world of late capitalism. The inauthenticity that Heidegger interprets as an ontological constant of Dasein's Being-in-the-world Marcuse identifies as the historical fundament of advanced industrial society. To be sure, the elements and terms of the critique vary, but the diagnosis of the age is essentially the same.[72] Moreover, as Marcuse began to doubt the "socially neutral" character of technology, he came to share Heidegger's view that science a priori presupposes an instrumentalist and manipulative relationship to nature. To illustrate his point, in *One-Dimensional Man* he approvingly cites Heidegger's essay, "The Question Concerning Technology": "Modern man takes the entirety of Being as raw material for production and subjects the entirety of the object-world to the sweep and order of production. . . . The use of machinery and the production of machines is not technics itself but merely an adequate instrument for the realization of the essence of technics in its objective raw material."[73] Marcuse is convinced that, whereas previously technology may have been socially neutral ("The machinery of the technological universe is indifferent towards political ends. . . . An electronic computer can serve equally a capitalist or socialist administration"), this is so no longer. Instead, *"when technics becomes the universal form of material production, it circumscribes an entire culture; it projects a historical totality—a 'world.' "*[74]

From here it is but a short step to Marcuse's controversial utopian appeal for a "new technology"—one that would aim at the pacification rather than the subjugation of nature. His argument bears distinct affinities with the later Heidegger's preference for "poesis" or "poetic revealing" as opposed to the "enframing" characteristic of modern "technics" (*das Gestell*). The discourse of German romanticism profoundly imprints the work of both thinkers. In Marcuse's case, recourse to Schiller's "play impulse," which proposes an aesthetic reconciliation of the antagonisms and divisions of modern society, is explicit:

> The liberated consciousness would promote the development of a science and technology free to discover and realize the possibilities of things and men in the protection and gratification of life, playing with the potentialities of form and matter for the attainment of this goal. Technique would then tend to become art, and art would tend to form reality: the opposition between imagination and reason, higher and lower faculties, poetic and scientific thought, would be invalidated.[75]

According to Marcuse, an emancipated technology conceived along these lines would mean that "science would arrive at essentially different concepts of nature and establish essentially different facts."[76] Marcuse thereby flirts with the notion of the "resurrection of fallen nature," a trope that is prominent in the doctrines Jewish mysticism, German romanticism, Marx's Paris Manuscripts, and the philosophy of Ernst Bloch.[77]

For Heidegger, prospects for authenticity are limited to a spiritual elite. For Marcuse, the capacity to transcend reification is the province of the theoretically gifted—an intellectual elite. During its North American exile, the Frankfurt School understood its labors as a *Flaschenpost* (message in a bottle): shunned by contemporary society, its message of emancipation would be taken up by an "imaginary future witness." As Horkheimer observed (without a trace of irony) in his programmatic essay on "Traditional and Critical Theory": "In the general historical upheaval truth may reside with numerically small groups of men."[78] Thus, Heidegger's ontological elitism found a parallel in critical theory's political elitism. In *Eros and Civilization*, Marcuse, driven to despair by the lack of prospects for radical social change, openly flirted with the idea of intellectual dictatorship: "How can civilization freely generate freedom, when unfreedom has become part and parcel of the mental apparatus? . . . From Plato to Rousseau, the only honest answer is the idea of an *educational dictatorship*, exercised by those who are supposed to have acquired knowledge of the real Good."[79] What began as a flirtation during the 1950s became a veritable obsession during the 1960s. In his controversial essay "Repressive Tolerance" (1965), he observes: "If the choice were between genuine democracy and dictatorship, democracy would certainly preferable. But democracy"—which, in Marcuse's view, had been effectively colonized by technocratic and political elites—"does not prevail." Hence, Marcuse openly entertained the idea of a "dictatorship of intellectuals," who, in good Platonic fashion, have seen the light about Reason and Happiness. After all, reasons Marcuse, would not such a dictatorship be more just than "representative government by a non-intellectual minority of politicians, generals, and businessmen?"[80]

Nevertheless, the theme of universal emancipation embraced by the Frankfurt School contrasts markedly with Heidegger's blatantly aristocratic perspective. For critical theory, the concept of emancipation remained general, never partial; to count as genuine, it needed to embrace everyone, not just a spiritual elite. Consequently, the critical theorists endorsed the traditional Marxist view that *formal* democracy must be sublated in the direction of *real* democracy. Or, as Walter Benjamin observed during the 1930s: "As long as there is still a beggar, there is myth."[81]

Arbeit Macht Frei:

Heidegger As Philosopher of

the German "Way"

An Aversion to Universal Concepts

Heidegger resigned from the position of university rector in May 1934. His brief, though concerted, foray into politics was a cause for considerable disillusionment. Heidegger was done in not only by philosophical hubris and his lack of prior political experience, but also by a basic incapacity for political judgment. As Karl Jaspers, paraphrasing Max Weber, remarked concerning Heidegger's case: children who play with the wheel of world history are smashed to bits. In many respects, Heidegger's political maladroitness was an outgrowth of the "factical worldview" he had cultivated since his early break with Catholicism (1919). At that time, Heidegger began to embrace a pseudoheroic, post-Nietzschean standpoint determined partly by Nietzsche's insight concerning the "death of God." According to Nietzsche, the death of God was symptomatic of the delegitimation of the highest Western values and ideals. What remained was a devil's choice between the abyss of nihilism and Nietzsche's own alternative: the superman who was "beyond good and evil."

Such were the "ontic" or historical origins of Heidegger's *Existenz-philosophie*. In a world whose highest ideals had been discredited, what was there left to trust but the "facticity" of one's own brute Being-in-the-world? This was Heidegger's rejoinder to Descartes' *ego cogito*

FIG. 5. Martin Heidegger, 1933. Photo courtesy of J. B. Metzlersche
Verlagsbuchhandlung and Carl Ernst Poeschel Verlag, Stuttgart, 1986.

sum. In Heidegger's view, even this Cartesian ontological minimum assumed too much. Moreover, by defining human nature in terms of "thinking substance" (*res cogitans*), Descartes and modern philosophy established a series of pernicious rationalist prejudices: they assumed that what was distinctive about humanity was its capacity for theoretical reason, a predisposition with which Heidegger strove concertedly to break. Thus, in *Being and Time*, Heidegger went to great lengths to demonstrate that even more primordial (*ürsprunglich*) than humanity's intellectual capacities were a series of pre-rational habitudes and dispositions: moods, tools, language (which always "speaks man"), practical involvements and situations, Being-with-others, and so forth.

Heidegger's philosophy betrays a fateful distrust of universal concepts, which are emblematic of a Western metaphysical tradition with which he hoped to break. Such concepts—"truth," "morality," "the good"—were representative of the theoretical tyranny of "representation" over "Being," a characteristically Platonic intellectual falsification. According to Heidegger's critique of metaphysics, the downfall of Western philosophy began when Plato shifted the locus of truth from the notion of "unconcealment" (*aletheia*) of things themselves to the notion of truth as "idea" or "representation." As Heidegger remarks, with Plato, "Truth becomes *orthotos*, correctness of the ability to perceive and to declare something."[1] Thus, whereas originally truth was something proper to the Being of beings, with Platonism (and in this respect, the entire tradition of Western metaphysics merely follows Plato's mistaken lead) its locus is transferred to the faculty of human judgment. Heidegger is merely being consistent, therefore, when in *Being and Time* he announces the need for a radical "destruction" of the history of Western philosophy.[2]

Needless to say, a rejection of universal concepts by no means entails a commitment to Nazism. Yet, with this radical philosophical maneuver, Heidegger left himself vulnerable to political movements whose major selling point—in opposition to the presumed decrepitude of Western liberalism—was an unabashed celebration of volkish particularism. Heidegger used the same normative criticisms he had brought to bear against Western rationalism as arguments against their corresponding political forms: cosmopolitanism, rights

of man, constitutionalism. Search as one may through Heidegger's voluminous philosophical corpus, one is extremely hard pressed to find a
positive word concerning the virtues of political liberalism. His philosophical and political predilections were related to one another necessarily rather than contingently.

In a book written shortly before his death in 1945, Ernst Cassirer
offered some perspicuous reflections on the relationship between
Heidegger's philosophy and the antidemocratic thought that was so
much in vogue during the waning years of the Weimar Republic. Cassirer began by contrasting Heidegger's "existential" point of departure
with Husserl's characterization of philosophy as "rigorous science"—an
aim that, according to Cassirer, was "entirely alien to Heidegger."
Heidegger, Cassirer continues,

> does not admit there is something like "eternal truth," a Platonic
> "realm of ideas," or a strictly logical method of philosophic
> thought. All this is declared to be elusive. In vain we try to build
> up a logical philosophy; we can only give an *Existenzialphilosophie.*
> Such an existential philosophy does not claim to give us an objec-
> tive and universal truth. No thinker can give more truth than his
> own existence; and this existence has a historical character. It is
> bound up with the conditions under which the individual lives. . . .
> In order to express his thought Heidegger had to coin a new
> term. He spoke of the *Geworfenheit* of man (being-thrown).[3]

Cassirer is quick to avow that Heidegger's ideas had little direct or
immediate bearing on German political thought during the pre-Nazi
period. But he also insists that the antirationalist animus that pervaded
Heidegger's doctrines was by no means ineffectual or without influence. Instead, as Cassirer observes, such approaches "did enfeeble and
slowly undermine the forces that could have resisted the modern political myths. . . . A theory that sees in the *Geworfenheit* of man one of
his principal characters [has] given up all hope of an active share in
the construction and reconstruction of man's cultural life. Such philosophy renounces its own fundamental theoretical and ethical ideals.
It can be used, then, as a pliable instrument in the hands of political
leaders."[4]

The epistemological emphasis on "facticity," which celebrates the particularism of one's own immediate heritage/life/milieu, is a logical corollary of a perspective that esteems the concrete over the abstract. In this regard, the central position that Heidegger in *Being and Time* accords to "mineness" (*Jemeinigkeit*) is also indicative and revealing. When in 1933 Heidegger turned down an offer for a position at the University of Berlin, he justified his decision by glorifying the provincial values of locality and region, which he contrasted to the corrupting influences of modern city life:

The world of the city runs the risk of falling into a destructive error. A very loud and very active and very fashionable obstrusiveness often passes itself off as concern for the world and existence of the peasant. But this goes exactly contrary to the one and only thing that now needs to be done, namely, to keep one's distance from the life of the peasant, to leave their existence more than ever to its own law, to keep hands off lest it be dragged into the literati's dishonest chatter about "folk character" and "rootedness in the soil."[5]

According to intimate Heinrich Petztet, the Freiburg philosopher felt ill at ease with big-city life, "and this was especially true of that mundane spirit of Jewish circles, which is at home in the metropolitan centers of the West."[6] In the late 1920s, Heidegger vigorously protested the growing "Jewification" (*Verjudung*) of German spiritual life.[7] Thus, in Heidegger's corpus, the boundaries between philosophy and *weltanschauung* are fluid and not impenetrable.[8] To date, the predominant formal-philosophical interpretations of his work have systematically neglected its ideological dimensions, to their own detriment. By proceeding from a philosophical standpoint that consistently valued the particular over the universal, Heidegger's thought was exposed from the outset to grave ethical and political deficits. This conclusion suggests that in seeking to account for Heidegger's 1933 political lapsus, the existential standpoint he cultivated in the early 1920s is as important as the historical-biographical contingencies stressed by his defenders.

In *My Life in Germany Before and After 1933*, Löwith recounts a 1936 controversy in a Swiss newspaper over whether Heidegger's political allegiances were consistent with his philosophy. A Swiss commentator had "regretted" the fact that Heidegger had "compromised" his philosophy by bringing it into contact with the "everyday"—that is, with contemporary German politics. Löwith, however, saw the matter quite differently. He realized that Heideggerianism, as a philosophy of *existence*, demanded contact with the everyday in order to satisfy its own categorial requirements. Thus, for Löwith, it was instead quite natural that "a philosophy that explains Being from the standpoint of time and the everyday would stand in relation to daily historical realities."[9] In Löwith's view, the radicalism of Heidegger's point of departure—naked "factical-historical life"—which devalued all traditional standpoints and received ideas, predisposed him to seek out radical political solutions. When later that same year Löwith had occasion to discuss the matter with Heidegger himself, Heidegger did not hesitate to avow that "his partisanship for National Socialism lay in the essence of his philosophy." It was, Heidegger explained, his theory of "historicity"—one of the central categories of Division II of *Being and Time*—that constituted the "basis of his political engagement."[10]

Historicity

In the massive secondary literature on *Being and Time*, the concept of historicity has suffered from relative neglect. Perhaps this is because it represents the aspect of Heidegger's treatise where the philosopher stands in the greatest proximity to contemporary politics—and, hence, the moment at which the ideological aspects of his thought are most exposed. The reasons for this neglect are, in part, comprehensible. To date, *Being and Time* has been interpreted primarily in a Kierkegaardian/existential vein. It portrays a highly individualized Dasein wrestling with a series of basic ontological questions: the struggle for authenticity, the meaning of death, the nature of "care." Yet the discussion of historicity, which in many respects represents a culmination of the book's narrative, emphasizes a set of concerns—"destiny," "fate," the nature of authentic historical community (*Gemeinschaft*)—that are difficult to reconcile with the Kierkegaardian interpretation of the work as basically concerned with Dasein as an isolated individual "Self." To be sure, were this Heidegger's standpoint, it would be very difficult to reconcile the idea of historical political commitment with his intentions, and one would have to view Heidegger's later political engagement as standing in contradiction with *Being and Time's* basic ideals. It has often been argued in the philosopher's defense that since Heidegger's actions on behalf of Nazism demanded a surrender of individuality to the ends of the historical community, his political choice stood at cross-purposes with his philosophy. According to this reading, therefore, Heidegger's political involvement represented an instance of *inauthenticity*. However, this interpretation forfeits its cogency once the concept of historicity—via which Heidegger unambiguously declares the centrality of collective historical commitment—is taken seriously.

As Löwith understood, it is but a short step from the facticity and particularism of individual *Existenz* to a celebration of volkish parochialism in collective-historical terms. For Heidegger, the mediating link between these two aspects of Dasein—the individual and the collective—was the conservative revolutionary critique of modernity. This strident lament concerning the world-historical decadence of bourgeois existence was first articulated in the work of Nietzsche, Spengler, and countless lesser *Zivilisationskritiker*. In Thomas Mann's *Confessions of an Unpolitical Man*, for example, the antinomy between *Kultur* and *Zivilisation* occurs more than one hundred times.

That the standpoint of *Being and Time* is informed by the conservative revolutionary worldview suggests that Heidegger's existential analytic, far from a purely "formal" undertaking, is in fact laden with ontic content—content derived from the *Zeitgeist* of the interwar years. The critique of "everydayness" in Division I—of "publicness," "falling," "curiosity," and the "they"—emerges precisely therefrom. Inattention to this dimension of Heidegger's work suggests the pitfalls of a purely text-immanent reading, in which the filiations between politics and philosophy are a priori extruded.

The intimate relationship between "fundamental ontology" and the "German ideology" should come as no surprise. Heidegger always insisted that ontological questioning can never be atemporal and never comes to pass in a historical void. Instead, it is unavoidably *saturated with historicity*. As he observes in *Being and Time*, "every ontology presupposes a determinate ontic point of view."

Outfitted with a measure of historical perspective, we are now aware of the extent to which the early Heidegger made this critique his own.[12] As Löwith comments:

Whoever . . . reflects on Heidegger's later partisanship for Hitler, will find in this first formulation of the idea of historical "existence" the constituents of his political decision of several years hence. One need only abandon the still quasi-religious isolation and apply [the concept of] authentic existence—"always particular to each individual"—and the "duty" that follows therefrom to "specifically German existence" and its historical destiny in order thereby to introduce into the general course of German existence the energetic but empty movement of existential categories ("to decide for oneself"; "to take stock of oneself in the face of nothingness"; "wanting one's ownmost destiny"; "to take responsibility for oneself") and to proceed from there to "destruction" now on the terrain of politics. It is not by chance if one finds in Carl Schmitt a political "decisionism"—in which the "potentiality-for-Being-a-whole" of individual existence is transposed to the "totality" of the authentic state, which is itself always particular—that corresponds to Heidegger's existentialist philosophy.[13]

Germanic Being-in-the-World

Heidegger's rectorship was an ill-fated affair, and he resigned from office after a year. In his official account of his term in office, which was prepared for a university denazification commission in 1945, Heidegger made himself out to be an intrepid foe of the politicization of scholarship. We now know that this explanation is largely a fabrication on his part and that in fact the opposite was the case: as rector, Heidegger proceeded too swiftly in the direction of the politicization of university life. Many members of the faculty were unwilling to follow him in this direction, and controversy ensued. Only when it became clear that Heidegger had failed to gain faculty support for an entire series of radical measures and reforms did he decide to step down.[14]

Heidegger was never a dyed-in-the-wool Nazi. Instead, he was convinced that Germany's "National Revolution" needed to be placed on an ontological rather than a biological footing. While he freely embraced arguments for German exceptionalism (that is, for Germany's singular, world-historical contribution to the history of the West), he never believed that this exceptionalism could be justified in racial or biological terms. For Heidegger, such justifications constituted a regression to the logic of nineteenth-century scientism or biologism. In his view, all questions of human *Existenz* ultimately stood or fell with the *Seinsfrage*—the question of Being—and, hence, could only be answered ontologically, never scientifically. Heidegger's fundamental ontology, in which a rediscovery of the "Greek beginning" played a central role, sought to combat and surmount the previous century's Darwinian revolution. The "ontological potential" of National Socialism could not, therefore, be explained in evolutionary or Social Darwinist terms. In Heidegger's view, the racial-biological interpretation of Nazism had succumbed to a self-misunderstanding. Ever the hermeneuticist, Heidegger believed that he understood Nazism better than the Nazis understood themselves. After all, if the ultimate questions of human existence, insofar as they pertained to the manner in which humanity allowed beings to manifest or show themselves, were *ontological questions*, who would be better placed to pass judgment on a political movement—or at least its standing in relationship to the "history of Being"—than a philosopher? It is in this vein that Heidegger's "arrogant" remark to Ernst Jünger—that Hitler had let him (Heidegger) down and, hence, owed him an apology—must be understood.[15] By this claim, Heidegger meant that it was not he who had erred by entrusting the Nazis with his support; it was Nazism itself that had gone astray by failing to live up to its true philosophical potential.

Despite these philosophical reservations, Heidegger's identification with the possibilities embodied in the new regime remained profound, as one can see by his May 1933 Rectoral Address, which concludes with an inspired paean to the "Glory and Greatness of the [National] Awakening."[16] However deluded his actions may seem in retrospect, it is clear that Heidegger thought of himself as Plato to Hitler's Dionysos (the tyrant of Syracuse), and that it was his intention, as a colleague would later remark, to provide the Nazi movement with the proper philosophical direction, and thus "to lead the leader" (*den Führer führen*).[17]

Along with the rectoral address, the 1934 lectures on "Logik" are philosophically significant insofar as they reveal how Heidegger understood the essential commonalities between fundamental ontology and the Third Reich. Instead of the biological National Socialism favored by the Nazi party hierarchy, Heidegger became an advocate of what one might call an "ontological National Socialism" or "ontological fascism." He was convinced that the Nazis' abrogation of liberal democracy and Germany's turn toward a one-party dictatorship were positive developments. Like his intellectual *compagnons de route*, Carl Schmitt and Ernst Jünger, the example of Mussolini's Italy had convinced him that fascism embodied *the* historically meaningful alternative to liberalism; it was merely a question of adapting fascist methods and goals to Germany's unique historical circumstances. That fascism, or a variant thereof, represented the best prospect for overcoming the abyss of European nihilism was a conviction Heidegger retained until the end of his days, despite his apparent postwar apoliticism.[18] Even in his later apologias and self-justifications, he never tried to conceal the fact that the Nazi seizure of power was a fundamentally constructive step that, regrettably, failed to live up to its ultimate metaphysical potential. In his view, National Socialism's empirical shortcomings left its historical "essence" unaffected. It was merely that, as he put it, the Nazis "were far too limited in their thinking" to provide their political revolution with the necessary ontological grounding.[19] The "ontological moment," or *Kairos*, had been there for the taking; yet, owing to human weakness (a weakness grounded in an inferior, "scientific" ideological perspective), the moment was never seized. As Heidegger remarked in a lecture course during the mid-1930s: "Hitler and Mussolini—who have, each in essentially different ways, introduced a countermovement to nihilism— have both learned from Nietzsche. The authentic metaphysical realm of Nietzsche has not yet, however, been realized."[20] The "countermovement to nihilism" that had been introduced by Hitler and Mussolini— fascism—was one that Heidegger wholeheartedly endorsed. That the two fascist dictators had not yet entered into the "authentic metaphysical realm of Nietzsche" indicated the space that still separated European fascism from the ontological goals that, in Heidegger's view, should have constituted its *raison d'être*.

In Heidegger's "Logik" lecture course, the names of Mussolini and Hitler also figure prominently. Heidegger invoked their achievements in order to illustrate the meaning of "historicity." For Heidegger, historicity signified *authentic historical existence*, as opposed to a merely passive

and inessential historical Being-at-hand. As such, the concept of historicity bears affinities with Hegel's conception of "world historical" as
well as Nietzsche's notion of "monumental history," which the author
of *The Use and Abuse of History* defines as "history in the service of life,"
or history as written and lived by the "experienced and superior man."[21]

The examples Heidegger employs to illustrate his thesis are telling.
Just as in *Being and Time* the contrast with inauthentic Dasein serves to
accentuate the uniqueness of authenticity, in the "Logik" he begins
with an analysis of pseudohistorical life.

In the nineteenth century, dominated intellectually by Darwin and
Spencer, the concept of natural history gained currency, and misguided
attempts arose to subsume human history under this fashionable social
evolutionary rubric. But according to Heidegger, though nature *evolves*,
it is devoid of history properly so-called or *historicity*, which entails a
sense of a "mission" and "destiny" (*Auftrag* and *Geschick*) to which a
people (*Volk*) must measure up.

For Heidegger, one essential manifestation of the spiritual decline of
the West was that the concept of history, in the sense of historicity, had
become meaningless. As Heidegger observed, nowadays one recounts
the history of capitalism and of the peasant wars; one even discusses
the history of the ice age and of mammals. But none of these conceptions allows room for history in the sense of historical *Existenz*. His
argument culminated in the following provocative claim:

> [It is said:] Nature, too, has its history. But then Negroes may be
> said to have history. Or then does nature not have history? It can
> indeed enter into the past as something passes away, but not
> everything that passes away enters into *history*. If an airplane
> propeller turns, then nothing actually "occurs" [*geschieht*]. Yet,
> when the same airplane brings the Führer to Mussolini, then
> history [*Geschichte*] occurs. The flight becomes *history*. . . . The
> airplane's historical character is not determined by the turning
> of the propeller, but instead by what in the future arises out of
> this circumstance.[22]

Despite their sensational side, certain of Heidegger's positions must
be given their due. That there are important differences between natural and human history is self-evident, for in recent years, sociobiology

has sought to efface the difference between them. However, the next set of distinctions he proposes—his condescension toward the history of capitalism and peasant wars—is more troubling. The topics themselves cannot be a priori condemned as inauthentic. Instead, the philosopher has prematurely accorded them short shrift.

The fact that Heidegger's judgments are often presumptuous—e.g., his supercilious contention that "Negroes," like nature, do not have a history—should not absolve one of the need to hazard judgments about the relative significance of historical events. A slack postmodernist relativism is not the proper antidote to Heidegger's Eurocentric arrogance. What is troubling about Heidegger's standpoint is not that he judges but the basis on which he distinguishes. His lock-step identification with the "German ideology" risks settling in advance all questions of relative historical merit. "Capitalism," "peasant wars," "Negroes"—once the world has been neatly divided into "historical" and "unhistorical" peoples and events, history's gray zones fade from view. That the "Volk" that, in Heidegger's view, possessed "historicity" in the greatest abundance—the Germans—had as of 1934 abolished political pluralism, civil liberties, and the rule of law and was in the process of consolidating one of the most brutal dictatorships of all time, cannot help but raise additional doubts about the "existential" grounds of Heidegger's discernment. Here, one could reverse the terms and claim that Germany of the 1930s suffered from an *excess* of historicity. Conversely, the historical events and peoples that Heidegger slights could readily be incorporated into progressive historical narratives.[23] That he fails to perceive these prospects is attributable to his renunciation of "cosmopolitan history" and his concomitant embrace of a philosophically embellished version of German particularism or so-called *Sonderweg*. From an epistemological standpoint, Heidegger's difficulties derive from his decision to base ethical and political judgments on *factical* rather than *normative* terms; that is, from the *Jemeinigkeit* or concrete particularity of German *Existenz*.

The more one reconsiders Heidegger's philosophy of the 1930s, the more one sees that one of its guiding leitmotifs is a refashioning of Western metaphysics in keeping with the demands of the Germanic Dasein.[24] He consistently rejects the "universals" that in the Western tradition occupied a position of preeminence in favor of ethnocentric notions derived from the annals of Germanic Being-in-the-world. The example of the airplane that "brings the Führer to Mussolini" is merely a paradigmatic instance of a more general trend.

Logic and Volk

Heidegger's lectures on "Logic" were held in the aftermath of his failed rectorship. In consequence, they express a political wisdom born of his disillusionment with the Nazi regime. Yet, upon reading them, it is apparent that Heidegger, far from having abandoned his belief in Nazism, is merely interested in propagating an "essentialized" interpretation of the movement's significance—an interpretation derived from the standpoint of the "history of Being" and the precepts of the philosopher's own "essential thinking."

Although the nominal topic of the 1934 lecture course is "logic," the traditional concerns of formal logic could not be more foreign to Heidegger's approach: "We want to shake logic *to its very foundations*," Heidegger declares. "The power of traditional logic must be broken. That means *struggle* [*Kampf*]."[25] Thereby, Heidegger signals a concern that had been characteristic of his lectures and writings throughout the 1920s and 1930s: a wish to break with the strictures of academic philosophy and a concomitant desire to rediscover philosophy's rootedness in human existence, whose ultimate expression, in keeping with the strictures of "historicity," is the life of the *Volk*. As he observes at one point: "We do not want a 'disinterested philosophy' [*Standpunktsfreiheit der Philosophie*]; instead, what is at issue is a *decision based on a determinate point of view* [*Standpunktsentscheidung*]."[26]

How is it that Heidegger is able to turn a lecture course on logic into a discourse about the virtues of *völkisch* Dasein? He is at pains to demonstrate that modern "logic" is a perversion of the Greek "logos." According to Heidegger, the Greek ideal had very little to do with the notion of propositional truth or the cogency of formal judgments. Such concerns represent Aristotelian accretions and misunderstandings that have been consecrated by the error-ridden Western metaphysical tradition. Heidegger claims that the original meaning of *logic* concerned language as a "site" for the emergence of Being. Yet Being never reveals itself arbitrarily. Thus, those to whom it exposes itself must be attuned to its "sendings" (*Schickungen*). In this respect, it goes without saying (at least for Heidegger) that certain peoples are linguistically and historically privileged. Ultimately, therefore, all *linguistic* questions turn out to be questions of human *existence*. As Heidegger remarks: "The question concerning the essence of language is not a question of philology or the philosophy of language; instead, it is a need of man insofar as man takes himself seriously."[27] Thus, when posed "essentially," existential questions also concern the historical self-understanding of a people or *Volk*. In this way, Heidegger is able to make the transition from logic and language to the hidden potentials of Germany's National Revolution. By "choosing themselves," as Heidegger puts it, the Germans are also opting for a new understanding of Being: an understanding that would be free of the divisiveness and debilities of the liberal era and that would finally prove adequate to the fateful "encounter between planetary technology and modern man."[28] Germany's momentous political transformation of 1933—historicity in the consummate sense—has gone far toward the necessary goal of establishing a unified political will among the German people. As Heidegger comments in the "Logik": "Insofar as we have become adapted to the demands of the university, and the university adapted to the demands of the state, we [at the university] also want the will of the state. However, *the will of the state is the will-to-domination of a Volk over itself*. We stand in the Being of the Volk. Our Being-a-Self [*Selbstsein*] *is* the Volk."[29]

Heidegger thereby advocates a type of intellectual *Gleichschaltung*. As a long-standing critic of academic freedom and the separation of science from broader existential concerns, in the Nazi revolution Heidegger saw an unprecedented opportunity to reintegrate knowledge with Volk and "state," thereby compelling it to serve a set of higher ontological goals. Only in this way would knowledge cease to be autonomous and "free-floating" as it was during the liberal era. By standing in the service of a higher "spiritual mission" (*geistigen Auftrag*) it would, Heidegger believed, regain a dignity and meaning it had not possessed since the Greeks. As Heidegger encourages his student listeners: "*The small and narrow 'we' of the moment of this lecture has suddenly been transformed into the we of the Volk*."[30]

A devotion to the precepts of intellectual *Gleichschaltung* already

characterized Heidegger's radicalism as rector. "The defining principle
of my rectorship," he once declared, "has been the fundamental transformation of scholarly education on the basis of the forces and demands of the National Socialist state."[31] In the "Logik" he complained
bitterly that to date university reforms had proved insufficiently radical,
that the "dissolution" of the old university structure had not proceeded
far enough.[32]

Heidegger believed that in contemporary Germany, few concepts
were more widespread yet poorly understood than the "Volk" idea. He
believed that it was his prerogative and calling to undertake a "phenomenological" clarification of its meaning and import. Correspondingly, much of the "Logik" is devoted to this task. According to
Heidegger, one of the linguistic and existential confusions of the early
days of the Nazi revolution derived from the fact that people invoked
the Volk concept in a wide variety of contexts and settings—*Volksgemeinschaft*, *Volkshochschule*, *Volksgericht*, and *Volksentscheidung* were just a
few of its many usages—without a deeper understanding of its essence.
It was fundamental ontology's task to bring clarity and precision to this
idea.

In a manner reminiscent of Aristotle, Heidegger proceeds by exam-
ining a variety of popular, yet misguided approaches to the question.
Frederick the Great, for example, referred to the Volk as "The beast
with many tongues and few eyes." Currently, observes Heidegger, there
are those who define the *Volk* as an "association of men" and others
who describe it as an "organism." Will such definitions suffice for our
contemporary historical needs, he inquires with mock seriousness?
"Perhaps for reading newspapers," he skeptically rejoins.[33]

The nature of the *Volk*, he continues, can be defined neither sociologically nor scientifically. Echoing his characterization of Dasein in
Being and Time, he observes that in interrogating the concept of the
Volk, we are concerned not with "what" questions, which would characterize the being of *things*, but with "who" or "we" questions: that is,
with *existential questions*—questions that address the historical identity
of the Germans. "The question: are we the *Volk* that we are? is far from
stupid," remarks Heidegger.[34] As it pertains to the historicity of German Dasein, the question cannot be answered in advance. Its future
determination will depend on a "decision" (*Entscheidung*) of the Ger-

man people as to whether they can measure up to their vaunted historical mission.

The Estate of Labor

Not all aspects of Heidegger's discussion of historicity are contaminated by the German ideology. At issue was a "crisis of historical existence" whose reality was widely acknowledged during the interwar
period. Heidegger's 1929 lecture course, *The Fundamental Concepts of
Metaphysics*, is preoccupied with the question of the present age as an
age of "affliction" or "destitution."[35] One manifestation of this all-encompassing destitution was a mood of generalized "boredom" (*Lang-
weile*): a sense of disorientation and inertia, combined with a corresponding lack of will. In Heidegger's existential idiom, "moods"
(*Stimmungen*), rather than concepts or ideas, are often the defining feature of an age.[36] Boredom, and the existential paralysis it entails, is a
manifestation of *inauthenticity*: it breeds a lack of "decisiveness" (*Entschlossenheit*) and culminates in the conformity of the "they" (*das Man*).

Yet time and again the conservative revolutionary idiom Heidegger
favors slips into a mode of proto-fascist yearning—in part because
Heidegger rules out nonradical alternatives as inferior "half-measures"
(*Halbheiten*).[37] Moreover, the more closely one examines the idea of
historicity, the more apparent is the degree to which philosophical and
historical dimensions are fused. A concept that, on first view, seems
largely formal, and thus potentially applicable to a variety of historical
circumstances, turns out to be inordinately content-laden. Ultimately,
Heidegger's formulation of historicity is irreconcilable with—and formulated explicitly in opposition to—political liberalism as a figure for
freedom of conscience, rule of law, and individual rights. Liberalism is
the paradigm that Heidegger wishes to surmount insofar as it is the
source of our current "destitution." This is true to the point that it
becomes very difficult to separate Heidegger's critique of "subjectivity"
(Descartes and his heirs) from his dubious political conclusions.[38]

As in *Being and Time*, the notion of *Stimmung* or "mood" plays a key
role in the "Logik." Heidegger observes that "the man who acts greatly
is defined by moods—by great moods—whereas small men are de-

fined only by temperaments." "Every great deed of a people [*Volk*] comes from its foundational mood [*Grundstimmung*]."[39] The rapid slippage between "ontological" and "ontic" levels of analysis is palpable: "The three-fold character of mandate, mission, and labor [*Auftrag, Sendung, und Arbeit*] is unified through mood," claims Heidegger. "To experience time by way of our appointed mission [*Bestimmung*] is the great and unique orientation of our Being qua historical Being. The fundamental nature of occurrence is our appointed mission in its three-fold sense: *mandate, mission, and labor.*"[40]

But it is Heidegger's emphasis on the importance of "labor" (*Arbeit*) that is the defining feature of his political worldview. During his time as rector, Heidegger ran afoul of his fellow faculty members due his attempt to make participation in "labor camps"—National Socialist sponsored public work projects that included obligatory ideological training—a requirement of university life. To Heidegger's colleagues, his vigorous endorsement of the camps seemed a lamentable concession to a regime that was both repressive and anti-intellectual. To Heidegger, conversely, their reaction was only a further instance of his colleagues' insufficient radicalism.[41]

Both Heidegger's 1933 rectoral address and his political speeches are fraught with references to the virtues of "labor" and of "labor service." "The Self-Assertion of the German University," for example, stresses the paramount importance of three types of service: knowledge-service, military service, and labor service. During this period, moreover, the notion of the "setting-to-*work*" ("in-Werk-setzen") of truth figures prominently in his philosophy. His political addresses of 1933–34 are preoccupied with the question of "labor camps"—the aforementioned Nazi-sponsored public work projects—that were meant to serve as a vehicle for the leveling of class differences as well as National Socialist ideological indoctrination.[42] Thus in "Labor Service and the University" Heidegger glorifies the virtues of "labor" in an existential idiom that is only a step removed from the Storm Trooper ethos convulsing Germany: "A new institution for the direct revelation of the *Volksgemeinschaft* is being realized in the work camp," declares Heidegger. "In the future, young Germans will be governed by the *knowledge of labor*, in which the *Volk* concentrates its strength in order to experience the hardness of its existence, to preserve the momentum of its will, and to learn anew the value of its manifold abilities." And in his 1934 speech, "National Socialist Education," he seeks to differentiate National Socialism's "spiritual" conception of labor from the outmoded and vulgar Marxist understanding of the term:

> Like these words "knowledge" and "Wissenschaft," the words "worker" and "work," too, have a transformed meaning and a new sound. The "worker" is not, as Marxism claimed, a mere object of exploitation. Workers [*Arbeiterstand*] are not the class of the disinherited who are rallying for the general class struggle. . . . *For us, "work" is the title of every well-ordered action that is borne by the responsibility of the individual, the group, and the State and which is thus of service to the Volk.*[43]

The labor camps praised by Heidegger, which were administered by the *Reichsarbeitfront*, were a linchpin in the Nazi plan for a homogeneous *Volksgemeinschaft*. In November 1933, under the direction of Albert Speer, the Nazis established an office for the "Beautification of Labor" as an offshoot of the "Strength Through Joy" leisure bureau—a fact that helps one appreciate the centrality of labor in the National Socialist worldview. Of course, one of the distinguishing features of Nazi rule was its grandiose efforts to secure *aesthetic self-legitimation*, the likes of which had not been seen since the age of absolutism, and the "Beautification of Labor" program represented an essential component of these efforts. Often, these beautification efforts were related to matters of efficiency, as in the slogan, "Good light, good work." As Anson Rabinbach has noted, "By combining industrial psychology with a technocratic aesthetic that glorified machinery and the efficiency of the modern plant, Beauty of Labor signified a new dimension of Nazi ideology."[44] But like so many other aspects of Nazism that targeted the working class, the program was long on form and short on substance. Thus, although lip service was paid to the "estate of labor," the traditional capitalist hierarchy between management and labor was rigidly maintained. German workers may, in certain instances, have enjoyed slightly improved working conditions. But in almost every substantive respect (wages, benefits, living conditions, and so forth), their lot under the Nazis failed to improve. Instead, the mostly cosmetic improvements were intended to facilitate their ideological integration within the Nazi behemoth. Although the "Beautification of Labor" program claimed that it sought to restore the "spiritual dignity" of work that was lacking under capitalism and communism, it entailed few real benefits for labor itself.

One historian has summarized the pivotal ideological function of "labor" in the early years of the Third Reich in the following terms:

> As a supplement, almost as a substitute for a labor policy, the Third Reich offered a labor ideology, combining simultaneous and roughly equal appeals to the pride, patriotism, idealism, enlightened self-interest, and, finally, urge to self-aggrandizement of those exposed to it. The centerpiece was the *labor ethos*, focusing not so much on the worker as on work itself. "Work ennobles" was a characteristic slogan. . . . Large factories even erected chapels whose main aisle led to a Hitler bust beneath the symbol of the Labor Front, flanked by heroic-sized worker figures; in effect, little temples to the National Socialist god of work.[45]

Heidegger's concern with the importance of labor in the new Reich was a matter of philosophical as well as political conviction. A longtime critic of the senescence and disorientation of German university life, he was of the opinion that the labor camps would serve to reintegrate knowledge with the life of the German Volk, whose simplicity and lack of sophistication he revered.[46] As Löwith remarked, Heidegger "failed to notice the destructive radicalism of the whole [Nazi] movement and the petty bourgeois character of all its 'strength-through-joy' institutions, because he was a radical petty bourgeois himself."[47] Heidegger, who hailed from the provincial lower classes, and who, despite his manifest brilliance, was denied a university chair until the age of thirty-nine, found much he could agree with in Nazism's dismantling of the old estates and commitment to upward social mobility.[48] In his view, the value of labor camps as a vehicle of ideological reeducation for politically reticent scholars could hardly be overestimated.

Heidegger's commitment to the goals of labor service may also be traced to the influences of conservative revolutionary ideology. Since Germany's defeat in World War I, which was abetted by class divisions as well as revolutionary upheaval during the war's final months, it had become a commonplace among radical conservatives that, in the future, the working classes must be integrated within the "national community." One of the classical expressions of this new orientation was Oswald Spengler's 1919 tract, *Prussianism and Socialism*. With the war effort's nationalization of the economy fresh in mind, Spengler argued that the virtues of Prussian nationalism must be combined with the economic advantages of "socialism," which he understood in terms of the *étatiste* ideal of a state-directed or planned economy. Only in this way could Germany secure the internal unity necessary for success in the *next* European war. As Spengler observes:

> We need a class of *socialist supermen*. . . . Socialism means: power, power and ever more power. . . . The way to power is foreordained: to combine the valuable part of German workers with the best representatives of the old Prussian devotion to state—both resolved to found a rigorously socialist state . . . both forged into unity through a sense of duty, through the consciousness of a great task, through the will to belong, in order *to dominate, to die, and to triumph.*[49]

During the early 1930s Heidegger had also fallen under the political influence of Ernst Jünger, whose 1932 study, *The Worker (Der Arbeiter)*, had been an immense success in right-radical circles. In *The Worker*, Jünger outlined a theory of a future totalitarian state. In it, the debilitating divisions of political liberalism would be surmounted. For Jünger, too, the "total mobilization" that marked the final stages of the German war effort during World War I—the fact that all aspects of economic, cultural, and domestic life were placed on common footing for the sake of a shared military goal—had set a significant precedent. Under conditions of the total state, argued Jünger, where geopolitical conflicts determined domestic political ends, the distinction between "soldiers" and "workers" would be effaced. Both groups would merely represent different aspects of a wholly militarized society. Jünger's dronelike "soldier-workers" represented an ideological antithesis to the timorous "bourgeois," concerned only with effete pursuits such as personal security and well-being. His idealized portrait of militarized "work-world" left a profound impression on Heidegger, who offered two seminars on Jünger during the 1930s, and who later avowed that during this period his understanding of politics had been predominantly shaped by Jünger's 1932 treatise.[50]

Germany's difficulties in adapting to the challenges of modern industrial society—which represented the antithesis of everything that it, qua *Kulturnation*, had stood for historically—are legendary. Following the traumas of war, defeat, and revolution, the mandarin intellegentsia, convinced of industrialism's inevitability, sought a way to reconcile traditional German values (Spengler's "Prussianism") with the imperatives of twentieth-century economic life. Heidegger alluded to this dilemma when he characterized National Socialism's "inner truth and greatness" as a solution to the fateful "encounter between planetary technology and modern man."[51] In *The Will to Power*—a radical conservative Bible—Nietzsche had already posed the problem of how one could maintain the values of heroism and cultural greatness in an era where qualitative differences were increasingly leveled by the dictates and rhythms of the machine. "In opposition to this dwarfing and adaptation of man to a specialized utility, a reverse movement is needed—the production of a synthetic, summarizing, justifying man for whose existence *this transformation of mankind into a machine* is a precondition, as a base on which he can invent his *higher form of being*."[52] For Nietzsche, the attainment of "great politics" did not mean a return to an idyllic, premodern past; it required reconciling the needs of the superman with the realities of modern technology. A few paragraphs later, Nietzsche issued his call for the "barbarians of the twentieth century": "A dominant race can grow up only out of violent and terrible beginnings. Problem: *where are the barbarians of the twentieth century?*" In National Socialism, his prophetic summons found an adequate response.[53]

From 1936 to 1940, Heidegger offered four lecture courses on Nietzsche's philosophy in which he demonstrated that he had internalized the lessons of conservative revolutionary theory of technology (*Technikgedanke*). As he observes in his 1940 course "European Nihilism":

What Nietzsche already knew metaphysically now becomes clear: that in its absolute form the modern "machine economy," the machine-based reckoning of all activity and planning, demands a new kind of man who surpasses man as he has been hitherto. . . . What is needed is a form of mankind that is from top to bottom *equal to the unique fundamental essence of modern technology and its metaphysical truth*; that is to say, that lets itself be entirely dominated by the essence of technology precisely in order to steer and deploy individual technological processes and possibilities. *The superman alone is adequate to an absolute "machine economy,"* and vice versa: he needs it for the institution of absolute domination over the earth.[54]

Toward the end of the same course, and with Germany's stunning Blitzkrieg victories fresh in mind, Heidegger provided further evidence that the Nazi war machine embodied the "form of mankind equal to modern technology and its metaphysical truth." It would be a fateful misunderstanding of Germany's glorious battlefield triumphs, notes Heidegger, to construe the Blitzkrieg strategy ("the total 'motorization' of the *Wehrmacht*") as an instance of "unlimited 'technicism' and 'materialism'"—that is, as developments on a par with the West's employment of technology. "In reality," insists Heidegger, "this is *a metaphysical act*."[55] The *Wehrmacht*'s stunning success proved that Germany alone had mastered the challenge posed by "planetary technology to modern man." Whatever Heidegger's philosophical differences with regime ideologues may have been at this point, he was convinced that Nazi Germany had gone far toward realizing the "dominion and form" (*Herrschaft* and *Gestalt*) of "the worker" as forecast by Jünger's prophetic 1932 essay.

In *Being and Time*, the instances of labor cited by Heidegger all pertained to the traditional work-world of artisans and handicraft. His diagnosis of the times had been resolutely anti-modern. By 1933, however, under the twin influences of Jünger and Germany's National Awakening, Heidegger's attitude toward technology underwent a decisive shift. In his view, the Germans—the most metaphysical of peoples since the Greeks—by allowing themselves to be entirely dominated by the "machine-economy," were well on their way to establishing their "absolute domination over the earth."

Labor and Authenticity

For decades, the themes of technology and labor had been scorned by Germany's intellectual mandarins. They were, at best, socialist concerns, beneath the dignity of sophisticated *Kulturmenschen*. Along with his fellow conservative revolutionaries, however, Heidegger was convinced that, to paraphrase Walther Rathenau, "economics had become destiny." Those who ignored this ultimatum of twentieth-century life did so at their own peril.

This insight helps account for Heidegger's abiding preoccupation with the concept of "work" during this period. Heidegger's focus on the importance of work led him to flirt with themes and concerns that had previously been the province of socialist thinkers. Ultimately, of course, his perspective remained rigorously *völkisch*, and it is in this sense that his attraction to Nazism as a form of national socialism must be understood.[56]

Heidegger's discussion of the ontological vocation of work is of considerable philosophical import. Significantly, he treats it in relationship to the problem of "temporality," one of fundamental ontology's central themes. In *Being and Time*, Heidegger criticized the modern concept of time, derived from the natural sciences and subsequently canonized by Descartes, as radically deficient. According to this conception, even human existence was understood on the model of "things," that is, as an inanimate "entity" that was merely "present-at-hand" (*vorhanden*).

In the "Logik" Heidegger polemicizes against modernity's inferior understanding of temporality, which is governed by an "empty" concept of time. Time "has become an empty form, a continuum that is *alienated from the Being of man*," Heidegger protests.[57] Whereas in 1927 the idea of authentic temporality was linked to the notion of Being-toward-death, in the "Logic," authentic temporality is tied to the concept of work. Along with "mandate" and "mission," work is an essential component of the "foundational mood" (*Grundstimmung*) of the German Volk. In the context at hand, what stands out is his quasi-Marxist characterization of work as an indispensable manifestation of authentic selfhood. "Time belongs characteristically and solely to man," observes Heidegger:

> According to the vital conception of time as our ownmost event, natural processes merely "expire" within the framework of time; but, stones, animals, and plants are not temporal in the sense that we are. They do not dispose over a concept of *mission*, they accept

no *mandate*, and *they do not work*. Not for lack of concern, but instead because they are incapable of work. The horse is only engaged in a human work-event. Machines, too, do not work. Work, understood in the physicalist sense, is a misunderstanding of the nineteenth century.[58]

In *Being and Time*, Heidegger's discussion of authenticity culminates in the concept of historicity. At issue is the idea of an authentic collectivity: a *Volk* or community that is capable of measuring up to its appointed historical destiny (*Geschick*).[59] It is by "historicizing" its existence that a *Volk* acts according to the strictures of authentic temporality. Here, we are reminded of Heidegger's contention in the "Logik" that not all peoples are capable of having "history"—that is, "history" conceived according to the requirements of authentic historicity.

What is new in the "Logik" is that for the first time Heidegger systematically ties both temporality and historicity to the concept of work. Work is thereby treated as an essential modality whereby humanity realizes itself historically. By considering work as an expression of authenticity, Heidegger approximates the early Marx's expressivist concept of labor in the Paris Manuscripts. Under the influence of Hegel and Schiller, Marx regarded labor as the highest expression of man's "species being." In this regard, it is hardly coincidental that a critique of "alienated labor" became the basis for his youthful critique of capitalism's degradation of everyday life.

Heidegger approximates the same expressivist concept of labor when he characterizes modern temporality, whose foremost expression is "work," as "alienated from the Being of man." Nevertheless, the Hegelian-Marxist, utopian ideal of a "reconciliation" between man and nature—in the Paris Manuscripts, Marx fantasizes about the eventual "humanization of nature and the naturalization of man"—is foreign to Heidegger's neo-Kierkegaardian, existential sensibility. Such utopian dreams, moreover, are fundamentally alien to the post-Spenglerian, apocalyptical "mood" that *Existenzphilosophie* consciously cultivates.

In an apologia written after the war for Freiburg University denazification proceedings, Heidegger explained that he became disillusioned with Nazism following the June 30, 1934, purge of the Röhm faction.[60] For Heidegger, the Röhm purge symbolized (as it did for many "old fighters") a "right turn" on the part of the new regime. It signaled an abandonment of the *älte Kämpfer*—many of whom upheld the "socialist" ideals of National Socialism—and an accommodation with traditional German elites: Hindenburg, the Wehrmacht, big industry. As such, Heidegger's avowal is a further indication of the depth of his commitment to the *ouvrièriste* wing of National Socialism in its early phase.

Since the "Logik" is a lecture course, rather than a public political statement (which might necessitate certain compromises with the regime), it presumably reflects Heidegger's genuine views. That is why it is so disturbing to find him, at least in one instance, flirting with the regime's racial-biological doctrines. Equally disturbing is the fact that Heidegger suggests that one might reconcile Nazism's racial precepts (the concepts of "blood" and "racial descent") with his own pet existential themes and ideals of "mood," "work," and "historicity":

> Blood, racial descent (*das Geblüt*) can only be [reconciled] with the foundational mood of man when it is determined by temperament and mood [*das Gemüt*]. The contribution of blood comes from the foundational mood of man and belongs to the determination of our Dasein through work. Work = the historical present. The present (*die Gegenwart*) is not merely the now; instead it is the present insofar as it transposes our Being in the emancipation of existence that is accomplished through work. As someone who works man is transported into the publicness of existence. Such being-transported belongs to the essence of our Being: that is, to our being-transported amid things in the world. . . . As something original, existence never reveals itself to us via the scientific cognition of objects, but instead in the essential moods that flourish in work and in the historical vocation of a Volk that predetermines all else.[61]

One of the Nazis' major domestic political concerns in the regime's initial years was whether they would be successful in integrating the German working classes—traditionally, staunch supporters of the political left—within the National Socialist *Volksgemeinschaft*. To that end, they established the German Labor Front to assure German workers that their role in the new state was an indispensable one. Both the

"Strength through Joy" and "Beautification of Labor" programs discussed earlier were an offshoot of the same effort.[62] In his celebration of the "joy of work" (*Arbeitsfreudigkeit*), Heidegger once again demonstrates the elective affinities between *Existenzphilosophie* and the National Socialist worldview:

> The question of the joy of work is important. As a foundational mood, joy is the basis of the possibility of authentic work. In work as something present, the making present of Being occurs. Work is presencing in the original sense to the extent that we insert ourselves in the preponderance of Being; through work we attain the whole of Being in all its greatness, on the basis of the great moods of wonder and reverence, and thereby enhance it in its greatness.[63]

However, Heidegger's encomium to the "joys of work" contains a hidden political agenda. Critics had frequently argued that the worldview expressed in *Being and Time* was excessively lachrymose. As evidence of the work's overriding mournfulness, detractors frequently invoked Heidegger's preoccupation with categories such as "Angst," "Being-toward-death," "Guilt," and "Falling." Indeed, much of Heidegger's existential ontology was indebted to a secularized Protestant sensibility that stressed the insurmountability of original sin and the irremediable forlornness of the human condition. In place of the Counter-Reformation *deus absconditus*, Heidegger substituted Nietzsche's declaration concerning the "death of God." But in the last analysis, the predominant view of the human condition was the same. Herbert Marcuse alluded to this problem when, in a 1971 interview, he remarked:

> If you look at [Heidegger's] view of human existence, of Being-in-the-world, you will find a highly repressive, highly oppressive interpretation. I have just gone through the table of contents of *Being and Time* and had a look at the main categories in which he sees the essential characteristics of existence or Dasein. I can just read them to you and you will see what I mean: Idle talk, curiosity, ambiguity, falling and Being-thrown, concern, Being-toward-Death, anxiety, dread, boredom, and so on. Now this gives a picture which plays well on the fears and frustrations of men and

women in a repressive society—a joyless existence: overshadowed by death and anxiety; human material for the authoritarian personality.[64]

The disconsolate worldview presented in *Being and Time* proved difficult to reconcile with the groundswell of enthusiasm that had been unleashed by Germany's National Awakening. By celebrating the "joy of work," Heidegger took steps to ensure the essential compatibility between fundamental ontology and the National Revolution.

Labor As Unconcealment

The "Logik" lectures contain many aspects that are frankly ideological; but it would be misleading to erect a firewall between Heidegger's ideological writings (the rectoral address and more narrowly political texts) and his more philosophical works. Such rigid distinctions between philosophy and ideology prove untenable. Although it may be tempting to downplay the significance of the "Logik" owing to the prominence of political references and elements, a close examination of other contemporary texts reveal merely differences in degree rather than differences in kind.

Moreover, the philosophically significant dimensions of the "Logik" build organically on the ontological foundations established in *Being and Time*. There is no absolute break between the two texts. Instead, Heidegger attempts, as he always did, to elaborate fundamental concepts in light of new developments that are both historical and conceptual in nature. The National Awakening of 1933 is certainly one such development of whose "epochal" nature Heidegger was convinced. At the same time, in the "Logik," he was engaged in a process of redefining the basic terms of his philosophy, as was the case throughout his productive life.

For this reason, his discussion of the concept of labor in the "Logik" lectures is of genuine philosophical significance. Although the concept appears nowhere in *Being and Time*, it figures prominently in "The Self-Assertion of the German University." There, under the guise of "labor service," it appears (along with "military service" and "service in

knowledge") as one of the three essential modes of comportment required by the new Reich.

In *Being and Time*, Heidegger is at pains to identify the fundamental
existential structures (*Existenzialien*) through which Being is revealed to
human experience. He considers the history of Western thought to be
largely unserviceable in this regard, due to its intellectualist and rationalistic biases. Already Aristotle had defined the vocation of man as
animal rationale. Subsequently, via the latinization of Greek thought and
culture, this standpoint was disseminated throughout the European
world, reaching a culmination of sorts with Descartes's definition of
the distinctively human as *res cogitans*: the "subject" qua disembodied
mind. In opposition to this rationalistic strain, Heidegger sought to
redefine human existence as "Dasein" (there-being): a mode of Being-
in-the-world that is not in the first instance characterized by intellectual
characteristics and habitudes, but by a series of more "primordial" capacities—moods, dealings with tools, Being-with-others, and so forth.

In *Being and Time*, the discussion of "tools" as a mode of Being
"ready-to-hand" (*Zuhandenheit*) anticipates the status of "labor" in the
"Logik." Heidegger's point is to show that our experience with useful
objects, such as tools, is prior to our conceptualization of objects as
mere things toward which we might assume a scientific or objectivating attitude (along the lines of Descartes's physicalist characterization
of objects—including the human body—as *res extensa* or extended substance). Instead, in our dealings with tools, at issue is a context of
relationships that remains implicit and unthematized unless something
is amiss: if the head falls off the hammer we are using, its unique and
explicit nature as an individual object becomes apparent to us in a way
it never was when we were preoccupied with the hammer as an object
of use. More generally, our relationship to the hammer and the whole
context of relationships it entails (other tools, co-workers, questions of
building and dwelling, and so forth) is an essential mode via which
Dasein's Being-in-the-world is constituted and disclosed. This context of
relationships tells us something essential about the ontological nature
of Dasein—why, for example, Dasein's Being-in-the-world is different
from the Being of things, tools, etc. Without the word ever being explicitly mentioned, the entire discussion, which is a significant one,

concerns the status of work in relationship to the Being-in-the-world of Dasein.

Something similar may be said about the status of labor in the "Logik" lectures. Yet, whereas in *Being and Time* "work" stands for a type of implicit knowledge or phenomenological precondition of human experience, in the "Logik" Heidegger elevates labor to an autonomous and central role in the uncovering of Being. In the "Logik," Heidegger exalts labor as a type of heroic ontological engagement that, in *Being and Time*, seemed reserved for "resolve" (*Entschlossenheit*) and Being-toward-death. His panegyrics to the ontological mission of labor aim to kill two birds with one stone: he seeks to surmount the customary dualism of intellectual and manual labor (another weighty bit of Cartesian detritus) and to demonstrate that the project of fundamental ontology is compatible with the worldview of the new regime—it is the philosophical or serious side of the National Revolution. During the 1930s, Heidegger often praised the essential role played by philosophers, statesmen, and poets in unveiling the truth of Being.[65] In the "Logik" lectures, he throws labor into the mix as a way of offsetting the sterile rationalism of traditional philosophy. Thus, just as he had shown in *Being and Time* how everyday Being-in-the-world is fraught with ontological implications, he seeks to demonstrate in the "Logik" that labor, far from representing an inferior mode of human Being-in-the-world, is an essential modality via which Being is revealed. In fact, in many respects the interventions of labor prove superior to the barren intellectualism characteristic of university scholarship, whose deficiencies Heidegger parodies in his Rectoral Address and elsewhere. As a modality of Being-in-the-world and as a creative approach to nonhuman being, labor transcends the objectivating standpoint of the natural sciences, according to which beings are merely objects of technical mastery cum exploitation. In unreflectively adopting the standpoint of the Cartesian "subject," modern philosophy has merely perpetuated ad nauseum this Cartesian original sin, resulting in the horrors of modern technology (*das Gestell*). For Heidegger, conversely, labor is ontologically significant insofar as, unlike "technology" qua "enframing," it is capable of *elevating* rather than degrading the otherwise inert "Being of beings." As he expresses this thought in the "Logik":

The Being of beings is not exhausted in the Being of objects. Such an erroneous view could only prosper—indeed, it must—where things are from the outset approached as "objects," a standpoint that presupposes the concept of man as "subject." Beings however never reveal themselves primordially via the scientific cognition of objects, *but in the labor that flourishes in essential moods and in the historical mission of a Volk that determines them.*[66]

To this end, the concept of "socialism" must be taken seriously, claims Heidegger. Not, however, in the customary senses of transforming economic relations or a diffuse interest in collective well-being. Instead, in Heidegger's view, socialism, when properly conceived, mandates the principle of "hierarchy according to career and achievement, and the inviolable honor of every [type of] labor."[67] At issue is not a Marxian socialism, but a *national socialism.*

Being and Time:

A Failed Masterpiece?

Antimodernism and "New Life"

For MANY YEARS, Heidegger's great work of 1927 has been enveloped in myth—a myth of purity carefully cultivated by the Master himself. According to this legend, *Being and Time*, a work of unequivocal genius, emerged virtually ex nihilo. In Heidegger's view, when questions of philosophical substance are at issue, scholarly influences or considerations of intellectual biography are beside the point. He once famously began a lecture course on Aristotle by observing, "He was born, he worked, he died"; the first and third terms of this sequence were, he intimated, irrelevant for an understanding of Aristotle's importance as a thinker. As Heidegger once explained to a friend, "My life is entirely uninteresting."[1] Heidegger wished instead to be judged solely on the basis of his work—admittedly, a very strange stance for the man who coined the term "thrownness" (*Geworfenheit*) to describe the fundamentally contingent, non-self-generated character of human Being-in-the-world; the man who in *Being and Time* avowed that the enterprise of fundamental ontology unavoidably derived from the existential basis of his own individual standpoint.[2] As Theodore Kisiel has formulated this problem: Heidegger's apparent indifference to autobiography "flies in the face of the most unique features of Heidegger's own philosophy, both in theory and in practice. For Heidegger himself resorted at times to philosophical biography by applying his own 'hermeneutics of facticity' to himself, to his situation, to what he himself

FIG. 6. Husserl and Heidegger, 1921. Photo courtesy of J. B. Metzlersche
Verlagsbuchhandlung and Carl Ernst Poeschel Verlag, Stuttgart, 1986.

called his 'hermeneutic situation,' precisely in order to clarify and advance his own thought."[2]

As Heidegger legend has it, between 1915 and 1927 the Freiburg sage published nothing. Finally, at the end of this twelve-year period of authorial abstinence, Heidegger's magnum opus miraculously emerged. This bit of received wisdom was famously codified in Heidegger's (fictionalized) "Dialogue Between a Japanese and an Inquirer," in which the Japanese's tentative observation, "And so you remained silent for twelve years," remains uncorrected by the "inquirer" (Heidegger himself).[4] This studied neglect of the circumstantial aspects of Heidegger's philosophy (a practice perpetuated by the editors of Heidegger's *Gesamtausgabe*, who, following the Master's wishes, have systematically refused to provide a critical apparatus for the edition) has made a systematic reconstruction of Heidegger's early philosophical project—its *Enstehungsgeschichte*—a challenging enterprise. Only in the last few years, with the appearance of Heidegger's early Freiburg lecture courses (1919–1923), has the situation begun to change significantly. On the basis of their publication, one can reproduce a semester-by-semester account of the intellectual path that culminated in *Being and Time*.[5]

Of course, even Heidegger himself was forced to avow that his life was not *entirely* uninteresting. Thus, throughout his life he selectively divulged useful biographical tidbits—albeit, often in a self-serving manner. In "My Way to Phenomenology" (1963) he tells the story of how, as an eighteen-year-old theology student, Franz Brentano's dissertation on *The Manifold Sense of Being in Aristotle* served as his initiation into the mysteries of philosophy. The question that aroused the young gymnasium student's interest was: "If being is predicated in manifold meanings, then what is its leading fundamental meaning? What does Being mean?"[6] It was at this point that Heidegger's basic philosophical question, the *Seinsfrage* or the "question of Being," was established.

Two years later (1909–10), Heidegger discovered Edmund Husserl's classic study, *Logical Investigations*, a book that remained checked out to his library carrel for the ensuing two years. Of particular value for Heidegger was Husserl's powerful refutation of psychologism: the doctrine that the workings of the human mind can be understood exclusively in physicalist terms. From the standpoint of a young theology student interested in the way that thought and language are grounded ontologically in the word of God, such scientistic pretensions were both arrogant and sacrilegious. The task of theology, with the auxiliary aid of philosophy and logic, was to ensure that scientific hubris became conscious of its own limitations. In *Logical Investigations*, Husserl, following the lead of Brentano, established the difference between the psychological and logical aspects of judgment. Whereas the former were relative and contingent, varying from individual to individual, the latter, he claimed, possessed timeless validity. The truth value of a syllogism, argued Husserl, is independent of the psychological factors and mechanisms whereby it is realized. At a time when philosophy's claims to autonomy were seriously under assault by the methods of the natural sciences, Husserl's idea of "phenomenology as rigorous science" (the title of the philosopher's celebrated 1909 *Logos* essay) played a crucial role in shoring up Heidegger's own youthful intellectual inclinations and intuitions. In 1916, Husserl left Göttingen for an appointment at Freiburg. Heidegger would serve as his assistant for four years (1919–1923).

Much has been made of Heidegger's Catholicism—his strict Catholic upbringing in provincial Messkirch (his father was the sexton at the local church), his seminary studies, his failed attempt to become a Jesuit circa 1915 (after three weeks of study, Heidegger was dismissed for reasons of health), and, finally, his painful break with the "religion of [his] youth" in 1917. Until recently, however, few have known how profoundly the twenty-year-old Heidegger was involved in the landmark debates over "modernism" (*der Modernismusstreit*) that rocked turn-of-the-century Germany. Heidegger was fond of citing Hölderlin's maxim, "As you began, so you shall remain." Unsurprisingly, insight into his profound youthful attachment to Catholicism goes far toward explaining his mature worldview.

Two years following German unification in 1871, Bismarck attempted to enforce Catholic allegiance to the new state via a series of compulsory and repressive mandates. The voluble *Kulturkampf* that resulted left wounds that would only heal very slowly. (Ironically, in the course of their struggle, German Catholics gained the support of many liberals who supported the principles of freedom of worship and conscience.) As Heidegger came of age circa 1910, Catholic mistrust of the German state remained keen; yet by then such mistrust had metamorphosed to an aversion to all aspects of modern society that threatened to bypass the values of religion and tradition. The historian Hans-Ulrich Wehler felicitously described Catholic immobilism during the Second Empire in the following terms:

> In the 1864 Syllabus of Errors, an index of eighty "errors of the time," orthodox Catholicism ranged itself implacably against liberalism, socialism and modern science. The call for increased ecclesiastical control of education and research reached totalitarian proportions. . . . The contempt felt by [the Roman Catholic Church] for the Protestant principle of toleration made coexistence with rival organizations or educational claims very difficult. Without doubt, Thomist neo-scholasticism, encouraged in its development by several popes since the mid-nineteenth century, also reinforced the anti-modernist character of Roman Catholicism at this time. This batch of theorems was opposed to the social mobility of the modern age and its notions of parliamentary representation and democratic equality. It cemented the backward-looking traditions of Catholicism and turned the values of a vanished world based on estates into an ideology. It sought to tie the nineteenth century into the strait-jacket of the medieval order while the tide of history moved in the opposite direction. Catholicism was even less likely than Protestantism to make an active and lasting contribution to the spread of parliamentary influence in Germany, to say nothing of its eventual democratization.[7]

The extent to which Heidegger's youthful outlook was permeated by such unyielding Catholic perspectives becomes clear if one peruses the eight articles he wrote for the conservative Catholic journal, *Der Akademiker*, during the years 1910–12. As his biographer Hugo Ott, who unearthed these early articles, observes: "What the *Der Akademiker* contributions display is their embeddedness in a closed system of the Catholic worldview from an integral, anti-modern perspective. Martin Heidegger carries the banner of ultraconservative Catholicism with intense seriousness and great enthusiasm in the fields of theology, philosophy, and ethics."[8] Once again, Heidegger's highly selective approach to autobiographical themes enters the picture, insofar as he inexplicably omitted his *Der Akademiker* essays from the collected works edition of his writings.

Der Akademiker was founded in the spirit of Pope Pius X's so-called "antimodernism" encyclical of 1907. In fact, the journal's first issue contained a Preface by Pius X offering words of encouragement to his German followers in their struggle against modernist mores and values. At the time he composed these articles, Heidegger stood under the influence of the antimodernist theologian Carl Braig. (Braig allegedly coined the word "modernism.") Heidegger acknowledged his profound intellectual debt to Braig nearly fifty years later when, in *Zur Sache des Denkens*, he praised Braig's "penetrating kind of thinking."[9] In his own highly polemical writings, Braig railed against a modernism that was "blinded to anything that is not its Self or that does not serve its Self." "Historical truth," Braig continues, "like all truth—and the most brilliantly victorious is mathematical truth, the strictest form of eternal truth—is prior to the subjective ego and exists without it. . . . As soon as the ego of reason regards the reasonableness of things, they are not in truth. . . . No Kant will change the law that commands man to act in accordance with the way things are."[10]

What Heidegger's own contributions to *Der Akademiker* may have lacked in originality, they made up for in polemical zeal. For example, in his very first article ("Per Mortem ad Vitem"), he attacks, in the spirit of Pius X and Carl Braig, the modernist fascination with the vagaries of subjectivity:

> In our day, one talks much about "personality." And philosophers find new value-concepts. Apart from critical, moral, and aesthetic evaluation, they operate also with the "evaluation of personality," especially in literature. The person of the artist moves into the foreground. Thus one hears much about interesting people. Oscar Wilde, the dandy; Paul Verlaine, the "brilliant drunkard"; Maxim Gorky, the great vagabond; the superman Nietzsche—all interesting people. And when one of these interesting people, in the hour of grace, becomes conscious of the great lie of his gypsy-life [*sic*], smashes the altars of false gods, and becomes Christian, then they call this "tasteless, revolting."[11]

To Ibsen, Heidegger attributes the view that, "Happiness is possible only through a life of deceit." He goes on to inquire, Do the great personalities we have mentioned find happiness? No, they find only death and despair insofar as "none of them had the truth." All remained wedded to "individualism," which is, Heidegger proclaims, a "false standard of life." Higher life, he continues, will only triumph if lower forms of life are destroyed: "the will of the flesh, the doctrine of the world, paganism." Heidegger's impassioned conclusion is that:

> The much-ballyhooed cult of personality can only flourish when it remains in intimate contact with the richest and deepest source of religio-ethical authority. This cannot, according to its nature, do without a venerable outer form. And the church will, if is to remain true to its eternal treasure of truth, justifiably combat the destructive influences of modernism, which is not conscious of the sharpest contradictions in which its modern views of life stand to the ancient wisdom of the Christian tradition.[12]

Yet Heidegger's critique of the modern apotheosis of self remains unmarred by anti-intellectualism. He always justifies his standpoint in the name of logic, rigor, and a more exalted conception of "truth"— one that has been ignored by the (frivolous) modern glorification of subjective experience. Accordingly, he takes modern thought to task for its lax subjectivism, its having made perplexity and disorientation into a positive value. "Today," Heidegger laments, "philosophy, a mirror of eternity, only reflects subjective opinions, personal moods and wishes." In opposition to the amorphous tendencies of the modern self, Heidegger recommends "a strict, ice-cold logic [that] is inimical to the *refined* feelings of the modern soul. To strictly logical thought, which hermetically seals itself off against any affective influence of the soul, to each truly presuppositionless scientific work, there belongs a certain base of ethical power."[13]

What is striking about these claims is the extent to which they anticipate Heidegger's mature positions and views. It is clear that Heidegger's lifelong ontological quest, centering on the question of Being, was first catalyzed in response to the disorienting pluralism and relativism of cultural modernity. His aversion to modern epistemology (the legacy of Descartes), beginning with *Being and Time* and culminating in the Nietzsche lectures of the 1930s, can in part be traced to the critique of modern thought articulated in these early writings. His pronounced disaffection with modern art and literature—in the 1966 *Der Spiegel* interview, Heidegger characterizes aesthetic modernism as essentially "destructive"—unambiguously originated in the *mentalité* of *Kultur-kampf.*[14] His semi-hysterical image of America as a relentless technologi-cal Moloch, as "the site of catastrophe," develops from attitudes and convictions first expressed in the *Der Akademiker* texts.[15] Finally, one may also trace Heidegger's attraction to National Socialism as a "pri-mordial" political phenomenon capable of redeeming Germany from the lacerations and divisions of modern "society" to the resolutely anti-modernist standpoint articulated in these early articles.[16] As early as 1924 Heidegger publicly declared the need to place "our German Da-sein on firm foundations."

Heidegger always insisted that the orientation of fundamental ontol-ogy derived from the domain of "factical" experience, from the domain of "life" in its sheer immediacy. In *Being and Time*, he goes so far as to invoke a determinate *"factical ideal* of Dasein that underlies the on-tological interpretation of Dasein's existence"; in other words, "fac-ticity," the domain of immediate experience, remains prior to first philosophy.[17] And in a revealing letter to Karl Löwith in the early 1920s, Heidegger insists that his philosophizing derives from the "fac-ticity" or existential immediacy of his own Being-in-the-world: "I work in a concretely factical manner, from out of my 'I am—from out of my spiritual, indeed factical heritage/milieu/life contexts, from out of that which thereby becomes accessible to me as the living experience in which I live.'"[18] All of these declarations indicate that the circumstantial aspects of Heidegger's thought, far from being epi-phenomenal or tangential, are of fundamental significance to under-standing his philosophy.

Further insight into the autobiographical components of the "factical ideal" underlying Heidegger's philosophy is provided by his recently published correspondence with Elisabeth Blochmann. Blochmann, who was half-Jewish, was originally a friend of Heidegger's wife, Elfride. She had studied philosophy with Georg Simmel in Strasbourg and fre-quented Youth Movement circles in which *Lebensphilosophie* (Nietzsche, Simmel, Dilthey) was fashionable.

Though their correspondence hints at the fact that Heidegger and Blochmann were more than friends (Heidegger was frequently inspired to uncharacteristic bursts of lyricism), tangible proof as to the precise nature of their relationship is lacking. Their exchanges began during the concluding months of World War I, a period of national despair. It was a time suited for radical questioning: the nostrums and rationalizations of prewar life and thought seemed patently inadequate. In Heidegger's view, the war had decimated everything except for the *"force of personality or belief in the intrinsic value or belonging central to the ego"*—a claim that betrays the marked influence of Husserl's transcendental phenomenology.[19] If any one book felicitously captured the *Zeitgeist*, it was Spengler's *Decline of the West*, and a confrontation with Spengler soon became a mandatory rite of passage for right-leaning German intellectuals. Although he regarded Spengler's historical typologies as ultimately superficial, Heidegger's own obsession with the imperatives of "destroying" and "destruction" (*destruieren, Abbau*)—a veritable leitmotif during this period—harmonized perfectly with the postwar cultural *Stimmung*.[20]

In the correspondence with Blochmann, the young *Privatdozent* bares his soul. As Heidegger writes in an impassioned letter of June 15, 1918:

> Spiritual life must again become truly real with us—it must be endowed with a force born of personality, a force that "overturns" and compels genuine rising—and this force is revealed as a genuine one only in simplicity, not in the blasé, decadent, enforced. . . . Spiritual life can only be demonstrated and shaped in such a way that those who are to share in it are directly gripped by it *in their most personal existence*. . . . Where belief in the intrinsic value of self-identification is truly alive, there everything that is unworthy in accidental surroundings is overcome from within and forever.[21]

Heidegger perceived the war as a great purgative out of which a new Germany might emerge. From a spiritual perspective, defeat on the battlefield would not constitute an irreversible setback; instead, it would serve to purify German culture of all that was artificial, tentative, and nonessential. It was the great acid bath out of which a deeper and more profound Germany would appear. A elemental Christian motif, reinterpreted through the prism of German romanticism and the war experience itself, underlay Heidegger's perceptions: from death and destruction, "new life" would be born. As he observes to Blochmann in his letter of January 1919: "The new life that we desire, or that desires us, has dispensed with being universal, i.e. being false and two-dimensional (superficial)—its asset is originality—not the artificially constructed, but the evident content of *total intuition*."[22] In keeping with his self-understanding as part of a new German spiritual elite, he described the war's "positive effects" in the following terms: "inwardly impoverished aesthetes and people who until now, as 'spiritual' people, have merely played with spirit the way others play with money and pleasure, will now collapse and despair helplessly—hardly any help or useful directives can be expected from them."[23]

The reference to "total intuition" highlights the new, nonuniversal approach to knowledge Heidegger saw emerging from the phenomenological method. The key intellectual discovery for him during this period was the nearly untranslatable notion of *Jeweiligkeit*, a concept that figured prominently in *Being and Time*: the incomparable uniqueness of the spatio-temporal present and the related question of how one might represent it through concepts. Heidegger's essential breakthrough to a new concept of temporality was contained in this idea. Traditional metaphysics strove to represent truth *sub specie aeternae*—that is, as something "universal"—to the detriment of the temporality and historicity of lived experience. By foregrounding the question of time, Heidegger sought to reverse this prejudice; subsequently, the appearance of Being in time, the uniqueness of the moment of its appearance (*Kairos, der Augenblick*), would occupy center stage in his thought. It was in this spirit that he chose as the epigraph for his post-habilitation trial lecture a saying from Meister Eckhart: *"Time is that which changes and pluralizes itself; eternity remains simple."*[24] The universalizing tendencies of traditional ontology remained indifferent to such concerns, and, hence, to experience as something meaningful, that is, *as something lived*. In a similar vein, in his habilitation study of the medieval philosopher Duns Scotus, Heidegger observed that, "What really exists is something individual [*ein Individuelles*]."[25] Only a radically transformed conception of temporality could resolve the dilemma of the philosophical concept's constitutional indifference to the singularity of experience.

From the very beginning, Heidegger's renewal of metaphysics was conceived of as part of an all-encompassing project of cultural and political renewal. In his first lecture course following World War I, *On the Vocation of Philosophy*, he announced prophetically: "The idea of science—and its genuine realization—signifies for the immediate consciousness of life a transformative intervention (however this may be conceived); it entails a change to a new attitude of consciousness and thereby a corresponding form of the movement of the life of spirit." He supplements the foregoing observations by declaring: "Every great philosophy fulfills itself in a worldview." In other words, unlike German idealism, *genuine* science does not leave the world around it unaffected.[26]

The Break with Catholicism

In 1917, Heidegger experienced a profound personal and religious crisis, an increasing sense of alienation from the religion of his youth. So momentous was this confessional parting-of-the-ways that Heidegger biographer Hugo Ott refers to it as "the first turn." Throughout his boyhood, Heidegger was dependent on the largesse of the Catholic Church in order to finance his studies; but this dependency bred resentment, insofar as the fellowships he received often came with strings attached. For example, following his dissertation on "The Doctrine of Judgment in Psychologism" (1911), Heidegger sought to continue his studies of phenomenology and logic. Yet, upon receiving a stipend from the Foundation in Honor of St. Thomas Aquinas, he was forced to devote his energies primarily to the study of scholasticism.

In 1916, Heidegger and Elfride Petrie were betrothed. They were married the following year. Elfride came from a staunchly Protestant background. For Heidegger, the engagement seems to have crystallized a process of confessional disillusionment that had played itself out during the previous years. Heidegger's father had been a sexton at the local church in Messkirch. For a period of thirteen years, his education had been generously funded by Catholic organizations and institutions. For these and other reasons, it would be difficult to overestimate the biographical significance of his formal break with Catholicism at the time of his engagement to Elfride.

Revealing testimony concerning this break was contained in the letter Heidegger wrote to one of his mentors, Freiburg University theology professor and priest Engelbert Krebs, in January 1919. As Heidegger avows:

> Over the last two years I have set aside all scientific work of a specialized nature and have struggled instead for a basic clarification of my philosophical position. This has led me to results that I could not be free to hold and teach if I were tied to positions that come from outside of philosophy.
>
> Epistemological insights that pass over into the theory of historical knowledge have made the system of Catholicism problematic and unacceptable to me—but not Christianity and metaphysics, although I take the latter in a new sense.[27]

Heidegger's letter indicates both the constraints he felt as a philosopher working within the strictures of Catholic theology and the expectation that, given this new freedom of research, he would be able to reconcile the demands of Christianity and metaphysics. Of equal importance, however, is his allusion to the "epistemological insights" of German historicism. Since completing his habilitation study on Duns Scotus, Heidegger had begun an intensive study of Dilthey, whose work had elevated the idea of "historical knowledge" to the status of a first principle of the human sciences. Dilthey's notion of "historicity," which would become one of the central categories of Being and Time, reinforced Heidegger's sense of the failings of traditional ontology—its aversion to temporality, its inordinate focus on "universality" and "eternity" at the expense of the singularity of the here and now. The idea of historicity helped drive home the notion of the irreducible uniqueness of events occurring in time.

As his alienation from Catholicism accelerated circa the mid-1910s, Heidegger undertook a confrontation with the essential texts of Protestant theology: the works of Augustine, Luther, Schleiermacher, and Kierkegaard. Yet he was less interested in the explicitly religious content of their thought than in its phenomenological aspects and significance—religious consciousness as a manifestation of intentional experience.[28] Thus, he was less interested in Christianity as a vehicle of religious experience than in its status as a paradigm of experience *simpliciter*: the phenomenological deepening of the self concomitant with the personal experience of faith, the cultivation of the inner self (*In-newerden*), the advent of "self-consciousness" in the sense of German Pietism later appropriated by Hegel. In his 1920 lecture course, "Introduction to the Phenomenology of Religion," in which Heidegger broaches many of these themes, he coins the term "Self-world" to describe the realm he is seeking.

Thus, in Heidegger's view, the classic texts of the Protestantism offered privileged insight into the irreducibly singular nature of an individual's encounter with God qua *lived experience*—experience that, as a result of Rome's neo-Thomist and ecclesiastical biases, seemed of lesser significance in Catholic traditions. As Heidegger himself laments circa 1916 with scholasticism in mind: "Dogmatic and casuistic pseudo-philosophies, which pose as philosophies of a particular system of religion (for example, Catholicism) and presumably stand closest to religion and the religious, *are the least capable of promoting the vitality of the problem.*" Insofar as scholasticism, following the mistaken lead of Aristotle, attempted to take its bearings from the natural world rather than the domain of inner life, it "severely jeopardized the immediacy of religious life and forgot religion for theology and dogmas."[29] From the phenomenological standpoint revered by the early Heidegger, scholastic ontology stood in urgent need of "dismantling." He believed that the phenomenological method alone could retrieve the experiential substrate in its primordial immediacy—a substrate that, throughout the history of metaphysics, had been repressed and distorted by the imposition of an alien ontology. In this way, Heidegger inquired into the primordial phenomenological relationship between self and world. In the words of one commentator: "On the threshold of his religious crisis of 1917, we find Heidegger already keenly interested in the phenomenology of religion, looking to it for insight into the notion of intentionality . . . as a vehicle for bringing a fossilized philosophy back to life."[30]

Encountering Phenomenology

"Phenomenology: that's Heidegger and me"—this was Husserl's succinct characterization of the movement during the early 1920s, a glow-

ing endorsement of Heidegger as his handpicked successor. His proph-
ecy was borne out in 1928 when Heidegger acceded to Husserl's chair
at Freiburg. In the early 1920s, students arrived intending to study with
Husserl and within weeks would switch to auditing Heidegger's lectures and seminars. At times, Husserl himself encouraged them to
make the shift. In her encomium written on the occasion of Heidegger's eightieth birthday, Hannah Arendt emphasizes the subterranean
renown that Heidegger enjoyed among German university students
well before the publication of *Being and Time*.[31]

In retrospective accounts of his philosophical path, Heidegger perennially downplayed the significance of his break with Husserl, insisting
instead on the elements of continuity between his early career as a
phenomenologist and his later status as a philosopher of Being. Yet,
from the time of their earliest collaboration, cracks in the alliance were
readily apparent. Husserl and Heidegger possessed fundamentally different conceptions of the mission of "science." Whereas for Husserl
phenomenology's ultimate goal was to place philosophy on a rigorous
objective footing (a longing for "apodeictic certainty" suffuses his early
treatises on method), Heidegger, as we have seen, was motivated by a
very different set of concerns. The celebration of "life" in its immediacy as an independent value and normative point of departure—an
orientation that was central to *Lebensphilosophie*—was entirely foreign
to Husserl's approach. Although Heidegger had distinct methodological reservations about vitalism, he remained in solidarity with many of
its critical aims. As he remarked in 1919: "Today the word 'lived experience' [*Erlebnis*] is so hackneyed and colorless that one would do best to
leave it to one side were it not so directly central."[32] Paradoxical though
it may seem, in their assessments of the great intellectual divide between rationalism and antirationalism, Husserl and Heidegger ultimately lay on opposite sides. Heidegger increasingly came to view
Husserl's emphasis on the nonsituated, transcendental ego as a type of
phenomenological *fundamentum inconcussum* as an unacceptable methodological failing. In Heidegger's view, it was Descartes's *res cogitans*
outfitted in phenomenological garb. Husserl understood phenomenology as a scientific redemption of the Enlightenment project that, while
avoiding all taint of physicalism and materialism, remained true to the
mission of first philosophy. As he remarked in a letter of 1935: "I want

to establish, against mysticism and irrationalism, a kind of *superrationalism* which transcends the old rationalism as inadequate and yet vindicates its inmost objectives."[33] The phenomenological intuition of essences (*Wesensschau*) would accomplish this end, thus avoiding a regression to the unverifiable conjectures of traditional metaphysics. Correspondingly, transcendental phenomenology embraced the modern scientific values of clarity, light, and reason. Or, as Husserl once declared: "Only one need absorbs me: I must win clarity, else I cannot live; I cannot bear life unless I can believe that I shall achieve it."[34] Heidegger, conversely, in his search for unfathomable depths of primordial experience, remained convinced that truths yielded by analytical reason were shallow and of little import. As a modality of lived experience, "judging" is a species of "un-living," polemicizes Heidegger. "The object-character (*das Gegenständliche*), the thing that is known, is as such dis-tant (*ent-fernt*), cut off from authentic lived experience."[35]

An anecdote from their early collaboration in Freiburg well illustrates the nature of their substantive differences. A student who was auditing classes with both men, but whose allegiances lay with Husserl, registered the following complaint: "Dr. Heidegger is taking a mediating position by asserting that the primal I is the qualified 'historical I,' from which the pure I is derived by repressing all historicity."[36] Therein lay their basic disagreement. Husserl assumed that the transcendental ego's purity depended on its being purged of all historical factors and influences. Historical contingency only sullied the purity of the transcendental standpoint. On one occasion, he went so far as to characterize "the pure ego and pure consciousness" as "the wonder of all wonders."[37] In *Formal and Transcendental Logic*, he insisted that, "Whether we like it or not, whether it may sound monstrous or not, the "I am" is the fundamental fact to which I have to stand up, before which, as a philosopher, I must never blink for a moment."[38] Only late in life with *The Crisis of the European Sciences and Transcendental Phenomenology* (1936) would Husserl belatedly prove receptive to the demands of history. There he argued (with astonishing naiveté) that Europe can avoid the abyss of impending nihilism only if it is able to reestablish the telos of first philosophy, whose thread has been lost amid a rising tide of scientist and vitalist intellectual currents. For Heidegger, conversely, the Self's receptivity to historicity (or temporality) was one of its indispensable attributes. As Heidegger observed: "In the theoretical attitude I am directed to something, but *I* have no living involvement (as a historical I) with this or that thing in the world."[39] In this way fundamental ontology, with its focus on the embodied attributes of "care," "mood," "solicitude, and "falling," would outstrip the transcendental "I" of Husserlian phenomenology.

A remarkable 1919 lecture course, *On the Vocation of Philosophy*, represents the germ of Heidegger's unique approach to the problems of first philosophy. Reading it gives one the sense of being privy to a portentous moment of intellectual discovery. Heidegger composed the lecture course in the midst of an emergency situation (*Notzustand*)—the revolutionary tumult of postwar Germany—and the semester in which it was delivered was appropriately known as the "war emergency semester" (*Kriegsnotsemester*). Here, Heidegger is preoccupied with the question of beginnings: only after this question has been satisfactorily treated will the vocation of science rest on sure footing. The transcript reveals Heidegger groping for a moment of phenomenological clarity that will found his philosophical project. He proceeds with a methodical rigor that suggests that the future of humankind depends on this discovery. In Heidegger's words: "We stand at a methodological crossroads where the life and death of philosophy is at stake; we stand before an abyss: either an abyss of nothingness, e.g., absolute objectivism (*Sachlichkeit*), or a successful leap into *another world*—or, more precisely, into the world for the first time."[40]

As Heidegger remarked in a letter to Löwith from the same period, his philosophy is inspired by a search for the *unum necessarum*—the "one thing that is necessary"; this pursuit is what motivates him in both philosophy and "existence." There is no way, he avowed, that the two can be separated. "I am not concerned," remarked Heidegger, "with a primary and isolated definition of philosophy—but rather only with that kind of definition that is related to the *existential interpretation of facticity*." In the letter, he returns to this point repeatedly:

I do not make a distinction between the scientific, theoretical life and one's own life. . . . The essential manner in which my facticity becomes existentially articulated is scientific research. . . . In this connection, for me the motive and goal of philosophizing is never to augment the store of objective truths, because the objectivity of philosophy . . . lies within the meaning of my existing.[41]

From these brief characterizations and self-descriptions one can see that Heidegger is driven by a concern to refound transcendental phenomenology in a manner that foregrounds the dimension of "factical/ existential" concern, or "life." The problem, however, was that in its current employment, the idea of life (*das Leben*) had succumbed to the fashionable, pseudopopular terms of value-philosophies and worldviews. One of Heidegger's major scientific aims was finally to place the diffuse and superficial orientations of *Lebensphilosophie* on a rigorous phenomenological footing.

In the early 1920s, Heidegger undertook a phenomenological search for what he calls an "Ur-etwas," a "primordial something." The encounter with this dimension of experience would propel the enterprise of fundamental ontology. Heidegger makes it clear that what he is searching for has nothing to do with the "sense data" (Locke) or "sensory manifold" (Kant) of modern epistemology. Epistemology's model of experience has always been *scientific experience*, a model that succumbs to the tyranny of the theoretical and thereby perpetrates the "de-living of life" (*Ent-leben des Lebens*).[42] Before "life"—that "primordial something"—can be experienced, it is made into an object of scientific cognition. For Heidegger, this primordial experiential stratum, though pre-theoretical, is *already meaningful*. (The positing of an abstract epistemological subject standing against an abstract object is a scientific construction). Fundamental ontology, conversely, does not foist an alien conceptual framework upon life. It is not primarily concerned with acts of "cognition," whereby experience is mechanically synthesized through concepts. Instead, it reads off meanings that are already there or experientially pregiven. At one point, Heidegger refers to his approach as "illuminating comportment," seeking thereby to distinguish it from the claims of epistemology.[43] Rather than proceeding by way of analysis and judgment, and thereby producing true propositions or statements (*Feststellungen*), fundamental ontology employs the method of "hermeneutical intuition."[44] Ultimately, this methodological breakthrough mandates a rejection of the Aristotelian primacy of *logos* (the rational account) in favor of the notion of *aletheia*—truth as a ontological chiaroscuro of "concealment" and "unconcealment." Fundamental ontology's "hermeneutical intuitions" (later: "formal indications") do not "still the stream of experience" but disclose meanings that are already present. Experience itself, the primordial encounter between self and world, far from being mute, and as always already meaningful, already contains an expressive dimension: it cannot help but speak to us if we reacquire the capacity to heed its signals. As Heidegger observes in a lapidary aside: "Philosophy as fundamental knowing is nothing other than the radical actualization of the facticity of life in its historicity."[45]

One of Heidegger's crucial discoveries of this period, one that would set him on the path toward *Being and Time*, was the idea of "facticity" (*Faktizität*) or "factical life." With this notion, he sought to identify (as earlier with the "primordial something") an irreducible and original (*ürsprünglich*) dimension of experience prior to the subject-object split. When one inquires into the incipient nature of experience as exemplified by the phrase, "there is . . ." (*es gibt*), one probes a level of primordial givenness that is prior to the differentiation of the world into discrete, individual objects. We inquire into something that simply "oc-curs" (*sich er-eignet*), we experience the world in its precategorial temporal "thereness" (*Jeweiligkeit*). We are interested not so much in the quiddity of beings (the level of pseudo-primordial questioning presupposed by metaphysics qua ontology)—their "whatness"—but in their *how-ness*, their basic existential modalities. For Heidegger, metaphysics, by preoccupying itself with the whatness or quiddity of beings (especially that of Dasein), inherently reifies experience; it defines Dasein's basic existential modalities as essentially thinglike and thereby freezes temporality. In the lexicon of "onto-theology," however, things have various functions (*telei* or aims) and so does "man," the "rational animal." Yet, by predefining human Being-in-the-world, metaphysics a priori eliminates a potential for primordial experience proper to the domain of "existence" or "factical life," a domain that for Heidegger is our "ownmost" (*eigenste*)—our most authentic or most proper sphere.

The ideological thrust of Heidegger's discussion is clear. As was standard procedure for the German intelligentsia during the Great War, he enlists philosophy in the service of a "critique of civilization." He views it as a weapon in the struggle against the values of "modernity" and the "West": "Everything modern," comments Heidegger, "is characterized by the fact that it slinks away from its own time in order thereby to produce an 'effect' (busy-ness, propaganda, proselytizing, economic cliques, intellectual profiteering)."[46] Such lamentations concerning modernity, reminiscent of similar polemics from the *Der Akademiker* texts, resurface in the criticisms of "curiosity"—one of the basic modalities of the "they-self"—in *Being and Time*. Thus, Heidegger defines curiosity as a perennial search for "novelty" or the new. It is an extension of modernity's preoccupation with "busy-ness" (*das Betrieb*), and, as such, an essential mode of self-forgetting Dasein—Dasein's refusal to be a Self. As Heidegger explains: "When curiosity has become free, it concerns itself with seeing not in order to understand what is seen . . . but *just* in order to see. It seeks novelty only in order to leap from it anew to another novelty. . . . It does not seek the leisure of tarrying observantly, but rather seeks *restlessness and the excitement of continual novelty of changing encounters*."[47] In the German, there is an added parallelism, insofar as curiosity—*Neugier*—is etymologically related to *neu* or new.

Philosophy, declaims Heidegger in 1923, has no interest in solving problems of "universal humanity and culture." Nor can its concern for "existence as the temporally determinate possibility of Dasein" become an "object of universal reasoning [*Räsonnements*] and public discussion." Staunchly opposed to the values of "public reason," Heidegger self-consciously embraces the particularist standpoint of factical experience, which is always that of an individual self: "The Being of factical life is characterized by the fact that it *is* in the How of the Being of self-possibility. The ownmost possibility of itself that Dasein (facticity) is . . . is called *existence*."[48] When facticity or existence is at issue, as is always the case with fundamental ontology, the Protestant leitmotif, *mea res agitur*—"my life is at stake"—always come into play.

Heidegger's discussion of facticity prefigures his later employment of Dasein: a being that is neither "subject" nor "object" but, qua "Being-in-the-world," ontologically prior to both. Facticity is the "site of Being" (later, Heidegger identified this site as the "clearing" or *Lichtung*) in the same way as Dasein is the site of Being in *Being and Time*. In *On the Vocation of Philosophy*, Heidegger's "Analysis of the Structure of Lived Experience" (*Analyse der Erlebnisstruktur*) distinctly foreshadows the "existential analytic" of *Being and Time*.

Phronesis *and* Existenz

"Being is said in many ways"—so begins chapter 7 of Aristotle's *Metaphysics*. This was the remark that catalyzed the young Heidegger's interest in philosophy. Yet he quickly became disillusioned with Aristotle's response. Although many things are predicated of Being, "obviously," concludes Aristotle, "that which 'is' primarily is the 'what', which indicates the substance of a thing."[49] Hence, for Aristotle, primary being—that which is "most real"—equals "substance" (*ousia*), which he goes on to define as that which remains the same throughout and despite all change. But early on, Heidegger felt that substance metaphysics—an orientation that dominated the history of ontology for 2,500 years—with its inordinate focus on the "whatness" of things, could not do justice to the wonder of "factical life"; nor could it account for the modalities of Dasein, whose essentially temporal nature defies fixedness or permanence. As the philosopher Werner Marx has appropriately observed: "When in our day a philosopher expressly poses the question of Being *no longer* as a question of essence and expressly thinks *no longer* in the sense of *ousia* or substance, we must regard this attempt as a veritable revolution."[50]

Nevertheless, despite his pronounced reservations about substance metaphysics, Heidegger was convinced that the regeneration of first philosophy could only be achieved by way of a systematic reappraisal of Aristotle's thought. Between 1921 and 1924, Heidegger taught no fewer than ten lecture courses or seminars related to Aristotle's philosophy; about half bore the understated, nondescript title, "Phenomenological Interpretations of Aristotle."

The key Aristotle text for Heidegger during this period—crucible years for the genesis of *Being and Time*—was Book VI of the *Nichomachean Ethics*. There Aristotle specified the different types of knowledge that were appropriate for various modalities of Being. *Nous* was a pure knowing suitable for cognizing unchanging first principles or pure

Being. *Poeisis* was a type of knowledge that resulted in the production of objects. And, most important from Heidegger's point of view, *phronesis* was a form of knowledge appropriate to men and women acting in concert with one another for the sake of living virtuously. In the *Nichomachean Ethics*, Aristotle went on to assay and categorize the essential human virtues. He stressed that in view of the multifarious and ever-changing nature of human affairs, knowledge of human action could never be absolute: "Let it be assumed that there are two rational elements: with one of these we apprehend the realities whose fundamental principles do not admit of being other than they are; and with the other we apprehend *things which do admit of being other*."[51] The second type of knowledge—*phronesis*—was proper to the domain of human practical life, and it inspired Heidegger's view that a hermeneutical, rather than metaphysical, approach would be the most fruitful point of departure for existential analysis. Unlike the material objects produced by *poeisis*, Dasein was the source of its own motion; and, as self-moving, it possessed, unlike physical objects, the capacity to be a "Self"—a potential that Heidegger came to view as one of the distinguishing features of *Existenz*. Only Dasein *exists*; things in the world simply *are*.

Heidegger came to view Aristotle's insight as the key to how one should conceptualize "factical life" or Being-in-the-world. Above all, Aristotle's directives reinforced his sense of how fundamental ontology ought *not* to proceed: it should *not* begin with a reliance on the precepts and prejudices of "substance metaphysics"; for by proceeding in this way, it would subject Dasein's Being to metaphysical standards and norms wholly inappropriate to it. Should it pursue this course, first philosophy would (as it so often had in the past) become an enterprise of mismeasure.

In Heidegger's view, the approaches of ontology (Aristotle) and epistemology (Descartes) were equally misguided. One emphasized the primacy of substance, the other that of the knowing subject. The authentic phenomenological point of departure—"factical life"—was *prior to both aspects*, Heidegger believed, just as a "phenomenological intuition" is neither entirely subjective nor objective. Only an approach that takes this fact into account can do justice to our primordial encounter with Being.

In retrospect, it must be said that the "existential analytic" or "Dasein-analysis" of *Being and Time* represents a strange hybrid. On the one hand, from the *Nichomachean Ethics*, Heidegger assimilated a standpoint that emphasized the *primacy of practical reason*. In consequence, he understood Dasein's Being in terms of the precedence of a series of "world-relations" related to Aristotlelian *pragmata*. Our relationship to the world of things is not primarily technical-scientific; it is not essentially concerned with "world mastery." Instead, "things" fundamentally represent a site or horizon of human interaction; they constitute a "world" in the nonphysicalist, existential sense. The things of our everyday dealings are not undifferentiated "objects" confronting a disembodied "subject"; they are not simply present-at-hand (*vorhanden*). Instead, as objects of use, they implicitly stand in an integral, even semi-fraternal relationship to the men and women who manipulate them. It is this dimension of *Being and Time* that stands resolutely opposed to the modern epistemological conception of the self as self-positing subjectivity.

At the same time, this worldly, affirmative, Aristotelian side of *Being and Time* is offset by another dimension: the Protestant-theological aspect that derives autobiographically from Heidegger's disillusionment with Catholicism circa 1917. These two dimensions comprise an uneasy admixture. Heidegger's Protestantism manifests itself in his discussion of "falling" (*Verfallen*) as one of the fundamental traits of Dasein. It is this dimension that accounts for fundamental ontology's bleakness: its Augustinian, angst-ridden view of human life.

Heidegger's Protestant-theological inclinations are especially prominent in a recently rediscovered 1922 draft of *Being and Time*, "Phenomenological Interpretations with Respect to Aristotle." As in *Being and Time*, Heidegger begins by characterizing "factical life" (Dasein) in terms of "care": "in the concrete temporalizing of its Being it is concerned about its Being, *even when it avoids itself.*" However, for reasons that are far from clear, in Heidegger's existential ontology self-evasion or faithlessness quickly predominates: "The most unmistakable manifestation of this is factical life's tendency towards making things easy for itself"—falling away from the tasks of being a Self or authenticity. In Heidegger's reading, the breach between fundamental ontology's existential radicalism and all competing paradigms of truth and meaning is well-nigh total:

When factical life authentically is what it is in this Being-heavy and Being-difficult, then the genuinely appropriate way of access to it and way of truthfully safe-keeping it can only consist in making it difficult. All making-easy, all misleading currying of favors with regard to needs, all metaphysical reassurances based on what is primarily book-learning—all of this leads already in its basic aim to a failure to bring the object of philosophy within sight and within grasp, let alone to keep it there.[52]

In its quest for authenticity, Dasein is perpetually thwarted by a "basic factical tendency of life: a tendency towards the *falling away* from one's own self and thereby towards *falling prey* to the world, and thus the *falling apart* from oneself." "The tendency towards falling is *alienating*," observes Heidegger, insofar as "factical life becomes more and more alien to itself in its being absorbed in the world."[53] In this way, Dasein's self-understanding becomes progressively "world-laden" (*welthaft*): it tends to view itself as an entity or thing rather than as a (self-moving) *Existenz*; it thus bypasses opportunities for authenticity or self-realization. In essence, *"life hides from itself."* Or, as Heidegger bluntly expresses a similar thought: "factical life . . . is for the most part *not lived as factical life*."[54] The seducements of alienation and falling away are most acute in the case of *death*. It is Dasein's attitude toward death as an ultimate instance or boundary situation (*Grenzfall*) that determines whether it is able to temporalize its existence authentically.

Why was Heidegger's view of Being-in-the-world so tendentiously grim? Does he, moreover, provide an adequate justification of his conception of human existence as characterized by the modalities of self-avoidance, alienation, and "falling?"

To take up the second question first: issues of justification have traditionally been one of fundamental ontology's major weaknesses. Heidegger's manner of philosophizing is, by contemporary standards, old school. He is uninterested in problems of ordinary language. Such problems are a priori devalued insofar as they derive from the inferior sphere of "everydayness." As we have seen, this sphere, which has been colonized by the "they-self," can make no serious contributions to matters of philosophical substance. The standpoint of the *sensus communis*, he believes, can only mislead. For Heidegger, philosophizing is an intrinsically aristocratic enterprise. As he remarked in his 1935 lecture course, "Truth is not for every man, but only for the strong."[55] In stark contrast with the pragmatist tradition (Peirce, Mead, and Dewey), his philosophical disposition is devoid of democratic sympathies. For Heidegger, the act of philosophizing suggests privileged access to a hermetic dimension of *Existenz*: the primordial experience of Being. In his estimation, almost all previous efforts in the realm of first philosophy are of such inferior worth that the very idiom of philosophical thought (*Denken*) must be recast from the ground up. Yet, as several critics have observed, by systematically shunning ordinary language and preferring unwieldy neologisms, a whiff of linguistic authoritarianism pervades Heidegger's approach. Such lexical pomposity seemingly demands of readers a posture of compliant submission; it has the perlocutionary effect of compelling them to acquiesce passively in the face of definitive and grandiose proclamations. In the last analysis, it seems impossible to separate Heidegger's philosophical authoritarianism from the question of his political authoritarianism. While the foregoing criticisms in no way disqualify the project of fundamental ontology, they do suggest some important caveats concerning its reception.

To be sure, the existential despondency that pervades the outlook of *Being and Time* is a peculiarly German inheritance. Many of the misanthropic tropes he employs are the stock and trade of German romanticism, stripped of the prospect of religious salvation and inscribed with an element of hard-edged, existential realism. Heideggerian *Angst* expresses the world-weariness of the romantic sensibility in an age when the hopes and consolations of an earlier era seem both anachronistic and unconscionably sentimental. In his philosophy, the romantic nexus between suffering and nobility of character has been filtered through the horrific images of Germany's war experience. As far as German traditions are concerned, this was a point of no return. Of course, Heidegger never experienced these horrors personally. For a time he served as a weatherman, providing meteorological data in the event of gas attacks. But soon he was accorded a medical discharge (heart palpitations once again; in later years, he became so self-conscious about his poor service record that he provided false accounts in curriculum vitae). Nevertheless, the *Kriegerlebnis* (war experience) soon became an obligatory point of reference for Germany's national conservatives. In particular, Heidegger's emphasis on Being-toward-death as a touchstone of authentic existence strongly betrays such historical influences and residues.

Heidegger's existential realism invites comparison with the political philosopher Carl Schmitt. Like Heidegger, following World War I Schmitt overcame a resolutely Catholic background to embrace political existentialism. Transposed to the sphere of international relations (*Völkerrecht*), political existentialism seemed to demand an end to "worldviews" (read: Wilsonianism) and a return to a purportedly non-ideological realism. Yet, insofar as Schmitt's "realism" was ideologically directed against the West's "universalism," it became a de facto legitimation of German particularism—an expression of the ideology of the German "way." Schmitt's political existentialism culminated in the following claim from *The Concept of Political* (which appeared in 1927, the same year as *Being and Time*): "The high points of great politics are the moments in which the enemy comes into view in concrete clarity as the enemy"—so much for Western shibboleths about cosmopolitanism or the "rights of man."[56] In *Political Romanticism*, his first book following the Great War, Schmitt sought to distinguish the romantic incapacity for authentic political decision—which he viewed as a nineteenth-century atavism—from the new German mentality that had been forged in the crucible of the war experience: masculinist, fearless, resolute, and hard—the ethos of Hitler's *Schützstaffel avant la lettre*. Heidegger, too, had imbibed much of this ethos: resoluteness (*Entschlossenheit*), in contrast with the vacillating ambiguity of the "they," was one of the hallmarks of authenticity.[57]

Fundamental ontology performed a Husserlian *epoché* (reduction) upon the totality of inherited worldviews and cultural traditions. Whereas transcendental phenomenology utilized the reduction for epistemological purposes (in order to secure the cognitive ideal of "pure knowing"), Heidegger, in keeping with his Scholastic training, employed it for ontological ends. But once "essence" (*essentia*) had been bracketed as redolent of "substance metaphysics," what was it that remained—the naked fact of existence in its unadulterated "thatness"? While there can be no doubting the boldness, novelty, and timeliness of this philosophical gesture, it ultimately led to an intellectual blind alley. In the tradition of onto-theology, existence was ensured of meaning insofar as it was provided with metaphysical guarantees or grounds: essence preceded existence, which secured a place for it (exist-ence) within a larger, meaningful whole. After the systematic decon-struction of the history of ontology, "factical life" became devoid of underlying support. In a representative play on words, Heidegger cele-brated this dilemma. *Grund* (reason or ground) had given way before the *Ab-grund* (groundlessness or abyss) of naked existence as such. At one point in *Being and Time*, Heidegger implored his readers to sum-mon up the "courage for *Angst*" (*Mut zur Angst*). Following this initial radical act of deconstruction, the ensuing discussion of "tradition" and "handing down" (*Überlieferung*) in Division II of *Being and Time* could not help but sound hollow and insincere.

Heidegger's solution to the problem of nihilism or meaninglessness followed the proverbial German formula of a *Flucht nach vorne*: he de-cided to seize the bull by the horns. Instead of fleeing the essential nihilism of the human condition by becoming "world-laden" (absorbed in the world), fundamental ontology would simply *embrace* it; "think-ing the abyss" became its badge of honor.

1927: Anno Mirabilis

In 1927, *Being and Time* appeared in Husserl's *Yearbook for Phenome-nological Research*. Its hasty composition was in part a response to exter-nal constraint: Heidegger was not yet a full professor (*Ordinarius*) at Marburg, and the publication of a significant work was a necessary precondition for promotion. (In 1926, he had been refused an appoint-ment at the University of Berlin due to a dearth of publications.) Heidegger wrote *Being and Time* in a remarkable creative burst be-tween the spring and fall of 1926. During the writing, he frequently expressed deep reservations about the project in his letters to Jaspers. "On the whole, this is for me a transitional work," observed Heidegger in May. Six months later, as the treatise neared completion, he confided to Jaspers that his estimation of the work's value was not "excessively high"; although, having completed it, he had "learned to understand . . . what greater ones have aimed at." Upon finishing it in December, he suggested to Jaspers that *Being and Time's* chief merit was that it allowed him to work through a number of pressing philosophical problems and themes; having finished it he could get on with more promising philosophical work.[58]

Heidegger's own methodological uncertainties were mirrored in the ambiguities of the book's structure. It opened with a suggestive quote from Plato's *Sophist* that placed the "question of Being" in the foreground and set the tone for the long introductory chapter, "The Exposition of the Question of the Meaning of Being": "For manifestly you have long been aware of what you mean when you use the expression 'Being.' We, however, who used to think we understood it, have now become perplexed." However, it proved difficult to reconcile the avowed focus on the *Seinsfrage* with the nature of the text that followed, which was preponderantly oriented toward *existential* rather than ontological concerns—i.e., concerns pertaining to the Being of *Dasein*. The question of Being resurfaces fleetingly at the book's conclusion as a type of promissory note. Tellingly, Heidegger had announced that *Being and Time* was only the first book of a two-part work; Part II, *Time and Being*, was never written. In essence, and strange as it may seem, Heidegger spent twelve years climbing a philosophical ladder that would lead to the publication of *Being and Time*; when he reached the top, it seems, he threw the ladder away.

In Heidegger's subsequent lectures and essays, the figure of Dasein is conspicuous by its absence. For example, his 1929 Freiburg University inaugural address, "What Is Metaphysics?", represents a watershed insofar as the question of Being receives unambiguous pride of place; the Being of Dasein has ceased to be the primary focus of his inquiry. Heidegger's discourse centers on the centrality of "nihilation" or "nothingness," the attitude we must assume in the face of our customary, complacent relationship to the Being of beings. The concept of "nothingness" thereby indicates the radical degree to which the totality of "beings" must be reduced or "bracketed" in order for philosophy to accede to the heartland of "Being."

Many of these issues surfaced in the legendary 1929 debate with Ernst Cassirer in Davos, Switzerland. Cassirer had been warned in advance about Heidegger's frankly nihilistic relationship to all inherited cultural forms and unconventional personal bearing: Heidegger viewed himself as a revolutionary and iconoclast, a rugged outdoorsman who was scornful of conventional academic mandarin mores. And although

Heidegger viewed the debate as insufficiently confrontational, contemporary observers were of an entirely different mind. The neo-Kantian Cassirer, author of a four-volume work called *The Logic of Symbolic Forms*, viewed culture as the indispensable bulwark that kept the fragile contingency of the human existence at bay. At one point in the debate, he sought to bring matters to a head by asking whether Heidegger wished to "destroy" the "entire absoluteness and objectivity" of culture in favor of the vagaries of human finitude. The battle lines thus drawn, Heidegger insisted that contemporary culture was a form of narcosis that prevented individuals from realizing their true freedom. Instead of seeking refuge in its stupefying blandishments, individuals, he insisted, must be returned to their existential nakedness and "the hardness of fate."[59]

The trend toward a direct meditation on Being unmediated by the habitudes of Dasein continued with the important essays of the early 1930s: "On the Essence of Truth," "Plato's Doctrine of Truth," and "Hölderlin and the Essence of Poetry." In all of these texts, the question of the "meaning of Being"—which Heidegger came to view as fatally tainted by anthropological suppositions—cedes to the question of the "truth of Being." Even when Dasein makes an ephemeral reappearance in later texts (e.g., the 1947 "Letter on Humanism"), Heidegger takes to hyphenating it—Da-sein—to emphasize that what is at stake is the "there" of "Being" rather than an entity one might confuse with *human* being. Upon reviewing these texts, there can be no doubt that the *Kehre* or "turn" in Heidegger's thought dates from shortly after the appearance of *Being and Time*—not, as is commonly assumed, from the late 1930s.

A major indication of this drastic shift of emphasis may be found in the 1943 afterword to "What Is Metaphysics?" Whereas in *Being and Time* Heidegger had claimed that "Only so long as Dasein is—that is, the ontic possibility of the understanding of Being—'is there' Being," in the 1943 postscript his characterization of the relationship between Being and beings underwent a complete volte-face, stressing the sovereign primacy of Being: "Being *indeed* essences without beings, but beings never are without Being," claims Heidegger.[60] And in the contemporaneous "Recollection in Metaphysics" (1941) he declares emphatically in the same spirit: "The history of Being is neither the history of man and of humanity, nor the history of the human relation to beings and to Being. The history of Being is *Being itself and only Being.*"[61] How might one account for this revolutionary change of direction in Heidegger's approach?

Reconstructing Heidegger's developmental path, it is clear that his motivating concern was a reformulation of the question of Being. Yet, along the way, and coincident with his fateful abandonment of the "religion of his youth," Heidegger became convinced, in good Lutheran fashion, that one could only gain phenomenological access to our primordial encounter with Being via the route of Dasein or human being. It was precisely in this sense that he affirmed in *Being and Time* that "*Only so long as Dasein is . . . is there Being.*" His preoccupation with the classic texts of Protestant theology during the late 1910s and early 1920s, as well as his ensuing concentration on Aristotle's *Nichomachean Ethics* (where the modalities of *areté* or human excellence are at issue), reaffirmed his conviction that he was pursuing the right course. Clearly, from an existential standpoint, the results were provocative, fascinating, and virtually without philosophical precedent; the end result is the "existential analytic" of *Being and Time*, the crowning achievement of Heidegger's early philosophy.

Yet, from a scholastic-ontological standpoint, the results were disappointing. Despite its pathbreaking nature, Heidegger's great work of 1927 made little headway in addressing (let alone resolving) the question of Being. Commentators were at pains to reconcile the two apparently competing agendas of *Being and Time*, one existential, the other ontological. Clearly, the goal of fundamental ontology was to *reconcile* these two areas of concern. But given *Being and Time*'s inordinate focus on the vagaries of existential analysis—on the various modes of Dasein's Being-in-the-world—there was little room left for an autonomous treatment of the *Seinsfrage*.

In her encomium on the occasion of Heidegger's eightieth birthday, Hannah Arendt proffered the following astute observations concerning the ontological impetus underlying the Master's philosophy:

> The storm that blows through Heidegger's thinking—like the one that still sweeps toward us from Plato's works after thousands of years—does not originate from the century he happened to live

in. It comes from the primeval (*aus dem Uralten*), and what it leaves behind is something perfect that, like all that is perfect, returns home to the primeval.[62]

With these words, Arendt has faithfully captured the motivations underlying the "turn" in Heidegger's thought from existence to Being.

Heidegger's fascination with Being's primeval origins would, of course, take him back well beyond Plato. Ultimately, he perceived Plato's doctrine of Being as insufficiently radical. According to Heidegger, with his theory of ideas, Plato had introduced a fatal separation between sensible and supersensible worlds, a division that would become the signature of Western metaphysics in its entirely—as well as the hallmark (at least in Heidegger's estimation) of its perdition. The theory of ideas sought the truth of Being not in Being itself, but in something "subjective": the *Eidos* (idea) qua "representation"; and what was "representation" other than a subjective construct? Heidegger sought to undo the fatal conflation of Being with representational thinking via the antisubjectivist orientation of the "turn." Ultimately, he sought inspiration and direction in the pre-Socratic doctrines of Parmenides and Heraclitus; he believed that their philosophy offered a glimpse of authentic "proximity" to Being (*Nähe*) in its pristine, antediluvian glory—a glimpse unequaled by the representatives of post-Socratic thought. Kisiel speaks felicitously of Heidegger's primordial fascination with "the It that empowers theoretical judgments" (as in: "it occurred to me" or "it so happened"): "Throughout his long career, Heidegger will never seek to surpass this central insight which gives priority to the impersonal event enveloping the I which 'takes place' in that Event."[63] To be sure, the results often sounded far-fetched and ponderous to modern ears; to wit, his portentous claim in a 1938 lecture course that "Being is the trembling of the Godding."[64] Although it would be foolish to minimize the importance of his multiple—at times breathtaking—changes of philosophical direction, one can safely say that Heidegger's fundamental question remained the one he first posed in his dissertation on Brentano: the question of Being. Thus, the line from Hölderlin he was fond of citing would be an especially appropriate epigram to characterize the thrust of his life's work: "As you began, so will you remain."

CONCLUSION

SHORTLY after I completed my earlier study of Heidegger's political thought, a favorably disposed reviewer concluded his evaluation of my findings by wondering whether, in using the precepts of democratic politics to assess Heidegger's philosophical legacy, I wasn't employing an alien measure.[1] If during the Cold War such ethical issues seemed unclear and confused—after all, didn't both the Western democracies and the Soviet Union act on the basis of a sinister *Realpolitik* that left the moral high ground vacant?— following the collapse of communism, they seem much less so.

Alternatively, one might employ a "historicist" standard to judge the philosophical and political choices Heidegger made in order to "sympathetically" reconstruct his motivations, thereby suspending critical judgment. But the failure of this approach has been demonstrated by Ernst Nolte's recent political biography of the Freiburg sage, in which the controversial historian, employing the historicist technique of "identification" (*Einfühlung*), concludes that in opting for National Socialism in 1933, Heidegger essentially made "the right choice."[2] Yet Heidegger's (and Germany's) "choice" was extremely prejudicial to the interests of Germany's 500,000 Jewish citizens; it was a choice that boded catastrophically for Europe's future. To suggest that writing history is merely a matter of "choosing sides" (as did some of Nolte's allies in the German *Historikerstreit*) is plainly inadequate.[3] The bankruptcy of historicism and the value relativism it promoted was sealed by the Nazi catastrophe. Though the measure of historical judgment is rarely unambiguous, the refusal to search for some adequate measure is the path to despair.

Would one not, then, be justified in turning the reviewer's question around to inquire: what better standard might there be to judge Heidegger's legacy—and that of his children—than a democratic one? For if one renounces historicism as a criterion of judgment, as well as the ethos of "authentic decision" that Heidegger and Carl Schmitt revered, what choices then remain? It is a troubling paradox, redolent of the era of German romanticism, to discover a thought so penetrating and rich, yet by the same token so bereft of constructive moral prescriptions; a thought that by virtue of its sweeping critique of the present age has virtually deprived itself of prospects for normative grounding.

Although there are few better guides to the history of philosophy than Heidegger and his disciples, they, like Hegel, often succumbed to the error of confusing the history of philosophy with history itself; yet the logics of the two realms, philosophy and history, often proceed in opposite directions. Thus, for each of Heidegger's children (Marcuse is a lesser offender), following the Master's lead, Descartes's philosophy ("Cartesianism") becomes a figure for modernity and all its glorious indigence. And while Descartes's impact on modern philosophy was certainly great, his actual *historical* influence in these standard polemical accounts is grossly exaggerated. At issue is one of the congenital debilities of the mandarin intellectual tradition: an aristocratic scorn for considerations of social history and a predilection for contentless speculative claims. As one critic has aptly remarked: "In the case of the old mandarins the conservative alliance between 'metaphysics' and 'social pessimism' . . . was strong enough to keep republican thoughts at a distance; and, when such thoughts did occur, they impelled transcendence in an 'authoritarian' direction."[4] As we have seen, even Herbert Marcuse, who sought to redress modernity's shortcomings from the standpoint of the political left, openly flirted with the idea of "educational dictatorship" once it became clear that the revolution he sought had failed to materialize.[5]

Paradoxically, in the case of Heidegger's children, their intellectual weak point was also their strength. They manifested a capacity for probing philosophical insight that one risks losing sight of today. As a generational cohort, they never shied away from posing the "ultimate" questions about the meaning of human existence—questions that their contemporaries the logical positivists, following Wittgenstein's famous prescription at the end of the *Tractatus* ("about that which one cannot speak one should remain silent"), wished to banish from the realm of serious intellectual discourse. And although today the positivist legacy has been largely discredited, traces of its influence remain strong among analytical philosophers, who, following the later Wittgenstein, narrowly insist on philosophy's "therapeutic" *raison d'être*. According to this standpoint, the idea of establishing an independent critical agenda lies beyond philosophy's purview. It should instead confine itself to the modest goal of resolving linguistic misunderstandings.

Yet this inordinately restrictive idea of philosophy's mission seems unjustifiably resigned. Just when things start to get interesting—when matters of philosophical substance are raised—it is suggested that philosophy beat a hasty retreat. Philosophy thereby surrenders—voluntarily and without a fight, as it were—its capacity for "strong evaluation": its ability to make significant distinctions in the realms of culture, morality, and truth.[6] One cannot help but sense that in the last analysis, the rash concessions linguistic philosophy has made to a Humean-derived epistemological and normative skepticism are extreme. Thus, whereas under positivism truth was narrowly associated with "protocol sentences" or basic logical truths, more recently it has been identified with the context-dependent vagaries of "use." In both cases, the autonomy of philosophy has been demeaned: in the case of positivism, it has been sacrificed to philosophy of science; in that of analytical philosophy, to the conditions of ordinary language use.

The "existential" paradigm initiated by Heidegger and refashioned by his intellectual heirs merits attention insofar as it has managed to preserve a distinctive manner of philosophical questioning, one of whose virtues is a willingness to remain out of sync with the predominantly utilitarian orientation of the "globalized" contemporary lifeworld. In a sense, then, the value of the existential tradition is as much "aesthetic" as it is "material." It consists of an approach to thinking that refuses to be measured by instrumental criteria of use-value or effectiveness. In part, then, its value consists in the fact that it promotes a space for reflection about ultimate values or "ends" untainted by the pressures of "everydayness." It thereby manages to recapture, however momentarily, the spiritual autonomy prized by the age of German classicism. Thus, as the theme of her last book, Hannah Arendt chose "the life of the mind" in order to emphasize a set of philosophical themes that endured above and beyond the changing winds of intellectual fashion.

If there is an obvious "deficit" characteristic of existential thought, this has to do with its lack of commitment to the values of "public reason"—an ethos that is the mainstay of a democratic political culture. As Kant once characterized the value of public reason: "The touchstone whereby we decide whether our holding a thing to be true is conviction or mere persuasion is external, namely the possibility of communicating it and of finding it to be *valid for all human reason.*"[7] The lack of confidence in public reason on the part of Heidegger and his philosophical heirs is surely in part a generational phenomenon overdetermined by the disorientation of the interwar years. To be sure, if ever there was an epoch in which claims to reason and reasonableness seemed more honored in the breach, this was surely one. Yet, for those of us who seek to ascertain the contemporary relevance of the "existential paradigm," this deficiency cannot be passed over in silence. Instead, it must form an essential part of the equation.

Once again, Marcuse's quasi-exceptional status—the fact that, unlike Heidegger's other disciples, he approached the Master's thought from the philosophical left—allowed him a measure of privileged insight concerning the intellectual bases underlying the fascist repositioning of Heidegger's philosophy circa 1933. Thus, among Heidegger's children, he was the first to perceive the elective affinities between Heidegger's thought and the Nazi cause he made his own for a time.

In "The Struggle Against Liberalism in the Totalitarian View of the State" (1934), Marcuse tellingly delineated the troubling family resemblances between Heidegger's philosophy and the illiberal worldview espoused by the Nazis and their supporters. In Marcuse's eyes, much hinged on Heidegger's self-conscious abandonment of the Kantian ideal of the "autonomy of reason" that had been promoted by classical German philosophy. As Marcuse remarks, "Kant had obligated man to self-given duty, to free self-determination as the only fundamental law." He believed in the existence of inalienable human rights, which *"man cannot surrender even if he so wills."* Existentialism, conversely, paved the way for its own sorry end, observes Marcuse, insofar as its *"struggle against reason [drove] it blindly into the arms of the reigning powers."*[8] Hegel continued to celebrate the "Idea" as "all that holds human life together and that has merit and validity," as the "consciousness of truth and right." But as Carl Schmitt knew well, on January 30, 1933 (the infamous date of the Nazi *Machtergreifung*) "Hegel died"—a development that Schmitt personally welcomed.[9] As of that fateful date, German Idealism's utopian dream of reconciling reality and the Idea went up in smoke. In keeping with this new mood of biopolitical realism, Heidegger, in his desire to recast truth as "concrete," declared that "The *Führer* himself is the German reality and its law."[10] Only an understanding of Heidegger's children that appreciates their relationship to the German catastrophe and the traumas it bred will prove capable of doing justice to their powerful and complex philosophical legacy.

Preface

1. *The Politics of Being: The Political Thought of Martin Heidegger* (New York: Columbia University Press, 1980).

2. *The Heidegger Controversy: A Critical Reader*, 2nd ed. (Cambridge: MIT Press, 1993).

3. This anecdote was related to me in Germany by a philosopher who was a close friend of Marcuse's.

Prologue: "Todesfuge" and "Todtnauberg"

1. Martin Heidegger, *Being and Time*, trans. J. Macquerrie and E. Robinson (New York: Harper and Row, 1962).

2. John Felstiner, *Paul Celan: Poet, Survivor, Jew* (New Haven: Yale University Press, 1995), p. 245.

3. The title of a recent biography of Heidegger by Rüdiger Safranski: *Heidegger: Ein Meister aus Deutschland* (Munich: Hanser Verlag, 1994). English translation: *Martin Heidegger: Beyond Good and Evil* (Cambridge: Harvard University Press, 1998). For a very different reading of the Celan-Heidegger encounter, see Richard Rorty, "A Master from Germany," *New York Times Book Review* (3 May 1998): 12.

4. This situation was especially characteristic of the early years of the regime. For more on this problem, see my article on the attitudes of Hans-Georg Gadamer and the German classics profession, "Fascism and Hermeneutics," *The New Republic* (May 15, 2000): 36–45. See also T. Laugstein, *Philosophie Verhältnisse im deutschen Faschismus* (Hamburg: Argument Verlag, 1990); and '*Die besten Geister der Nation': Philosophie und Nationalsozialismus*, I. Korotin, ed. (Wien: Picus Verlag, 1994).

5. See, for example, Herbert Marcuse, in a plaintive and moving letter to Heidegger written in 1948: "Many of us have long awaited a statement from you, a statement that would clearly and finally free you from such identification [with the regime]. . . . Common sense (also among intellectuals) . . . refuses to view you as a philosopher, because philosophy and Nazism are irreconcilable. In this conviction common sense is justified. Once again: you (and we) can only combat the identification of your person and your work with Nazism (and thereby the

dissolution of your philosophy) if you make a public avowal of your changed views"; cited in Wolin, ed., *The Heidegger Controversy: A Critical Reader* (Cambridge, Mass.: MIT Press, 1993), 161.

6. On this problem in Heidegger, see Berel Lang, *Heidegger's Silence* (Ithaca: Cornell University Press, 1997). See also A. Milchman and A. Rosenberg, eds., *Martin Heidegger and the Holocaust* (Atlantic Heights, N.J.: Humanities Press, 1996).

Chapter 1—Introduction: Philosophy and Family Romance

1. Needless to say, there is inevitably something arbitrary about such hypothetical kudos. The other likely contenders would be Leo Strauss, Antonio Gramsci, and Carl Schmitt. The thought of the latter two has been compromised as a result as a result of proximity to left- and right-wing political extremism. Strauss—for all his astuteness as a reader of philosophical texts—like his fellow German-Jewish émigrés, seems strangely out of touch with the demands of modern politics, despite his fleeting influence on American neoconservatism. On this connection, see Shadia Drury, *Leo Strauss and the American Right* (New York: St. Martin's Press, 1997). For a comparison of Strauss and Arendt, see *Hannah Arendt and Leo Strauss: German Emigrés and American Political Thought After World War II*, eds. P. Kielmansegg et al. (Cambridge: Cambridge University Press, 1995).

2. Walter Benjamin, *The Origin of German Tragic Drama*, trans. J. Osborne (London: New Left Books, 1977), p. 182; emphasis added.

3. For a classic study of modern poetry along these lines, see Harold Bloom, *Anxiety and Influence* (New York: Oxford University Press, 1997).

4. For an important discussion of this problem in Heidegger's work, see Jürgen Habermas, "Martin Heidegger: Work and *Weltanschauung*," in *The New Conservatism: Cultural Criticism and the Historians' Debate*, trans. S. Nicholsen (Cambridge: MIT Press, 1989), 140–172.

5. For a discussion of nihilism as a generational phenomenon, see Robert Wohl, *The Generation of 1914* (Cambridge: Harvard University Press, 1979).

6. Hugo Ott, *Martin Heidegger: A Political Life* (New York: Basic Books, 1993); Victor Farias, *Heidegger and Nazism* (Philadelphia: Temple University Press, 1989). On this question, see also Michael Zimmerman, *Heidegger's Confrontation with Modern Technology* (Bloomington: Indiana University Press, 1989).

7. "Herbert Marcuse-Martin Heidegger: An Exchange of Letters," in Wolin, ed., *The Heidegger Controversy*, 161. This fascinating letter has recently been reprinted in Herbert Marcuse, *Technology, War, and Fascism*, D. Kellner, ed. (New York: Routledge, 1997), 263–67.

8. Martin Heidegger, "Why We Remain in the Provinces," in *The Weimar Sourcebook*, M. Jay, A. Kaes, and E. Dimendberg, eds. (Berkeley and Los Angeles: University of California, 1992), 426–28.

9. Martin Heidegger, "German Students," in Wolin, ed., *The Heidegger Controversy*, 47.

10. Karl Löwith, *My Life in Germany Before and After 1933* (Urbana: University of Illinois Press, 1994), 60.

11. Letter from Arendt to Jaspers, *Hannah Arendt-Karl Jaspers Correspondence*, 48.

12. Edmund Husserl, Letter of May 4, 1933, in *Martin Heidegger im dritten Reich* ed. B. Martin (Dormstadt: Wissenschaftliche Buchgesellschaft, 1989), 149.

13. Ulrich Sieg, "Die Verjudung des deutschen Geistes," *Die Zeit* 52 (22 December 1989): 19.

14. "Ein Gespräch mit Max Müller," *Freibürger Universitätsblätter* 92 (June 1986): 13–31.

15. Léopoldine Weizmann, "Heidegger: était-il Nazi?" *Etudes*, 638.

16. The story of Heidegger's denunciation of Baumgarten is told by Victor Farias in *Heidegger and Nazism* 209–211. See also Thomas Sheehan, "Heidegger and the Nazis," *New York Review of Books* (15 June 1988): 38–47.

17. Karl Jaspers, "Letter to the Freiburg University Denazification Committee," in *The Heidegger Controversy*, 159.

18. Oral communication from Heidegger biographer Dr. Hugo Ott. For an account of Heidegger's breakdown, see Ott, *Martin Heidegger: A Political Life*, 309–51.

19. On this problem see Johannes Fritsche, *Historical Destiny and National Socialism in Heidegger's* Being and Time (Berkeley and Los Angeles: University of California Press, 1999); Richard Wolin, *The Politics of Being: The Political Thought of Martin Heidegger* (New York: Columbia University Press, 1990); and Tom Rockmore, *On Heidegger's Nazism and Philosophy* (Berkeley and Los Angeles: University of California Press, 1992).

20. See Arendt, "'What Remains? The Language Remains': A Conversation with Günter Gaus," in *Essays in Understanding: 1930–1954*, J. Kohn, ed. (New York: Harcourt Brace, 1994), 1–23.

21. See Löwith, "European Nihilism: Reflections on the Spiritual and Historical Background of the European War," in R. Wolin, ed., *Martin Heidegger and European Nihilism* (New York: Columbia University Press, 1995) pp. 173–224; and Löwith, *From Hegel to Nietzsche* (New York: Columbia University Press, 1991), *passim*.

22. Hannah Arendt, *The Human Condition* (Chicago: University of Chicago Press, 1958), 1–2. In the passage cited, Arendt surely exaggerates the pervasiveness of the longing to "escape from men's imprisonment to the earth." Though at times such attitudes may have been expressed, they seem to have been a distinctly minoritarian view. Moreover, it was often difficult to draw a clear-cut distinction between the longing for "escape" and the glorification of new technological possibilities. *Pace* Arendt, the predominant sentiment at the time praised humanity's capacity to explore unknown horizons. Hence, the prevalent comparisons with the Columbian "age of explorations."

23. Hans Jonas, *The Imperative of Responsibility: In Search of an Ethics for the Technological Age* (Chicago: University of Chicago Press, 1984), 201–2.

24. The phrase "planetary technology," employed by Heidegger on numerous occasions, bespeaks his profound indebtedness to the apocalyptical prognostications of Ernst Jünger, who first coined this epithet in the early 1930s. For more on Jünger, see Elliot Neaman, A Dubious Past: Ernst Jünger and the Politics of Literature After Nazism (Berkeley: University of California Press, 1999).

25. Anson Rabinbach, In the Shadow of Catastrope: German Intellectuals Between Apocalpyse and Enlightenment (Berkeley and Los Angeles: University of California Press, 1997), 27.

26. Georg Lukács, The Theory of the Novel (Cambridge: MIT Press, 1971), 21.

27. Nietzsche, The Will to Power, trans. W. Kaufmann and R. J. Hollingdale (New York: Vintage, 1967), 7, 9. For an important study of the reception of Nietzsche's philosophy in a German context, see Steven Aschheim, The Nietzsche Legacy in Germany: 1890–1990 (Berkeley and Los Angeles: University of California Press, 1992).

28. Ernest Gellner, Words and Things: A Critical Account of Linguistic Philosophy and a Study in Ideology (London: Victor Gollancz, 1959), 20.

29. See Richard Wolin, "The House that Jacques Built: Deconstruction and Strong Evaluation," in The Terms of Cultural Criticism: The Frankfurt School, Existentialism, and Poststructuralism (New York: Columbia University Press, 1992).

Chapter 2—The German-Jewish Dialogue: Way Stations of Misrecognition

1. Arno J. Mayer, Why Did the Heavens Not Darken? (New York: Pantheon, 1988), 39.

2. Franz Neumann, Behemoth: The Structure and Practice of National Socialism (New York: Harper and Row, 1966), 121; emphasis added. Neumann's study was first published in 1942; a second edition appeared in 1944. In a parallel deflection of German historical culpability, George Mosse has observed: "Ironically, before the first World War it was France rather than Germany or Austria that seemed likely to become the home of a successful racist and National Socialist movement." See Mosse, Towards the Final Solution: A History of European Racism (New York: Howard Fertig, 1974), 14.

3. Cited in George Mosse, German Jews Beyond Judaism (Bloomington: University of Indiana Press, 1985), 14.

4. See Hannah Arendt-Karl Jaspers Correspondence, 1926–1969, L. Kohler and H. Saner, eds. (New York: Harcourt Brace, 1992), 198.

5. H. I. Bach, The German Jew: A Synthesis of Judaism and Western Civilization, 1730–1930 (Oxford: Oxford University Press, 1984), 143.

6. Sigmund Freud, The Standard Edition of the Complete Psychological Works (London: Hogarth, 1959), 273–74. Although he went on to speculate: "Because I was a Jew I found myself free from many prejudices which restricted others in the use of their intellect; and as a Jew I was prepared to join the Opposition and to do

without agreement with the 'compact majority.'" For more on Freud's relationship to Judaism, see Yosef Yerushalmi, *Freud's Moses: Judaism Terminable and Interminable* (New Haven: Yale University Press, 1991).

7. Kafka, *Dearest Father* (New York: Schocken, 1964), 173.

8. Bach, *The German Jew*, 167.

9. Kafka, *Letters to Milena* (New York: Schocken, 1990), 219. In a letter to Gershom Scholem, Walter Benjamin emphasized Kafka's importance as a denizen (and bard) of modernity. Kafka is an individual "confronted with that reality of ours which realizes itself theoretically, for example, in modern physics, and practically in the technology of modern warfare. What I mean to say is that this reality can virtually no longer be experienced by an individual, and that Kafka's world, frequently of such playfulness and interlaced with angels, is the exact complement of his era which is preparing to do away with the inhabitants of this planet on a considerable scale." See Benjamin, *Illuminations* (New York: Schocken, 1969), 143.

10. Stephen Magill, "Defense and Introspection: German Jewry, 1914," in Bronsen, *Jews and Germans from 1866–1933* (Heidelberg: Carl Winter, 1979), 220.

11. Kafka, *Letters to Friends, Family, and Editors* (New York: Schocken, 1978), 289.

12. Saul Friedländer, *Nazi Germany and the Jews* (New York: HarperCollins, 1996), 84.

13. Cited in Jacques Le Rider, *Modernité viennoise et crises de l'identité* (Paris: Presses Universitaires de France, 1990), 215.

14. Cited in Hans-Ulrich Wehler, *The German Empire: 1871–1918* (Leamington Spa: Berghahn, 1985), 219.

15. Ernst Jünger, "Uber Nationalismus und Judenfrage," *Suddeutsche Monatshefte* 27 (1930): 845. Upon hearing a similar sentiment expressed by a German mandarin-type during the late 1940s, the philosopher Jürgen Habermas notes that he paid little heed, since he was too engrossed in reading authors such as Husserl, Max Scheler, Georg Simmel, and Ludwig Wittgenstein.

16. See Richard Wagner, *Judaism in Music and Other Essays* (Lincoln: University of Nebraska Press, 1995); see also Otto Dov Kulka, "Richard Wagner und die Anfänge des modernen Antisemitismus," in *Bulletin des Leo Baeck Instituts* 4 (December 1961): 281–300.

17. Cited in Habermas, *Philosophical-Political Profiles*, 41. For more on Schmitt's anti-Semitism, see Raphael Gross, *Carl Schmitt und die Juden* (Frankfurt am Main: Suhrkamp Verlag, 2000).

18. See Ray Monk, *Ludwig Wittgenstein: The Duty of Genius* (London: Jonathan Cape, 1990), 394.

19. Isaiah Berlin, "Jewish Slavery and Emancipation," *Jewish Chronicle* (21 September 1951).

20. Gershom Scholem, *On Jews and Judaism in Crisis* (New York: Schocken, 1978), 80.

21. Ibid., 83.

22. Dan Diner, "Negative Symbiosis: Germans and Jews after Auschwitz," in P. Baldwin, *Reworking the Past: Hitler, the Holocaust, and the Historians' Debate* (Boston: Beacon Press, 1990).

23. Enzo Traverso, *The Jews and Germany*, trans. D. Weissbort (Lincoln: University of Nebraska Press, 1995), 40.

24. Fritz Stern, *Dreams and Delusions: The Drama of German History* (New York: Alfred Knopf, 1987), 111.

25. See Shulamit Volkov, "The Dynamics of Dissimilation: Ostjuden and German Jews," in *The Jewish Response to German Culture: From the Enlightenment to the Second World War*, J. Reinharz and W. Schatzberg, eds. (Hanover and London: University Press of New England, 1985), 195–211; and Amos Funkenstein, "Dialectics of Assimilation," *Jewish Social Studies* 1 (winter 1995): 1–14.

26. Martin Buber, "Jüdische Renaissance," *Ost und West* 1 (1901): 7–10.

27. Moritz Goldstein, "Deutsch-jüdischer Parnass," *Der Kunstwart* 25 (March 1912): 283.

28. Ismar Schorsch, "German Judaism: From Confession to Culture," in *Die Juden im Nationalsozialistschen Deutschland, 1933–1943*, A. Paucker, ed. (Tübingen: J.C. B. Mohr, 1986), 68. For a lucid survey of these trends, see Michael Brenner, *The Renaissance of Jewish Culture in Weimar Germany* (New Haven: Yale University Press, 1996).

Chapter 3—Hannah Arendt: Kultur, "Thoughtlessness," and Polis Envy

1. Thomas Mann, "Germany and the Germans" (Washington: Library of Congress, 1945), 18.

2. Heidegger, *Introduction to Metaphysics* (New Haven: Yale University Press, 1959), 150; Heidegger, "Only a God Can Save Us," in R. Wolin, ed., *The Heidegger Controversy*, 111.

3. For a comparison, see Ian Kershaw and Moishe Lewin, eds., *Stalinism and Nazism: Dictatorships in Comparison* (Cambridge: Cambridge University Press, 1997).

4. For an important recent study of anti-Semitism that, in many respects, picks up where Arendt's analysis leaves off, see Albert Lindemann, *Esau's Tears: Modern Anti-Semitism and the Rise of the Jews* (Cambridge: Cambridge University Press, 1997).

5. Karl Löwith, *My Life in Germany Before and After 1933*, 45.

6. See Hannah Arendt/Martin Heidegger, *Briefe: 1925–1975* (Frankfurt: Klostermann Verlag, 1998), 21–25.

7. Elzbieta Ettinger, *Hannah Arendt/Martin Heidegger* (New Haven: Yale University Press, 1995), 15.

8. Martin Heidegger, "Why We Remain in the Provinces," 426.

9. Heidegger, "The Self-Assertion of the German University," in *The Heidegger Controversy*, 34.

10. Cited in Claudia Schorcht, *Die Philosophie an den Bayerischen Universitäten 1933–45* (Erlangen: Harald Fischer, 1990), 161.

11. For an account of this episode, see Rüdiger Safranski, *Martin Heidegger: Beyond Good and Evil*, 327.

12. Ettinger, *Hannah Arendt/Martin Heidegger*, 15.

13. Hannah Arendt/Martin Heidegger, *Briefe, 1925–1975* (Frankfurt am main: Klostermann, 1998) 76.

14. Ibid., 66.

15. Ibid., 150.

16. Hannah Arendt/Heinrich Blücher, *Briefe, 1936–1968* (Munich: Piper Verlag, 1996), 208.

17. See Sartre's classical account in *Anti-Semite and Jew* (New York: Grove Press, 1960).

18. Arendt, *The Jew as Pariah*, R. Feldman, ed. (New York: Grove Press, 1978), 92.

19. Arendt, *Essays in Understanding, 1930–1954*, Jerome Kohn, ed. (New York: Harcourt Brace, 1994), 6, 12.

20. *The Diaries of Franz Kafka*, 111.

21. Richard Bernstein, *Hannah Arendt and the Jewish Question* (Cambridge: MIT Press, 1996), 28.

22. Arendt, *The Jew as Pariah*, 247.

23. Bernstein, *Hannah Arendt and the Jewish Question*, 29.

24. See David Sorkin, *The Transformation of German Jewry, 1780–1840* (New York: Oxford University Press, 1987), 23: "Underlying the discussions of emancipation was an image of a corrupt and debased Jewish people. Because of this image, emancipation was to become linked to the notion of the Jews' moral regeneration. The emancipation debate essentially turned on whether this regeneration was possible, who was to be responsible for it, and when and under what conditions it was to take place."

25. Wilhelm Marr, *Vom Jüdischen Kriegsschauplatz: Eine Streitsschrift* (Berne, 1879), 19; cited in Peter Pulzer, *The Rise of Political Anti-Semitism in Germany and Austria* (Cambridge: Harvard University Press, 1988), 48.

26. Hermann Cohen, "Germanness and Jewishness," in *Reason and Hope* (New York: W. W. Norton, 1971), 187.

27. Heinrich von Treitschke, *A History of Germany in the Nineteenth Century*, vol. 4, (Chicago: University of Chicago Press, 1975), 556.

28. Cited in Habermas, *Philosophical-Political Profiles*, 22.

29. Peter Pulzer, *The Rise of Political Anti-Semitism in Germany and Austria*, 68. See also Steven Aschheim, *Brothers and Strangers: The East European Jew in German and German Jewish Consciousness, 1800–1923* (Madison: University of Wisconsin Press, 1982), 78: "The historical image of the Jew had never died in Germany and was available for exploitation in appropriate structural crises. Onto the traditional

fear and distrust of the Talmud and ghetto Jew was grafted the notion of the modern Jew, characterless and destructive in intent."

30. In his dissertation written the previous year, *The Role of the Individual in Fellow Being*, Karl Löwith also directly challenged Heidegger's concept of "Being-with" in *Being and Time*. However, Arendt does not refer to Löwith's dissertation in *Love and Saint Augustine*. For Löwith's critique, see Chapter 4.

31. Arendt, *Love and Saint Augustine* (Chicago: University of Chicago Press, 1995), 178. I thank Samuel Moyn for pointing out this aspect of Arendt's critique.

32. See Fritz Ringer, *The Decline of the German Mandarins: The German Academic Community, 1890–1933* (Cambridge: Harvard University Press, 1969).

33. Arendt, *Love and Saint Augustine*, 100; emphasis added.

34. Ibid., 102.

35. Arendt, *The Human Condition*, 53; emphasis added.

36. Arendt, *Rahel Varnhagen: The Life of a Jewess*, ed. L. Weissberg, trans. R. and C. Winston (Baltimore: Johns Hopkins, 1997), 91.

37. Arendt, *Essays in Understanding*, 11. For Heidegger's letter to Husserl, see Bernd Martin, ed., *Martin Heidegger und das dritte Reich* (Darmstadt: Wissenschaftliche Buchgesellschaft, 1989), 149.

38. Arendt, *Rahel Varnhagen*, 85; emphasis added.

39. Ibid., 88.

40. For Weber's discussion of the Jew as pariah, see his *Ancient Judaism* (New York: Free Press, 1967).

41. Arendt, *Rahel Varnhagen*, 91.

42. Arendt, "What Is Existenz Philosophy?" *Partisan Review* 13(1) (1946), 46; emphasis added.

43. Thomas Mann, *Addresses Delivered at the Library of Congress, 1942–1949*, 51, 65.

44. Arendt/Heidegger, *Briefwechsel*, 75.

45. Hannah Arendt/Karl Jaspers, *Correspondence* (New York: Harcourt and Brace, 1925), 142.

46. Arendt, "What is *Existenz* Philosophy?" 48; emphasis added.

47. Arendt, "Martin Heidegger at Eighty," in M. Murray, ed., *Martin Heidegger and Modern Philosophy* (New Haven: Yale University Press, 1978), 302. See also Theodor Adorno, *The Jargon of Authenticity*, trans. K. Tarnowski (New York: Seabury, 1975). For Hugo Ott's refutation of Heidegger's anti-Nazism, see Ott, *Martin Heidegger: A Political Life*, 235–260.

48. Cited in Seyla Benhabib, "The Personal Is Not the Political," *The Boston Review* 24(5) (October–November 1999): 46; emphasis added.

49. Hannah Arendt/Karl Jaspers, *Correspondence*, 457.

50. Hannah Arendt/Martin Heidegger, *Briefe*, 94.

51. Seyla Benhabib, "The Personal Is Not the Political," 47.

52. Arendt, *Eichmann in Jerusalem* (New York: Penguin, 1963), 117, 125–26; emphasis added.

53. Yehuda Bauer, *History of the Holocaust* (New York: F. Watts, 1982), 166–67.

54. Scholem, "An Exchange of Letters between Gershom Scholem and Hannah Arendt," in *The Jew as Pariah*, 243.

55. Michael Marrus, "A History of the Holocaust: A Survey of Recent Literature," *Journal of Modern History* 59 (March 1987): 149.

56. For a fictionalized account of Rumkowski's reign, see Leslie Epstein, *The King of the Jews* (New York: Coward, McCann & Geoghegan, 1979).

57. For the remark about Eichmann as a "convert to Judaism," see Arendt, *Eichmann in Jerusalem*, 40.

58. Ibid., 58.

59. Hannah Arendt/Karl Jaspers, *Correspondence*, 586.

60. Raul Hilberg, *The Politics of Memory: The Journal of a Holocaust Historian* (Chicago: Ivan Dee, 1996), 149–50.

61. For more on this issue, see Bernstein, *Hannah Arendt and the Jewish Question*, 137–53.

62. Hans Mommsen, "Hannah Arendt and the Eichmann Trial," *From Weimar to Auschwitz*, (Princeton: Princeton University Press, 1991), 271, 255.

63. Tocqueville, *The Old Regime and the French Revolution*, trans. S. Gilbert (Garden City: Anchor Books, 1955).

64. Arendt, "Organized Guilt and Universal Responsibility," *The Jew as Pariah*, 230; emphasis added. For more on the so-called functionalist approach to Nazism, see Ian Kershaw, *The Nazi Dictatorship: Problems and Perspectives of Interpretation* (London: E. Arnold, 1993); Christopher Browning, *Ordinary Men: Police Battalion 101* (New York: HarperCollins, 1992), especially chapter 5 ; Hans Mommsen, *From Weimar to Auschwitz*; and Omer Bartov, *Murderers in Our Midst: The Holocaust and Modern Mass Death* (New York: Oxford University Press, 1995).

65. Arendt, "Organized Guilt and Universal Responsibility," 229.

66. Ibid., 231.

67. Ibid., 234.

68. Ibid., 232; emphasis added.

69. Of course, this is not to claim that other groups did not suffer immensely. Yet, even Romany and homosexuals, who were also killed in great numbers, were not the explicit targets of an *Endlösung* or Final Solution.

70. As Dan Diner has remarked, "Blücher's inspiration and influence on Hannah Arendt is still a subject for research. . . . Especially in the last and third part of *Origins*, the discursive structure of an ex-communist narrative makes itself conspicuous"; Diner, "Hannah Arendt Reconsidered: On the Banal and the Evil of Her Holocaust Narrative," *New German Critique* 71 (spring-summer 1997): 187. In a 1963 letter to Jaspers, Arendt remarks that Blücher's "opinion of the Jewish people is not always what one might wish"; Arendt/Jaspers, *Correspondence*, 511.

71. Arendt/Jaspers, *Correspondence*, 542.

72. Margaret Canovan, *Hannah Arendt: A Reinterpretation of Her Political Philosophy* (Cambridge: Cambridge University Press, 1992), 20.

73. Steven Aschheim, *Culture and Catastrophe* (London: MacMillan, 1996), 111–12.

74. See for example, Richard Bernstein, *Hannah Arendt and the Jewish Question*, especially chapter 7.

75. Arendt, *Eichmann in Jerusalem*, 26.

76. Diner, "Hannah Arendt Reconsidered," 185.

77. See, for example, Dana Villa's *Arendt and Heidegger: The Fate of the Political* (Princeton: Princeton University Press, 1996), whose main failing is a blissful lack of awareness concerning the historical and cultural matrix in which the political thought of Arendt and Heidegger developed and, as such, is paradigmatic of the aforementioned decontextualized approaches. Thus, Villa, following Arendt and Heidegger, uncritically appropriates a mass of pejorative characterizations of modern society (e.g., trafficking in timeworn clichés such as "the alienation of modern man"), judgments that must be documented, verified, and elaborated instead of merely assumed. The problem is that Arendt's celebration of "aestheticized politics" and "action for action's sake"—positions she freely endorses in *The Human Condition*—stands in perilous proximity to the "actionist" and "decisionist" critiques of liberal democracy accepted by the political right during the 1920s. The more closely one examines the (to be sure, intellectually fascinating) antimodernist biases of Arendt's political thought, the harder it is to reconcile it with any historically known incarnation of democratic practice, ancient or modern. (Her belated endorsement of council democracy represents a partial exception to this verdict.) By failing to take seriously the frankly antiliberal context in which Arendt's political philosophy emerged, Villa's interpretation unreflectively inherits a welter of dilemmas proper to German antidemocratic thought of the 1920s. Finally, the attempt to view Arendt as a "postmodernist" (as in the claim that her political thought attempts to "think political action and judgment *without grounds*") seriously misconstrues the classicist biases of her approach to political theory.

78. On this point, see Pierre Bourdieu's important study, *The Political Ontology of Martin Heidegger*, trans. P. Collier (Stanford: Stanford University Press, 1991).

79. Arendt, *The Human Condition*, 23.

80. Karl Marx, "Theses on Feuerbach," in *The Marx-Engels Reader*, R. Tucker, ed. (New York: Norton, 1978), 143.

81. Herbert Marcuse, "The Foundations of Historical Materialism," in *Studies in Critical Philosophy*, trans. J. de Bres (Boston: Beacon, 1972), 13–14. See also Michael Walzer's criticisms of Arendt's "republicanism," her prejudicial attempt to privilege citizenship or political "virtue" at the expense of "work" and "sociality": "In practice, work, though it begins in necessity, takes on a value of its own—expressed in commitment to a career, pride in a job well done, a sense of camaraderie in the workplace. All of these are competitive with the values of citizenship"; Walzer, "The Concept of Civil Society," in M. Walzer, ed., *Tower Is a Global Civil Society* (Providence: Berghahn Books, 1995), 10.

82. Charles Taylor, *Sources of the Self: The Making of Modern Identity* (Cambridge: Harvard University Press, 1989), 292. See the revealing remarks by Philip

Ariès: "The historians taught us long ago that the King was never left alone. But in fact until the end of the seventeenth century, *nobody was ever left alone*. The density of social life made isolation virtually impossible, and people who managed to shut themselves up in a room for some time were regarded as exceptional characters"; *Centuries of Childhood*, trans. R. Baldick (New York: Knopf, 1962), 398.

83. John Milton, *Paradise Lost*, VIII, ll. 192–94.

84. For a convincing rebuttal of the claim that liberal political thought remains devoid of virtue, see Peter Berkowitz, *Virtue and the Making of Modern Liberalism* (Princeton: Princeton University Press, 1999).

85. Arendt, *The Human Condition*, 31.

86. See François Furet, *Interpreting the French Revolution* (Cambridge: Cambridge University Press, 1979).

87. To be sure, Arendt's Aristotle has been Heideggerianized. As Villa remarks, "Thus, when Arendt takes up Aristotle's distinction between acting and making [*phronesis* and *poesis*], she is in fact reformulating *praxis* as authentic *existenz*" (*Arendt and Heidegger*, 140). See also Benhabib, *The Reluctant Modernism of Hannah Arendt*, 107: "Arendt, as opposed to Heidegger, found in Aristotle's concept of praxis the key to a new revaluation of human action as interaction unfolding within a space of appearances."

88. On this point, see the important book by Donald Sassoon, *One-Hundred Years of Socialism* (New York: The New Press, 1996).

89. J. Cohen and A. Arato, *Civil Society and Political Theory* (Cambridge: MIT Press, 1992), 177.

90. Karl Jaspers, *Notizen zu Martin Heidegger* (Munich: Piper Verlag, 1988), 274.

91. Her veneration of workers' councils, however, harbors some serious misrepresentations of the movement's content and orientation. As Arato and Cohen point out in *Civil Society and Political Theory* (p. 199): "Her argument [with reference to workers' councils] is entirely fictitious, though, since the movements from 1848 to 1956 to which she refers cannot be represented as having no social and economic interests and demands, and even less as not playing a major part in the economic reproduction of society." For a more recent account of the ways in which Arendt's political thought has influenced the German left after reunification, see Jan Müller, "Intellectuals and the Berlin Republic," *New German Critique* 72 (1998): 178–81.

92. Heidegger, *Hölderlins Hymnen "Germanien" und "Der Rhein"* (Frankfurt: Klostermann, 1980), 210.

93. Heidegger, *Introduction to Metaphysics*, 133.

94. Ibid., 153.

95. Arendt, *The Human Condition*, 211.

96. Arendt, *On Revolution* (New York: Penguin, 1963), 275.

97. Ibid., 279–80.

98. Canovan, *Hannah Arendt*, 135.

99. Arendt, *The Human Condition*, p. 205; emphasis added.

100. Nietzsche's vindication of "great politics" appears in his late works, such

as *Beyond Good and Evil* (New York: Vintage, 1968): "The time for petty politics is over; the very next century will bring the fight for the dominion of the earth— the *compulsion* to great politics"; section 208. For a parallel critique of Arendt's political philosophy, see Sheldon Wolin, "Hannah Arendt: Democracy and the Political," in *Hannah Arendt: Critical Essays*, L. and S. Hinchman, eds. (Albany: State University of New York Press, 1994), 289–307.

101. Hannah Arendt, "Karl Marx and the Tradition of Western Political Thought"; cited in Canovan, *Hannah Arendt*, 142.

Chapter 4—Karl Löwith: The Stoic Response to Modern Nihilism

1. Löwith, *From Hegel to Nietzsche: The Revolution in Nineteenth-Century Thought*, trans. David Green (New York: Columbia University Press, 1989); *Meaning in History* (Chicago: University of Chicago Press, 1949); *Max Weber and Karl Marx* (London: Allen and Unwin, 1982). See also Löwith, *Nature, History, and Existentialism*, A. Levinson, ed. (Evanston: Northwestern University Press, 1966); Leo Strauss's extremely favorable review of *From Hegel to Nietzsche*, in *Social Research* 8 (4) (1941).

2. Löwith, "The Historical Background of European Existentialism," *Nature, History and Existentialism*, 7.

3. Goethe, letter to Zelter, June 6, 1825, *Goethes Briefe und Briefe an Goethe*, vol. 4 (Munich: Beck, 1988), 146.

4. Charles Baudelaire, "Fusées," in Oeuvres Complètes (Paris: Gallimard, 1975), 665–66.

5. Nietzsche, *The Will to Power*, 861–862, 866, 868; emphasis added.

6. For an excellent discussion of Löwith's endorsement of the so-called secularization thesis (with a sideways glance at Heidegger and Carl Schmitt) focusing on political implications, see Jeffrey Barash, "The Sense of History: On the Political Implications of Karl Lowith's Concept of Secularization," *History and Theory* 37 (February 1998): 69–83. See also Robert Wallace, "Progress, Secularization, and Modernity: the Löwith-Blumenberg Debate," *New German Critique* 22 (1981): 63–79. For an influential rejoinder to Löwith, see Hans Blumenberg, *The Legitimacy of the Modern Age*, trans. R. Wallace (Cambridge: MIT Press, 1983), especially 27–35.

7. Löwith, "Welt und Menschenwelt," *Sämtliche Schriften* I (Stuttgart: Metzler, 1981), 302.

8. Löwith, *Meaning in History*, v, vi. For a good treatment of Löwith's intellectual trajectory in relationship to Stoicism, see Josef Chytry, "Zur Wiedergewinnen des Kosmos: Karl Löwith contra Martin Heidegger," in *Zur philosophischen Aktualität Heideggers*, D. Papenfuss and Otto Pöggeler, eds. (Frankfurt: Klostermann, 1990), 71–99.

9. Friedrich Nietzsche, *Thus Spoke Zarathustra*, trans. R. J. Hollingdale (New York: Penguin, 1969), Part I, section 5. *Human, All-Too-Human* dates from 1880.

10. "As Löwith remarks in "The Historical Background of European Existentialism," (pp. 15–16): "From Napoleon and Bismarck, Nietzsche learned that the democratic leveling of Europe would some day culminate in dictatorship. . . . Thus [his] ideas paved the way for the Third Reich."

11. Löwith, *Nietzsche's Philosophy of the Eternal Recurrence of the Same*, trans. Harvey Lomax (Berkeley and Los Angeles: University of California Press, 1997), 8.

12. For an important critique of Löwith's later thought, see Jürgen Habermas, "Karl Löwith: Stoic Retreat from Historical Consciousness," in *Philosophical-Political Profiles*, 79–98.

13. Hans-Georg Gadamer, *Truth and Method* (New York: Seabury, 1975), 481.

14. Löwith, "Natur und Humanität des Menschen," *Sämtliche Schriften* I, 294.

15. Löwith, "Welt und Menschenwelt," 295.

16. See Heidegger, "The Age of the World Picture," in *The Question Concerning Technology and Other Essays*, W. Lovitt, ed. (New York: Harper & Row), 115–54.

17. Löwith, "Welt und Menschenwelt," 295.

18. Ibid., 307.

19. Max Weber, "Science as a Vocation," in H. Gerth and C. W. Mills, eds. *From Max Weber: Essays in Sociology* (New York: Oxford, 1946), 156

20. Karl Löwith, "Curriculum Vitae," in *Mein Leben in Deutschland vor und nach 1933* (Stuttgart: Metzler Verlag, 1986), 147.

21. See Dieter Henrich, "Sceptico Sereno," in *Natur und Geschichte: Karl Löwith zum 70. Geburtstag* (Stuttgart: Kohlhammer, 1967), 458–463.

22. Hans-Georg Gadamer, "Karl Löwith," in *Philosophical Apprenticeships* (Cambridge: MIT Press, 1985), 171.

23. Löwith, *Das Individuum in der Rolle des Mitmenschen* (Darmstadt: Wissenschaftliche Buchgesellschaft, 1969), 1.

24. Ludwig Feuerbach, "Principles of the Philosophy of the Future," in W. Schirmacher, ed., *German Socialist Philosophy* (New York: Continuum, 1994), 77.

25. Ibid., 41. For an excellent survey of leading twentieth-century philosophies of intersubjectivity, see Michael Theunissen, *The Other: Studies in the Social Ontology of Husserl, Heidegger, Sartre, and Buber*, trans. C. McCann (Cambridge: MIT Press, 1986).

26. For Husserl's remarks, see his letter of May 4, 1933, in Bernd Martin, ed., *Martin Heidegger und das "dritte Reich,"* 149.

27. Löwith, *Mein Leben in Deutschland vor und nach 1933*. The text dates from 1940. The Harvard prize committee had made it clear that it was in not interested in "philosophical reflections about the past," but in testimony that was "factual" (*wahrheitsgetreu*). Needless to say, Löwith failed to win the prize. His reflections on the great personages and events of the period undoubtedly proved too substantial for the tastes of the Harvard prize committee. The manuscript then lay dormant for some forty-six years until it was discovered by Löwith's widow and published in 1986. For an English translation, see *My Life in Germany Before and After 1933*, trans. E. King (Urbana: University of Illinois Press, 1994).

28. Löwith, *Mein Leben in Deutschland*, 19.

29. Ibid., 25. For a recent survey of this trend in intellectual history, see Arthur Herman, *The Idea of Decline in Western History* (New York: The Free Press, 1997).

30. For an excellent account of Nietzsche's conception of "great politics," see Bruce Detwiler, *Nietzsche's Aristocratic Radicalism* (Chicago: University of Chicago Press, 1990).

31. See Fritz Ringer, *Decline of the German Mandarins*,

32. Löwith, *Mein Leben in Deutschland*, 44–45, 57

33. Löwith, "The Political Implications of Heidegger's Existentialism," in Wolin, *The Heidegger Controversy*, 182–83.

34. Cited in Löwith, *Martin Heidegger and European Nihilism*, R. Wolin, ed. (New York: Columbia University Press, 1995), 236.

35. For an analysis of National Socialism as "revolution of nihilism" (written by a disillusioned former party member), see Hermann Rauschning, *The Revolution of Nihilism* (New York: Alliance, 1939).

36. For a systematic discussion of this problem in Heidegger's thought, see Johannes Fritsche, *Historical Destiny and National Socialism in Heidegger's Being and Time* (Berkeley and Los Angeles: University of California Press, 1999).

37. Löwith, "The Political Horizon of Heidegger's Existential Ontology," in *Martin Heidegger and European Nihilism*, 212.

38. Hugo Ott, *Martin Heidegger*, 307.

39. Arendt, "What is *Existenz* Philosophy?" 34–56.

40. Heidegger's letter to Sartre was originally published in the *Frankfurter Allgemeine Zeitung* (1 January 1994): 27. For Frédéric Towarnicki's own account of their encounter, see his memoir, *Martin Heidegger: Souvenirs et Chroniques* (Paris: Rivages, 1999).

41. Hans-Georg Gadamer, "Das Sein und das Nicht-Sein," in Traugott König, ed., *Sartre: Ein Kongress* (Hamburg: Rowohlt, 1988), 37.

42. Jean-Paul Sartre, "The Humanism of Existentialism," in G. Guignon and D. Pereboon, eds., *Existentialism: Basic Writings* (Indianapolis: Hackett, 1995), 271.

43. Heidegger, "Letter on Humanism," in *Basic Writings* (New York: Harper Row, 1977), 208, 213–214. For more on antihumanism as a philosophical trope, see my discussion in, "Antihumanism in the Discourse of Postwar French Thought," *Labyrinths: Explorations in the Critical History of Ideas* (Amherst: University of Massachusetts Press), 175–209.

44. Heidegger's letter to Schmitt has been reprinted in *Telos* 72, (2)20 (summer 1987): 132.

45. On Schmitt's relationship to liberalism, see John McCormick's important study, *Carl Schmitt's Critique of Liberalism* (Cambridge: Cambridge University Press, 1998). See also William E. Scheuerman, *Carl Schmitt: The End of Law* (Lanham, Maryland: Rowman & Littlefield, 1999). For a discussion of Schmitt within the context of Weimar legal culture, see Peter C. Caldwell, *Popular Sovereignty and the*

Crisis of German Constitutional Law: The Theory and Practice of Weimar Constitutionalism (Durham: Duke University Press, 1997).

46. With reference to Mussolini, see Carl Schmitt, *The Crisis of Parliamentary Democracy*, trans. E. Kennedy (Cambridge: MIT Press, 1985), p. 82: "Just as in the sixteenth century an Italian has once again given expression to the principle of political realism."

47. Schmitt, *Der Begriff des Politischen* (Berlin: Duncker and Humblot, 1979), 67. English translation: *The Concept of the Political*, trans. G. Schwab (Chicago: University of Chicago Press, 1996). For Nietzsche's discussion of the importance of "grasping the value of having enemies," see *Twilight of the Idols*, trans. R. J. Hollingdale (New York: Penguin, 1968), 43–44.

48. I discuss the relation between these two phases of Schmitt's development in "Carl Schmitt, Political Existentialism, and the Total State," in *The Terms of Cultural Criticism*, (New York: Columbia University Press, 1992), 83–102; and in "Carl Schmitt: the Conservative Revolutionary Habitus and the Aesthetics of Horror," in *Labyrinths: Explorations in the Critical History of Ideas*, 103–22. For an excellent treatment of Jünger, see Elliot Neaman, *A Dubious Past* (Berkeley: University of California Press, 1999).

49. Löwith, *Martin Heidegger and European Nihilism*, 215.

50. It went through three editions during Löwith's lifetime and in 1984 was included as the titular essay of volume 8 of his collected works.

51. On these points, see Heidegger's essays, "The Age of the World-Picture" and "The Question Concerning Technology," in W. Lovitt, ed., *The Question Concerning Technology and Other Essays* (New York: Harper and Row, 1977). See also his important text of 1936–38—touted by some as the missing sequel to *Being and Time—Beiträge zu Philosophie* (Frankfurt: Klostermann, 1989); *Contributions to Philosophy*, trans. P. Emad and K. Maly (Bloomington: Indiana University Press, 1999).

52. Löwith, *Martin Heidegger and European Nihilism*, p. 43.

53. Heidegger, "Hölderlin and the Essence of Poetry," in *Existence and Being* (Chicago: Regnery-Gateway, 1949), 287. See also the following remarks from *Hölderlins Hymnen "Germanien" und "Der Rhein,"* 51–52: "The historical Dasein of nations—their emergence, flowering, and decline—originates from poetry; out of the latter [originates] authentic knowledge in the sense of philosophy; and from both of these, the realization of a Volk as Volk through the state—politics. This original, historical age of peoples is therefore the age of poets, thinkers, and state-founders, that is, of those who authentically ground and establish the historical Dasein of a Volk."

54. Heidegger, "Letter on Humanism," in D. Krell, ed., *Basic Writings* (New York: Harper and Row, 1977), 210, 216.

55. Löwith, *Martin Heidegger and European Nihilism*, 86. Heidegger citation from "The Anaximander Fragment," 19.

56. Heidegger, "The Word of Nietzsche: 'God is Dead,'" in *The Question Concerning Technology*, 112; emphasis added.

57. Löwith, *Martin Heidegger and European Nihilism*, 43.

58. Ibid., 251 (translation altered).

59. Reprinted in *The Heidegger Controversy*, 91–116.

60. Ibid., 106.

61. Löwith, *Martin Heidegger and European Nihilism*, 90–91.

62. For the controversy surrounding this claim from *An Introduction to Metaphysics* (New Haven: Yale University Press, 1959), 159, see Jürgen Habermas, "Martin Heidegger: On the Publication of the Lectures of 1935," in *The Heidegger Controversy*, 186–197.

63. Löwith, *Martin Heidegger and European Nihilism*, 78–79.

64. Cited in H. W. Petzet, *Encounters and Dialogues with Martin Heidegger*, trans. P. Emad (Chicago: University of Chicago Press, 1993), 91.

65. Habermas, "Karl Löwith," in *Philosophical-Political Profiles*, 85.

66. In "Karl Löwith," Habermas formulates the dilemma in the following terms: "Precisely from the eminently practical experience of the risks that appear to be posed by modern consciousness, Löwith wants to get back to an attitude toward the world that is theoretical in the classical sense [i.e., *theoria* or contemplation] because it is elevated above practice and free from the restrictions of pragmatic consciousness" (p. 84). Habermas goes on to observe caustically that Löwith's embrace of the "cosmos" is a standpoint one might expect to find in the pages of the *Eranos Jahrbuch*.

67. See, for example, R. R. Palmer, *The Age of Democratic Revolutions*, 2 vols. (Princeton: Princeton University Press, 1959).

68. See Löwith's *Jacob Burckhardt, Sämtliche Schriften*, vol. 7 (Stuttgart: Metzler, 1984), first written in 1935. For Löwith's reflections on suicide, see "Töten, Mord, und Selbstmord: Die Freiheit zum Tode" and "Die Freiheit zum Tode," in *Mensch und Menschenwelt*, 399–425.

69. Heidegger, "Overcoming Metaphysics," in *The Heidegger Controversy*, 67–90.

70. For an important vindication of "modernity" in this sense, see Habermas, "Modernity: An Unfinished Project," in *Habermas and the Unfinished Project of Modernity*, eds. D'Entreves and Benhabib (Cambridge: MIT Press, 1997), 38–55.

71. For a classic discussion of this evolutionary trend, see T. H. Marshall, *Citizenship and Social Class* (Cambridge: Cambridge University Press, 1950).

Chapter 5—Hans Jonas: The Philosopher of Life

1. Heidegger, "Letter on Humanism," in *Basic Writings* (New York: Harper and Row, 1977), 210.

2. Jonas, "Heidegger and Theology," in *The Phenomenon of Life: Towards a Philosophical Biology* (New York: Delta Publishing, 1966), 247.

3. Löwith, *My Life in Germany Before and After 1933* (Urbana: University of Illinois Press, 1994).

4. Jonas, "Is Faith Still Possible? Memories of Rudolf Bultmann and Reflections on the Philosophical Aspects of His Work," in *Mortality and Morality* (Evanston: Northwestern University Press, 1996), 146.

5. Jonas, *Wissenschaft als persönliches Erlebnis* (Göttingen: Vandenhoeck und Ruprecht, 1987), 20–21.

6. Jonas, The Gnostic Religion (Boston: Beacon, 1958).

7. Jonas, "Gnosticism," in *The Encyclopedia of Philosophy* (New York: MacMillan, 1967), 340.

8. Ibid., 337.

9. Ibid., 340.

10. Bacon, *Novum Organum*, in E. Burtt, ed. *The English Philosophers From Bacon to Mill* (New York: Random House, 1939), p. 28.

11. Jonas, "Gnosticism, Existentialism, and Nihilism," in *The Phenomenon of Life*, 214.

12. Ibid., 233.

13. Ibid., 44–45.

14. Nietzsche, *The Will to Power*, 8.

15. Jonas, *The Phenomenon of Life*, 3.

16. Ibid., 4.

17. Jonas, "Evolution and Freedom: On the Continuity Among Life-Forms," in *Mortality and Morality*, 66.

18. Ibid., 68.

19. Ibid.

20. Ibid., 69.

21. Simmel, "Metropolis and Mental Life," *The Sociology of Georg Simmel* (New York: The Free Press, 1950), 409–410.

22. Cited in Christian Zimmerli, "Prophet in dürftiger Zeit," *Focus* 19 (May 10, 1993): 82.

23. Jonas, *The Imperative of Responsibility* (Chicago: University of Chicago Press, 1984), 9.

24. Jonas, *Mortality and Morality*, 101.

25. Ibid.

26. Jonas, *The Imperative of Responsibility*, 26–27.

27. Ibid., 27.

28. Ibid., 131.

29. Ibid., 104ff.

30. Ibid., 137; emphasis added.

31. Herbert Schnädelbach, *Philosophy in Germany: 1831–1933* (Cambridge: Cambridge University Press, 1984), 140. For an extreme case of correlating vitalism and fascism, see Georg Lukács, *The Destruction of Reason* (London: Merlin, 1982), passim.

32. Jonas, *The Imperative of Responsibility*, 138. For a good discussion of Green Party politics, see A. Markovits and P. Gorski, *The German Left: Red, Green, and Beyond* (New York: Oxford University Press, 1993), 117.

33. Ibid., 139, 142; emphasis added.

34. For an impressive account of these changes, see Donald Sassoon, *One-Hundred Years of Socialism: The Western European Left in the Twentieth Century* (New York: New Press, 1997).

35. Jonas, *The Imperative of Responsibility*, 143, 145.

36. Ibid., 146–47.

37. Ibid., 147. See Erik Jacob, *Martin Heidegger und Hans Jonas* (Tübingen: Francke Verlag, 1996), 355: "For Jonas the ideology of Marxism, as a result of its theoretical principles, would be better able to meet the demands of an ethic of responsibility than a liberal system with a market economy and democracy: an economy of needs would replace the profit economy, a rational and centrally organized bureaucracy would replace free, profit-oriented entrepreneurship."

38. Ibid., 149, 151.

39. Jonas, "Dem bösen Ende näher," *Der Spiegel* 20 (1992): 95.

40. Ibid., 99, 101.

41. Ibid., 101.

42. Jonas, "The Concept of God After Auschwitz," in *Mortality and Morality*, 139.

43. Ibid., 142.

44. Jonas, "Heidegger's Entschlossenheit und Entschluss," in Neske and Kettering, eds. *Antwort: Martin Heidegger im Gespräch* (Pfullingen: Neske Verlag, 1988), 225.

45. Ibid., 227.

Chapter 6—Herbert Marcuse: From Existential Marxism to Left Heideggerianism

1. Paul Piccone and Alexander Delfini, "Marcuse's Heideggerian Marxism," *Telos* 6 (1970): 36–46. For a good assessment of Marcuse's relationship to the New Left, see Paul Breines, "Marcuse and the New Left in America," in J. Habermas, ed., *Antworten auf Herbert Marcuse* (Frankfurt: Suhrkamp Verlag, 1968), 134–151.

2. Marcuse confirms this portrait of his political development in a 1978 interview: "I was involved briefly, as a member of the soldiers' council in Berlin in Reineckendorf in 1918. I left that soldiers' council very, very quickly when they began electing former officers to it. Then I belonged to the SPD (Social Democratic Party) for a short time, but I left that too after January 1919. I believe my political stance was fixed at that time, in the sense that I was uncompromisingly against SPD policy. In this sense I was a revolutionary." See Marcuse, "Theory and Politics: A Discussion," *Telos* 38 (Winter 1978–79): 125. For the German original,

see Jürgen Habermas et al., *Gespräche mit Herbert Marcuse* (Frankfurt: Suhrkamp, 1978), 9–62.

3. Ibid., 125. In his contribution to a Heidegger memorial volume in 1977, Marcuse expressed a similar insight:

> *Being and Time* appeared in the dissolution-phase of the Weimar Republic: the proximity of the Nazi regime, the coming catastrophe, was generally sensed. Yet, at the time the major philosophical trends in no way reflected this situation. Heidegger's work appeared to me and my friends as a new beginning: we experienced his book (and his lectures, of which we possessed transcripts) as, finally, a *concrete* philosophy: here was talk of Existence, of our existence, of anxiety, care, boredom, etc. And we experienced yet another "academic" emancipation: Heidegger's interpretation of Greek philosophy and German idealism gave us new insight into lifeless texts.

See G. Neske, ed., *Erinnerungen an Martin Heidegger* (Neske Verlag: Pfullingen, 1977), 162.

4. Marcuse, "Contributions to a Phenomenology of Historical Materialism," *Telos* 4 (Fall 1969): 4; emphasis added. As a cursory examination of this essay bears out, the preponderance of citations and references refer to Marx (especially to the recently published MEGA edition of his and Engels' work).

5. Frederick Olafson, "Heidegger's Politics: An Interview," in R. Pippin et al., eds., *Marcuse and the Promise of Critical Theory* (South Hadley, Mass.: Bergin and Garvey, 1988), 96. For a more philosophically sophisticated analysis of the problem of pseudo-concreteness of the phenomenological approach, it is worth consulting Marcuse's critique of Sartre, in which a number of similar charges are made and substantiated. See Marcuse, "Sartre's Existentialism," *Studies in Critical Philosophy*, trans. J. de Bres (Boston: Beacon Press, 1972), 157–190.

6. See the account of Bernstein's position in James Joll, *The Second International, 1889–1914* (New York: Harper, 1966), 93: Above all, Bernstein "maintained that Marx was wrong in his predictions about the future development and impending collapse of the capitalist order. In spite of the growth of trusts and cartels, capitalism was not becoming exclusively a system of large concerns, the members of lower middle class were not everywhere being forced to become members of the proletariat; there was no absolute and rigid division between classes, and therefore it was false to interpret the political situation solely in terms of a class struggle; the standard of living of the working class was in fact rising and they were not being forced into the ever increasing misery which Marx had prophesied."

7. Georg Lukács, Preface (1962) to *The Theory of the Novel*, trans. Anna Bostock (Cambridge: MIT Press, 1971), 11.

8. Karl Marx, *Capital*, vol. 1, in *The Marx-Engels Reader*, R. Tucker, ed. (New York: Norton, 1978), 324.

9. Marcuse, "Contributions to a Phenomenology of Historical Materialism," 5.

10. Marcuse, "The Foundation of Historical Materialism," *Studies in Critical Philosophy*, 34. For a description of "automatic Marxism," see Russell Jacoby, "Towards a Critique of Automatic Marxism, *Telos* 10 (winter 1971): 119–146.

11. *The Marx-Engels Reader*, 143. Although the "Theses on Feuerbach" were written in 1845, they remained unpublished until Engels discovered them among Marx's papers nearly four decades later.

12. Heidegger, *Being and Time*, trans. J. Macquarrie and Robinson (New York: HarperCollins, 1962), 358.

13. For an analysis that makes this claim, see Günther Stern, "On the Pseudo-Concreteness of Heidegger's Philosophy," *Philosophy and Phenomenological Research* 9 (1948): 337–370.

14. Marcuse, "Contributions," 3. Marcuse's article first appeared in an issue of *Philosophische Hefte* (1928), which was devoted entirely to *Being and Time*.

15. Marcuse, "Contributions," 16; emphasis added.

16. Heidegger, *Being and Time*, 46.

17. Marcuse, "Contributions," 32; emphasis added.

18. Ibid., 6; emphasis added. For one of the most extensive discussions of some of the uncanny philosophical parallels between Lukács and Heidegger, see Lucien Goldmann, *Lukács and Heidegger*, trans. W. Boelhower (London: Routledge, 1977). For more on Goldmann, see Mitchell Cohen, *The Wager of Lucien Goldmann* (Princeton: Princeton University Press, 1995).

In a conversation with Marcuse in April 1976, he confirmed to me the formative philosophical role that *History and Class Consciousness* had played in his intellectual development. In *Herbert Marcuse and the Crisis of Marxism* (pp. 387–88), Douglas Kellner reports a similar response: "Marcuse stressed the importance of *History and Class Consciousness* for developing Marxism and noted its impact on his own thought. Marcuse also said that he believed that Lukács and Korsch were the 'most intelligent' Marxists to write after the deaths of Luxemburg and Liebknecht, and that in his 1930s work, with the Frankfurt Institute for Social Research, he took a more favorable position toward *History and Class Consciousness* than Horkheimer and his other colleagues."

19. Marcuse, "Über die konkrete Philosophie," *Archiv für Sozialwissenschaft und Sozialpolitik* 62 (1929), 120.

20. Marcuse, "Contributions," 15.

21. Ibid., 6

22. Ibid., 12, 16; emphasis added.

23. Lukács, *History and Class Consciousness*, xxii; emphasis added. In *The Destruction of Reason*, trans. P. Palmer (Atlantic Heights, N.J.: 1980), Lukács's judgment of Heidegger was far less charitable. He viewed Heidegger's philosophy as an expression of despair that was typical of the bourgeois imperialist era. In Lukács inimitable words (p. 503): "One may say without undue exaggeration that in the period of the imperialistic bourgeoisie's struggle against socialism, Heideg-

ger was related to Hitler and Rosenberg as Schopehauer, in his own day, was related to Nietzsche."

24. *The Marx-Engels Reader*, 145.

25. Marcuse, "Contributions," 11; emphasis added.

26. Ibid., 17.

27. Marcuse, "Über die konkrete Philosophie," 126.

28. Ibid., 18, 21.

29. Ibid., 124, 127.

30. Adorno, review of Marcuse, "Hegels Ontologie und die Grundlegung einer Theorie der Geschichtlichkeit," *Zeitschrift für Sozialforschung* (1) (1932): 409–410.

31. Marcuse, "The Foundation of Historical Materialism, 3.

32. Two of the more important studies are Istvan Meszaros, *Marx's Theory of Alienation* (New York: Harper & Row, 1970) and Bertell Ollman, *Alienation: Marx's Conception of Man in Capitalist Society* (Cambridge: Cambridge University Press, 1976). See also Alvin Gouldner, *The Two Marxisms* (New York: Seabury, 1977); and the introductory discussion in Leszek Kolakowski, *The Main Currents of Marxism*, vol. 1, trans. P. Falla (New York: Oxford University Press, 1978), 132–146.

33. *The Marx-Engels Reader*, 72.

34. Cited by Marcuse in "The Foundation of Historical Materialism," 12.

35. Ibid., 5, 6, 10.

36. For an overview of this debate, see Seyla Benhabib, Translator's Introduction, Herbert Marcuse, *Hegel's Ontology and the Theory of Historicity* (Cambridge: MIT Press, 1987), ix–xl. In "Marcuse and Hegel on Historicity" (in *Marcuse and the Promise of Critical Theory*), Robert Pippin makes a strong case for the centrality of *Hegel's Ontology* in relationship to Marcuse's later work (in particular, *Reason and Revolution*). But on the whole I think Pippin attributes more developmental significance to Marcuse's habilitation study than it can bear. Moreover, his reflections omit the important question of Marx's influence. For another important survey of the early Marcuse's relationship to Heidegger, which is highly critical of Heidegger's influences, see Alfred Schmidt, "Existential Ontology and Historical Materialism in the Work of Herbert Marcuse," in *Marcuse and the Promise of Critical Theory*, 47–67. Marcuse's writing style was as a rule remarkably lucid. *Hegel's Ontology* constitutes a significant exception. As Benhabib remarks (p. xxxiv): "Those readers familiar with the German original will know the tortured and convoluted character of Marcuse's style, a combination, undoubtedly, of academic conformism, Heideggerian neologisms, and philosophical profundity at times bordering on obscurity."

37. Quoted in Benhabib, xii.

38. Marcuse, "Das Problem der geschichtlichen Wirklichkeit: Wilhelm Dilthey," *Die Gesellschaft* 8 (4) (1931): 350–367.

39. For more on these parallels, see Pippin, "Marcuse and Hegel on Historicity," 69–74.

40. G.W.F. Hegel, *Phenomenology of Spirit*, trans. A. V. Miller (New York: Oxford University Press, 1978), 298.

41. Marcuse, *Hegel's Ontology*, 283, 289.

42. Hegel, *Phenomenology of Spirit*, 314, 252.

43. Marcuse, *Hegel's Ontology*, 290.

44. Marcuse, "On the Philosophical Foundation of the Concept of Labor in Economics," trans. D. Kellner, *Telos* 16 (summer 1973), 11; emphasis added.

45. Ibid., 13; emphasis added.

46. Friedrich Schiller, *On the Aesthetic Education of Man: A Series of Letters*, trans. R. Snell (New York: Frederick Ungar, 1965), 80.

47. Cited in Martin Jay, *The Dialectical Imagination* (Boston: Little and Brown, 1973), 57.

48. Schiller, *On the Aesthetic Education of Man*, 39.

49. Ibid., 26.

50. Ibid., 77.

51. Marcuse, "On the Philosophical Foundation of the Concept of Labor in Economics," 25. Here, the parallels with aspects of Kojève's argument in his *Introduction to the Reading of Hegel* are striking. For Kojève, "desire" is an expression of human lack. Of course, the ultimate source of Marcuse's and Kojève's argument may have been the same: the master-slave section of Hegel's *Phenomenology of Spirit*.

52. Marcuse, "On the Philosophical Foundation of the Concept of Labor in Economics," 25; emphasis added.

53. Aristotle, *Nichomachean Ethics* (Indianapolis: Robbs-Merrill, 1962), 1176A.

54. Ibid., 15; emphasis added.

55. Marcuse, *One-Dimensional Man* (Boston: Beacon Press, 1964), 16. Suffice it to say that speculation concerning the "abolition of labor" stands in marked contrast to Marx's characterization of labor as a fundamental mode of man's species-being in the Paris manuscripts. To be sure, Marcuse's suggestion that, "Technology would become subject to the free play of faculties in the struggle for the pacification of nature and society," points in the direction of his romantic argument for a new technology that would engage nature in a manner that was nonobjectivating and nonmanipulative.

56. See Benhabib, Introduction to Marcuse, *Hegel's Ontology*, xxx: "Depending on what degree of individual self-reliance and autonomy of thought Heidegger could tolerate among his disciples, he might have had grounds to reject this work as a *Habilitationsschrift*, which he fully endorsed even if it appears that historically he never had to do so. Marcuse's proto-Marxist reading of Hegel and Dilthey could have hardly escaped Heidegger's acute knowledge of and sense for the history of philosophy."

57. Olafson, "Heidegger's Politics," 99.

58. Heidegger, "Schlageter," in R. Wolin, ed., *The Heidegger Controversy*, 42. As he remarks in one address commemorating a popular Nazi martyr: "As he stood

defenseless facing the rifles, the hero's inner gaze soared above the muzzles to the daylight and mountains of his home that he might die for the German people and its Reich with the Alemannic countryside before his eyes. . . . He was not permitted to escape his destiny so that he could die the most difficult and greatest of all deaths with a hard will and a clear heart."

59. Olafson, "Heidegger's Politics," 101.

60. Marcuse, *Eros and Civilization: A Philosophical Inquiry into Freud* (New York: Vintage, 1962), 216.

61. Marcuse, "The Struggle Against Liberalism in the Totalitarian View of the State," in *Negations: Essays in Critical Theory* (Boston: Beacon Press, 1968), 40.

62. Heidegger, *Being and Time*, 345.

63. Although Marcuse never fully developed these criticisms, they display a remarkable affinity with Jonas's critique of the vacuousness of Heideggerian "decisiveness." See Jonas, "Heideggers Entschlossenheit und Entschluss," in Kettering and Neske, eds., *Antwort: Martin Heidegger im Gespräch* (Pfullingen: Neske Verlag, 1988), 221–31.

64. Olafson, "Heidegger's Politics," 100; emphasis added.

65. Marcuse, letter to Heidegger of August 28, 1947, in *The Heidegger Controversy*, 160.

66. Heidegger, letter to Marcuse of January 20, 1948, in *The Heidegger Controversy*, 162–63.

67. For an exposition of this idea, see Helmut Dubiel, *Theory and Organization* (Cambridge: MIT Press, 1982) and Rolf Wiggershaus, *The Frankfurt School: History, and Political Theory*, trans. M. Robertson (Cambridge: MIT Press, 1993).

68. For the argument about labor, see Marcuse, *Eros and Civilization*, 196–202; for the argument about death, see 202–214.

69. For one of Heidegger's most powerful articulations of this idea, see "The Overcoming of Metaphysics," in *Heidegger Controversy*, 67–90.

70. Marcuse, *One-Dimensional Man*, 9, 10, 11.

71. Marcuse, *An Essay on Liberation* (New York: Penguin, 1969), 19, 25; emphasis added.

72. "Left Heideggerianism"—a Heideggerianized Marxism—became a prominent intellectual current in France during the 1960s under the influence of *Arguments* group thinkers such as Kostas Axelos and Edgar Morin. See, for example, Axelos's *Alienation, Praxis, and Techne in the Thought of Karl Marx* (Austin: University of Texas Press, 1976).

73. Heidegger, "The Question Concerning Technology," in *The Question Concerning Technology and Other Essays* (New York: Harper & Row, 1977); cited by Marcuse in *One-Dimensional Man*, 153–54. To my knowledge, this is the only time Marcuse ever directly cited Heidegger following the war.

74. Marcuse, *One-Dimensional Man*, 154; emphasis added.

75. Marcuse, *An Essay on Liberation*, 24.

76. Marcuse, *One-Dimensional Man*, 166–67.

77. For an important critique of Marcuse's notion of a "new science," see Jürgen Habermas, "Science and Technology as Ideology," *Towards a Rational Society,* trans. J. Schapiro (Boston: Beacon, 1970), 81–122.

78. Max Horkheimer, *Critical Theory,* trans. M. O'Connell (New York: Seabury, 1973), 241.

79. Marcuse, *Eros and Civilization,* 206; emphasis added.

80. Marcuse, "Repressive Tolerance," in Barrington Moore Jr. et al., *Critique of Pure Tolerance* (Boston: Beacon Press, 1966), 121.

81. Walter Benjamin, *Das Passagenwerk,* vol. 2 (Frankfurt: Suhrkamp Verlag, 1982), 505.

Chapter 7—Arbeit Macht Frei: Heidegger As Philosopher of the German "Way"

1. On this point, see Heidegger, "Plato's Doctrine of Truth," in *Philosophy in the Twentieth Century,* W. Barrett and H. D. Aiken, eds. (New York: Random House, 1962).

2. Heidegger, *Being and Time,* 41–49.

3. Ernst Cassirer, *The Myth of the State* (New Haven: Yale University Press, 1946), 293.

4. Ibid.

5. Heidegger, "Why We Remain in the Provinces," 428.

6. Heinrich Petzet, *Encounters and Dialogues with Martin Heidegger* (Chicago: University of Chicago Press, 1993), 9.

7. Ulrich Sieg, "Die 'Verjudung des deutschen Geistes: Ein unbekannter Brief Heideggers,'" *Die Zeit* 52 (29 December 1989): 19.

8. On this point, see the important essay by Jürgen Habermas, "'Work' and 'Weltanschauung: The Heidegger Constroversy from a German Perspective," in *The New Conservativism: Cultural Criticism and the Historians' Debate,* S. W. Nicholsen, ed. (Cambridge: MIT Press, 1989), 140–173.

9. Löwith, "The Political Implications of Heidegger's Existentialism," in *The Heidegger Controversy,* 182–83. For the full text of Löwith's memoirs, see *My Life in Germany Before and After 1933,* trans. E. King (Urbana: University of Illinois Press, 1994).

10. Löwith, "My Last Meeting with Heidegger in Rome, 1936," in *The Heidegger Controversy,* 142.

11. Heidegger, *Being and Time,* 358.

12. See, for example, Pierre Bourdieu, *Heidegger's Political Ontology;* and Winfried Franzen, "Die Suche nach Härte und Schwere: Über ein zum NS-Engagement disponierendes Motiven Heideggers Vorlesung 'Die Grundbegriffe der Metaphysik' von 1929/30," in *Heidegger und die praktische Philosophie,* A. Gethmann Siefert and O. Pöggeler, eds. (Frankfurt: Suhrkamp Verlag, 1988), 78–92. For an analysis of similar motifs that can be traced back to the middle of the nineteenth century, see Karl Löwith, "European Nihilism: Reflections on the Spiritual and

Historical Background and of the European War," in *Martin Heidegger and European Nihilism*, 173–283. See also the fascinating discussion of Heidegger, Schmitt, and Jünger in Karl Heinz Bohrer, *Asthetik des Schreckens* (Munich: Hanser, 1977).

13. Löwith, "The Political Implications of Heidegger's Existentialism," 173–74. For an early treatment of the conservative revolutionaries and their parallel worldviews, see Christian von Krockow, *Die Entscheidung* (Frankfurt: Campus Verlag, 1990).

14. For the story of Heidegger's rectorship, see Hugo Ott, *Martin Heidegger: A Political Life*, 235–262.

15. Ernst Jünger, "Le Traveilleur Planétaire," in M. Haer, ed. *Martin Heidegger* (Doris: Editions de l'Herne, 1983), 150.

16. Heidegger, "The Self-Assertion of the German University," in *The Heidegger Controversy*, 38

17. Otto Pöggeler, "Den Führer führen?" *Neue Wege mit Heidegger* (Freiburg/Munich: Karl Albert, 1992), 203–54.

18. For the best account of the later Heidegger's political convictions, see his interview with *Der Spiegel*, "Only a God Can Save Us," in *The Heidegger Controversy*, 91–116.

19. Ibid., 111.

20. Cited in Pöggeler, "Den Führer führen?," 44.

21. For Nietzsche's concept of monumental history, see "The Uses and Disadvantages of History for Life," *Untimely Meditations* (New York: Cambridge University Press, 1983), 94.

22. Heidegger, *Logica*, 42. These lectures should not be confused with Heidegger's 1925–26 Marburg lectures of the same title (*Gesamtausgabe* vol. 21).

23. Marx does precisely this for the history of capitalism. Ernst Bloch's study of *Thomas Münzer: Theologe der Revolution* (Munich: Kurt Wolff, 1921) does this for the peasant wars.

24. Though the literature on this topic has become voluminous, see Hans-Ulrich Wehler, *The Second Empire* (Leamington Spa: Berg, 1985); and David Blackbourn and Geoff Eley, *The Peculiarities of German History* (New York: Oxford University Press, 1984).

25. Heidegger, *Logica Lecciones de Martin Heidegger*, V. Farias, ed. (Barcelona: Anthropo, 1991), 2.

26. Ibid., 38.

27. Ibid., 6.

28. Heidegger, *Introduction to Metaphysics* (New Haven: Yale University Press, 1959), 199.

29. Heidegger, *Logica*, 16.

30. Ibid., 18.

31. Cited in Ott, *Martin Heidegger*, 247.

32. Heidegger, *Logica*, 32.

33. Ibid., 22.

34. Ibid., 28.

35. Heidegger, *The Fundamental Concepts of Metaphysics*, trans. W. McNeill (Bloomington: Indiana University Press, 199), 152–59.

36. See the discussion of "mood" in *Being and Time*, 172ff.

37. See, for example, Heidegger, *Introduction to Metaphysics*, 199.

38. See the characterization of Descartes in *Being and Time*, 122–34. See also the long discussion of Descartes's place in the history of modern thought in Heidegger, *Nietzsche: Nihilism* (New York: HarperCollins, 1982), 96–101.

39. Heidegger, *Logica*, 82.

40. Ibid.

41. The story of Heidegger's involvement in the Nazi labor camps is told by Ott in *Martin Heidegger*, 224.

42. Both the rectoral address and Heidegger's political addresses from the years 1933–34 are contained in *The Heidegger Controversy*. For more on the role of the labor camps under Nazism, see Peter Duden, *Erziehung durch Arbeit* (Wiesbaden: Westeuropaische Verlaganstalt, 1988).

43. *The Heidegger Controversy*, 42, 59.

44. Anson Rabinbach, "The Aesthetics of Production in the Third Reich," *Journal of Contemporary History* 11 (1976): 44. On the more general question of the pride of place Nazism accorded to aestheticized politics, see Peter Reichl, *Der schöne Schein des dritten Reiches* (Munich: Hanser, 1991). For an examination of Nazi attitudes toward the working class, see Timothy Mason, *Nazi, Fascism, and the Working Class* (Cambridge: Cambridge University Press, 1995).

45. David Schoenbaum, *Hitler's Social Revolution: Class, Status in Nazi Germany, 1933–1939* (New York: Norton, 1980), 75–76.

46. On this point, see Heidegger, "Why We Remain in the Provinces," note 5 above.

47. Löwith, *My Life in Germany Before and After 1933* (Urbana: University of Illinois Press, 1994), 60.

48. See Schoenbaum, *Hitler's Social Revolution*, passim.

49. Oswald Spengler, *Preussentum und Sozialismus* (Munich: Beck, 1925), 99; emphasis added.

50. See Ernst Jünger, *Der Arbeiter: Herrschaft und Gestalt* (Stuttgart: Klett-Cotta, 1981). A translation of Jünger's essay "Total Mobilization" may be found in *The Heidegger Controversy*, 119–39. For Heidegger's indebtedness to Jünger, see his remarks in "The Rectorate 1933/34: Facts and Thoughts," in *Martin Heidegger and National Socialism*, G. Neske and E. Kettering, eds. (New York: Paragon House, 1990). For a recent study of Jünger, see Elliot Neaman, *A Dubious Past: Ernst Jünger* (Berkeley and Los Angeles: University of California Press, 1999).

51. See note 31 above.

52. Nietzsche, *The Will to Power*, W. Kaufmann, ed. (New York: Vintage, 1967), 866; emphasis added. Also see Nietzsche's discussions of mechanism and machine at 888 and 889. On Nietzsche's reception by the conservative revolutionaries, see Steven Aschheim, *The Nietzsche Legacy in Germany, 1890–1990* (Berkeley: University of California, 1992). For the more general question of the way in which

German fascism reconciled itself to modern technology, see Jeffrey Herf, *Reactionary Modernism* (Cambridge: Cambridge University Press, 1984).

53. Nietzsche, *The Will to Power*, 868; emphasis added. Nietzsche concludes these reflections as follows: "Obviously they [the new barbarians] will come into view and consolidate themselves after tremendous socialist crises—they will be the elements capable of the greatest severity toward themselves and able to guarantee the greatest will."

54. Heidegger, *Nietzsche: Europäischer Nihilismus, Gesamtausgabe* 48 (Frankfurt: Klostermann, 1986): 205; emphasis added. The extant English translation published by HarperCollins is based on an earlier German that does not contain many of the passages in question.

55. Ibid., 333.

56. For an important discussion of "national socialism" (lower case) in the French context, see Eugen Weber, "Nationalism, Socialism, and National Socialism," in *My France: Politics, Myth, Culture* (Cambridge: Harvard University Press, 1991), 261–284.

57. Heidegger, *Logica*, 82.

58. Ibid., 84–85.

59. For a discussion of this theme, see Johannes Fritsche, *Historical Destiny and National Socialism in Heidegger's* Being and Time (Berkeley and Los Angeles: University of California Press, 1999), especially Chapter 3.

60. Martin Heidegger, *Das Rektorat 1933–34: Tatsachen und Gedanken* (Frankfurt: Klostermann, 1983), 40.

61. Ibid.

62. For a good treatment of the "Beautification of Labor" program, see Anson Rabinbach, "The Aesthetics of Production in the Third Reich," in *International Fascism: New Thoughts and Approaches*, G. Mosse, ed. (Beverly Hills: Sage, 1979), 189–222.

63. Heidegger, *Logica*, 102.

64. Herbert Marcuse, "Heidegger's Politics: An Interview," in *Marcuse: Critical Theory and the Promise of Utopia* (South Hadley, Mass.: Bergin and Garvey, 1987), 99.

65. See, for example, *Introduction to Metaphysics*, where Heidegger speaks of the equiprimordial role of philosophers, statesmen, and poets. Similar remarks may be found in his 1934 lecture course, *Hölderlins Hymnen "Germanien" und "Der Rhein"* (Frankfurt: Klostermann, 1980).

66. Heidegger, *Logica*, 104; emphasis added.

67. Ibid., 120.

Excursus: Being and Time: *A Failed Masterpiece?*

1. Heinrich Petzet, *Auf einen Stern Zugehen: Begegnungen und Gespräche mit Heidegger* (Frankfurt: Societäts Verlag, 1983), 9.

2. See Heidegger, *Being and Time*, trans. J. MacQuarrie and E. Robinson (New York: Harper and Row, 1962), 310.

3. Theodore Kisiel, "Heidegger's Apology: Biography As Philosophy and Ideology," *Graduate Faculty Philosophy Journal* 14 (2), 15 (1) (1991): 364.

4. "Dialogue Between a Japanese and an Inquirer," in *On the Way to Language*, trans. P. Hertz (New York: Harper and Row, 1971), 6.

5. This path has recently been painstakingly and magisterially reconstructed in Theodore Kisiel, *The Genesis of Heidegger's* Being and Time (Berkeley and Los Angeles: University of California, 1993).

6. Heidegger, "My Way to Phenomenology," in *On Time and Being* (New York: Harper and Row, 1972), 74.

7. Hans-Ulrich Wehler, *The German Empire: 1971–1918*, trans. K. Traynor (Leamington Spa: Berg, 1985), 116–17.

8. Hugo Ott, "Heidegger's Contributions to *Der Akademiker*," in *Graduate Faculty Philosophy Journal* 14 (2), 15 (1) (1991): 482.

9. Heidegger, *Zur Sache des Denkens* (Tübingen: Martin Niemeyer, 1964), 82.

10. Carl Braig, "Was soll der Gebildete von dem Modernismus wissen?"; cited in Dieter Thomä, *Die Zeit des Selbst und die Zeit danach* (Frankfurt: Suhrkamp Verlag, 1990), 35.

11. Heidegger, "Contributions to *Der Akademiker*," 487.

12. Ibid., 493, 495.

13. Ibid., 497.

14. Heidegger, "Only a God Can Save Us," in *The Heidegger Controversy*, 106.

15. See Heidegger, *Hölderlin's Hymne 'Der Ister'* (GA 53) (Frankfurt: Klostermann, 1975), 85; Heidegger, *An Introduction to Metaphysics*, 45–46.

16. Cited in Kisiel, "Heidegger's Apology," 395.

17. Heidegger, *Being and Time*, 310. For the best discussion of Heidegger's understanding of "life," see his important lecture course of 1919, *Zur Bestimmung der Philosophie*, GS 57 (Frankfurt: Klostermann, 1987).

18. The letter of August 19, 1921 is reprinted in Löwith, *Martin Heidegger and European Nihilism*, Richard Wolin, ed. (New York: Columbia University Press, 1995), 236.

19. Heidegger-Blochmann *Briefwechsel*, J. Storck, ed. (Marbach am Necker: Deutsche Schillergesellschaft, 1989), 7; emphasis added.

20. Heidegger discusses Spengler in the as yet unpublished 1920–21 lecture course, "Phänomenologie der Religion." For a discussion, see Kisiel, *Genesis*, 161–63.

21. Heidegger-Blochmann *Briefwechsel*, 7.

22. Ibid., 15.

23. Ibid., 12.

24. Heidegger, "Der Zeitbegriff in der Geschichtswissenschaft," GA 1, *Frühe Schriften* (Frankfurt: Klostermann Verlag, 1978), 194.

25. Heidegger, "Die Kategorien- und Bedeuteungslehre Duns Scotus," GA 1, *Frühe Schriften* (Frankfurt: Klostermann Verlag, 1972), 194.

26. Heidegger, *Zur Bestimmung der Philosophie*, GA 56/57 (Frankfurt: Klostermann, 1988), pp. 3, 8.

27. The letter is cited in Thomas Sheehan, "Reading a Life: Heidegger and Hard Times," in *The Cambridge Companion to Heidegger*, C. Guignon, ed. (Cambridge: Cambridge University Press, 1993), 71–72.

28. Karl Barth's "dialectical theology" would also have a profound influence on Heidegger, but his important interpretation of *The Epistle to the Romans* was not published until 1921.

In the later "Dialogue on Language," Heidegger emphasizes the importance of his encounter with Protestant theology and Dilthey's historicism: "Later, I met the term 'hermeneutics' again in Wilhelm Dilthey in his theory of the historical human sciences. Dilthey's familiarity with hermeneutics came from the same source, his theological studies, especially his work with Schleiermacher"; *On the Way to Language* (New York: Harper and Row, 1972), 10.

29. Cited in Hugo Ott, "Zu den katholischen Wurzeln im Denken Martin Heidegger's. Der theologische Philosoph," in *Akten des römischen Heidegger Symposions* (1992), 82.

30. Kisiel, *Genesis*, 71.

31. Arendt, "Martin Heidegger at Eighty," in M. Murray, ed. *Heidegger and Modern Philosophy* (New Haven: Yale University Press, 1979), 303.

32. Heidegger, *Zur Bestimmung der Philosophie*, 66.

33. Cited in H. Spiegelberg, *The Phenomenological Movement*, vol. 1 (The Hague: Martinus Nijhoff, 1976), 84.

34. Husserl, "Persönliche Aufzeichnungen," *Philosophy and Phenomenological Research* (16) (1956): 297.

35. Heidegger, *Zur Bestimmung der Philosophie*, 74.

36. Gerda Walther to Alexander Pfänder, June 20, 1919, cited in Kisiel, *Genesis*, 58.

37. Husserl, *Ideen* III (*Husserliana* V) (The Hague: Martinus Nijhoff, 19), 75.

38. Husserl, *Formal and Transcendental Logic* (The Hague: Martinus Nijhoff, 1969), 209. As far as Husserl's own ego is concerned, Gadamer tells the story of how at the end of a long-winded lecture (there was seldom room for discussion in his seminars), Husserl observed:" My, we certainly had a fascinating discussion today!" See Gadamer, *Philosophical Apprenticeships* (Cambridge: MIT Press, 1985), 36.

39. Heidegger, *Zur Bestimmung der Philosophie*, 74.

40. Ibid., 63.

41. Heidegger to Löwith, August 19, 1921, in Löwith, *Martin Heidegger and European Nihilism*, 235–36, 237.

42. Heidegger, *Zur Bestimmung der Philosophie*, 89–90.

43. Heidegger, *Phänomenologische Intepretationen zu Aristotles*, GA 61 (Frankfurt: Klostermann, 199), 54.

44. Heidegger, *Zur Bestimmung der Philosophie*, 117.

45. Heidegger, *Phänomenologische Intepretationen zu Aristoteles*, 111.

46. Heidegger, *Ontologie: Hermeneutik der Faktizität*, 19.

47. Heidegger, *Being and Time*, 216; emphasis added.

48. Heidegger, *Ontologie: Hermeneutik der Faktizität*, 18, 16.

49. Aristotle, *Metaphysica*, trans. D. Ross (Clarendon Press: Oxford, 1928), 1028a, 15.

50. Werner Marx, *Heidegger and the Tradition*, trans. T. Kisiel (Evanston: Northwestern University Press, 1971), 5.

51. Aristotle, *Nichomachean Ethics*, trans. M. Ostwald (Indianapolis: Bobbs-Merrill, 1962), 1139, 6; emphasis added.

52. Heidegger, "Phenomenological Interpretations with Respect to Aristotle," *Man and World* 25 (1992): 359–60.

53. Ibid., 363–64.

54. Ibid., 364–65.

55. Heidegger, *An Introduction to Metaphysics*, (New Haven: Yale University Press, 1959), p. 133.

56. Schmitt, *The Concept of the Political*, trans. G. Schwab (Chicago: University of Chicago Press, 1993), 67. Since the English translation is faulty (for example, in the sentence cited, the word "great" is simply left out), I have relied on the German edition, *Der Begriff des Politischen* (Berlin: Duncker und Humblot, 1963), 67.

57. K-H Bohrer, *Ästhetik des Schreckens* (Munich: Henser Verlag, 1978).

58. See Heidegger-Jaspers, *Briefwechsel* (Munich: Piper, 1992), 70.

59. See "A Discussion Between Ernst Cassirer and Martin Heidegger," in *The Existential Tradition*, N. Langiulli, ed. (New Brunswick: Transaction, 1997). At the same time, one may discern an interim phase of his philosophical development during the mid-1930s, in which he proposes for consideration the alternative idea of the "setting-to-work of truth," chiefly in the realms of politics and in art. The two most representative texts of this phase are "The Self-Assertion of the German University" (Heidegger's 1933 rectoral address) and "The Origin of the Work of Art." For a more detailed discussion of this theme, see the important study by Winfried Franzen, *Von der Existentzialontologie zur Seinsgeschichte* (Messenheim am Glan: Anton Heim 1975). See also Alexander Schwan, *Politische Philosophie im Denken Heideggers* (Köln and Opladen: Westdeutscher Verlag, 1965).

60. Heidegger, *Wegmarken* (Frankfurt: Klostermann, 1967), 304.

61. Heidegger, *The End of Philosophy* (New York: Harper & Row, 1973), 82.

62. Arendt, "For Martin Heidegger's Eightieth Birthday," in Neske/Kettering, *Martin Heidegger and National Socialism* (New York: Paragon House, 1990), 217.

63. Kisiel, *The Genesis of Heidegger's* Being and Time, 25.

64. Heidegger, GA 65 (Frankfurt: Klostermann, 1965), 239.

Conclusion

1. Mitchell Aboulafia, review of *The Politics of Being: The Political Thought of Martin Heidegger*, *International Journal of Philosophy* (1991).

2. Nolte, *Heidegger: Politik und Geschichte im Leben und Denken* (Berlin and Frankfurt: Propyläen, 1992).

3. Here, I am thinking predominantly of Andreas Hillgruber's claim in *Zweierlei Untergang* that it is the "duty" of the German historian to identify with the brave German troops fighting to stave off the Red Army on the Eastern front. For a discussion of these matters, see Charles Maier, *The Unmasterable Past: History, Holocaust and German National Identity* (Cambridge: Harvard University Press, 1988); see especially chapter 4. For more on the background of historicism, see George Iggers, *The German Conception of History* (Middletown, Conn.: Wesleyan University Press, 1983).

4. See Hauke Brunkhorst, *Der Intellektuelle im Land der Mandarine* (Frankfurt: Suhrkamp Verlag, 1987), 9.

5. See Chapter 6.

6. For a classical articulation of this position, see Charles Taylor, "What Is Human Agency," in *Human Agency and Language: Philosophical Papers* I (Cambridge, Cambridge University Press, 1985), 15–45.

7. Immanuel Kant, *The Critique of Pure Reason*, trans. N. K. Smith (London: Oxford University Press), 645. In her later writings (e.g., her unfinished lectures on Kant's political philosophy), Arendt seemed to be moving closer to a Kantian standpoint, taking as her benchmark the *Third Critique*. Thus, in the essay "The Crisis of Culture," she discusses the relationship between aesthetic and political judgment, claiming that both pertain to phenomena proper to the "public world" (i.e., art and politics). It is in this context that she enthusiastically cites Kant's suggestion in the *Critique of Judgment* that:

> The power of judgment rests on a potential agreement with others, and the thinking process which is active in judging something is not, like the thought process of pure reasoning, a dialogue between me and myself, but finds itself always and primarily, even if I am quite alone in making up my mind, in an anticipated communication with others with whom I know I must finally come to some agreement. This means . . . that such judgment must liberate itself from the "subjective private conditions," that is, from the idiosyncrasies which naturally determine the outlook of each individual in his privacy and are legitimate as long as they are only privately held opinions, but which are not fit to enter the market place, and lack all validity in the public realm."

Arendt, *Between Past and Future* (New York: Penguin, 1968), 220.

8. Marcuse, "The Struggle Against Liberalism in the Totalitarian View of the State," in *Negations: Essays in Critical Theory*, trans. J. Shapiro (Boston: Beacon Press, 1968), 41, 40; emphasis added.

9. Carl Schmitt, *Staat, Bewegung, Volk* (Hamburg: Hanseatischer Verlag Anstalt, 1933), 32.

10. Cited in *The Heidegger Controversy*, 47.